AF352529

BLOOD NOVELS

Blood Novels

*Gender, Caste, and Race in
Spanish Realism*

JULIA H. CHANG

UNIVERSITY OF TORONTO PRESS
Toronto   Buffalo   London

ISBN 978-1-4875-4301-3 (cloth)   ISBN 978-1-4875-4302-0 (EPUB)
ISBN 978-1-4875-4303-7 (PDF)

Toronto Iberic

Library and Archives Canada Cataloguing in Publication

Title: Blood novels : gender, caste, and race in Spanish realism / Julia H. Chang.
Names: Chang, Julia H., author.
Series: Toronto Iberic ; 75.
Description: Series statement: Toronto Iberic ; 75 | Includes bibliographical
   references and index.
Identifiers: Canadiana (print) 20220160082 | Canadiana (ebook) 20220160309 |
   ISBN 9781487543013 (cloth) | ISBN 9781487543020 (EPUB) |
   ISBN 9781487543037 (PDF)
Subjects: LCSH: Spanish fiction – 19th century – History and criticism. |
   LCSH: Blood in literature. | LCSH: Women in literature. | LCSH: Caste
   in literature. | LCSH: Social status in literature. | LCSH: Race in
   literature. | LCSH: Realism in literature.
Classification: LCC PQ6144 .C53 2022 | DDC 863/.509 – dc23

We wish to acknowledge the land on which the University of Toronto Press
operates. This land is the traditional territory of the Wendat, the Anishnaabeg, the
Haudenosaunee, the Métis, and the Mississaugas of the Credit First Nation.

This book has been published with the help of a Harriet S. Turner grant from the
Asociación Internacional de Galdosistas and a grant from the Hull Memorial
Publication Fund of Cornell University.

University of Toronto Press acknowledges the financial support of the Government
of Canada, the Canada Council for the Arts, and the Ontario Arts Council, an agency
of the Government of Ontario, for its publishing activities.

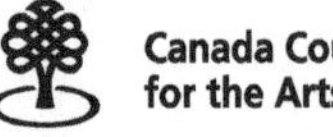

For my family

Contents

Preface

Childbirth has commonly been used as a metaphor for writing a book. A friend once told me that finishing a big project produced a sense of loss she termed post-partum depression. Having done and endured all these things, I can say for myself that writing a book has been nothing like childbirth. But pregnancy, labour, and the long post-partum period did impact the direction of my work in rather unexpected ways.

To be sure, I never set out to write a book about blood – I started with a project on a Hispanic concept of purity. Back then, my interest in blood (i.e., bloodlines) was an offshoot of a larger investigation that probed the interconnectedness of caste (*casta*) and chastity (*castidad*) in nineteenth-century Spanish realism. The existing scholarship, I found, tended to focus on the concept of chastity, particularly in relation to women and bourgeois domesticity, while caste was largely overlooked. But realism's women, commonly described as beautiful, pure, and chaste, were tainted in other ways – their bloodlines were impure.

In the course of writing and revising, my body was thrust into a mode of perpetual endurance for which I was underprepared: I sustained four pregnancies – two miscarriages, two full-term births. These were times of deep physical loss; expansion and contraction; love and woundedness; intimacy and alienation. I became acutely aware of my body's recalcitrance, its temporality, the way it registered loss, its power and limitations. Through these particularly physical, sanguinary, and fluid experiences, intellectually something shifted inside me. As I started to conduct new research, I became increasingly invested not only in what Michel Foucault terms a "symbolics of blood," that is, "the way [blood] functions in the order of signs (to have a certain blood)," but also the kind that ultimately occupies the outside of the "threshold of modernity" (143): physical blood. For Foucault, blood is, above all, a metaphor. Its discursive power is what matters most: "blood was *a reality with a symbolic function"* (147). In picking up what Foucault left behind – material blood – I started to see my literary corpus anew. Blood worked like an undertow that pulled me further and further into the novels' aesthetic surfaces and narrative innerworkings with a kind of bodily consciousness I could not turn off.

I term these key works of Spanish realism "blood novels" for making bloodlines central to their plots and for giving material blood a certain visceral immediacy and aesthetic force. These novels – especially the works by Benito Pérez Galdós – were just as concerned with stained bloodlines as a woman's problem, as they were physical blood loss as a sign of gendered (and more implicitly) racial precarity. Stepping back, I began to see a prominent feature of Spanish realism that had not been seriously assessed before: blood's duality, that is, the tension between discursive and material blood, captures the very tenets of literary realism. A project about purity thus became a book about blood.

In this book, I engage with blood's gendered cultural significance in Spain, stemming from, but not limited to, the historical preoccupation with blood purity, known as *limpieza de sangre*. I argue that the history of *limpieza* profoundly shaped the unique contours of Spanish realism, particularly those novels authored by men. As this male-dominated genre attempted to capture the material world on the page, women and their bodies served as (unruly) *materia prima*. Feelings of patriarchal ambivalence – disgust, curiosity, fear, desire – imbue these sanguinary narratives that revolve around bodies gendered feminine. Blood's gendered significance is nothing new, but these novelists' preoccupation with this issue – making blood the matter of women and feminized bodies – is a critical dimension of Spanish realism that has long been ignored and one that I explore over the course of the book, ultimately culminating in the Coda, where I, perhaps surprisingly, dialogue with contemporary feminist theorists in generative ways.

"We're all bored of gender," a professor in graduate school once told me. Later on, a fellow student followed suit: "I feel sorry for you. Gender is such a '90s topic." Whether the study of gender was passé or not, Judith Butler's theory of performativity (1990) felt so definitive and timeless that it seemed futile (or reactionary) to attempt to think against it or outside of it. Everyone *knew* that gender was performative (even if the concept was grossly misused); Butler had deciphered the science of gender, and now we could all move on. In my first year of teaching as an assistant professor, I dutifully assigned Butler's *Gender Trouble* (1990) and taught it as though it were law. One particularly sceptical graduate student challenged me and asked what contemporary theories of gender successfully critiqued Butler. I shrunk a little inside myself, taken aback by his boldness. But also, admittedly, I came up short. I had grown very protective of feminist studies as something I had been told was, time and time again, an unfashionable or unserious scholarly pursuit. It took me time to understand that I was too steeped in the widely accepted discursive/performative narrative of gender that questioning it felt like an act of disloyalty to the field.

Stacy Alaimo and Susan Hekman's important edited volume *Material Feminisms* came out in 2008, when I was still taking coursework, but my own arrival to it was rather belated.[1] Their intervention signalled an important sea change in the field of feminist theory that has been crucial to the evolution of my own thinking. The essays collectively critique the linguistic-discursive turn or the constructivist undercurrent of feminist theory and set out, instead, to integrate "the material and discursive, the human and the nonhuman, the natural and the cultural, while challenging these dichotomies and the givenness of categories" (11). The move to undo this dichotomous relationality, I believe, lends itself to nuanced theories of gendered embodiment and, perhaps somewhat surprisingly, sheds new light on Spanish literary realism, a genre so bound to the written word yet helplessly enamoured of the material world. In looking at the productive *tension* between the discursive and the material, this book recuperates the agential, recalcitrant capacity of the matter that counts as reality and the novel's reflexivity on the limitations of representational power.

In attempting to advance a culturally situated analysis of blood – at once material and discursive – I wondered if this too was a passé topic. Within Iberian Studies, it still feels anachronistic to talk about blood purity in the era of so-called modernity. While from a gender studies perspective, it might sound dated to research, say, menstrual blood. Once I saw realism's blood, however, I simply could not unsee it. I could not, for example, read an account of a character's fatal postpartum hemorrhage (Galdós *Fortunata y Jacinta*) in quite the same way, and I wondered how I had previously glossed over such a momentous scene. Bleeding gendered feminine, I think, is an act that still horrifies us. It is a site of abjection. It can be leveraged in the name of sex essentialism that feminists rightfully denounced. To be sure, this is not a book that privileges the experiential even as it stems from it. Rather, this critical engagement with my own positionality and lived, embodied experience – my own reckoning with blood loss – became, as it turns out, the key to a feminist methodology that brought me to these rather unconventional readings of exemplars of Spanish realism. My hope is that this book provides a unique kind of entry into these works we thought we knew well and gesture towards news ways of understanding how and why blood came to matter.

Acknowledgments

As I neared the completion of this book, our structural inequities and political failures allowed COVID-19 to ravage the world. The awareness I had gained around my own bodily precarity and now those of my children and my parents stood at the forefront of my thoughts. During a virtual Passover Seder, a relative asked where we might find strength during times of hardship. In that moment of introspection, my mind filled with thoughts of my mother and her mother. I was humbled imagining their hardship during the Korean War. I consider myself lucky by comparison, even as I continue to manage chronic illness and raise two little ones during a pandemic. Crucially, I have done none of these things alone. I have been the recipient of immeasurable acts of care and gestures of kindness, incurring many debts along the way. Naming them here is testament to the communal labour that makes intellectual life possible. I apologize for any inadvertent omissions.

First and foremost, I would like to recognize my family, without whom none of this would have been possible. To my mother, Yongshin Sabina Park, for every sacrifice made (known and unknown to me) – every flight, pot of soup, jar of fermented vegetables, hand-stitched blanket and garment. She has never ceased the labour of mothering – nourishing our souls through our bellies – especially when the pressures of being an academic parent felt like too much to bear. To my stepfather, Dr. Moon Kim, for his kind-heartedness. To my sister, Debbie Chang, whose artistic talent unfurled before my eyes as a child, awakening my own inclination towards the arts. To my father, Young Soo Chang, who, perhaps unbeknownst to him, passed down his knack for languages and his adventuresome spirit. To my parents-in-law, Ellen and Stuart, for giving us regular reprieve from round-the-clock parenting. To Noemi and Isaac for grounding me and for being the source of unbounded, unmediated joy in times of darkness. Last but not least, I am eternally grateful to my husband and co-parent Eli – our anchor and my optimist. Thank you for, among many things, believing in me when I was unable to believe in myself. None of this would have been possible without you.

In keeping with the theme of care, I would like to recognize those that provided essential care work in some of the most demanding moments of these past few years. To Kate Dimpfl, body worker and doula extraordinaire, Dr. Marta Guzman and her Women of Color support group, and our mother's helper Emily Spafford.

There is no way to measure the significance of old friends who preserve a part of me I may otherwise I have lost in this process. To Daniel Dobrott and Stephanie Villaseñor, thank you for the meals, groceries, care packages, visits, and above all, for holding up a mirror to me. And to Javier Gonzáles, whose friendship kept me afloat in Madrid. *Gracias mil.*

I have written this book in the company of so many amazing scholars whose labour and care have deeply enriched my thinking. I am indebted to the invaluable mentorship of two inspiring women in the field: Jo Labanyi and Akiko Tsuchiya. Before I knew them personally, their feminist scholarship served as a guiding light whilst I fumbled my way through graduate school. Both scholars participated in a book manuscript workshop that proved immensely helpful in moving this project towards publication. I would not have found my footing in the field of Modern Iberian Studies without them.

This manuscript has been enriched by the insightful feedback of numerous friends and colleagues who read drafts of individual chapters. Many thanks to Ananda Cohen Aponte, Ernesto Bassi, Andrew Campana, Elisha Cohn, Jeffrey Coleman, Shawn McDaniel, N. Michelle Murray, Deborah Starr, and Julie Ann Ward. I want to express my gratitude to the two anonymous reviewers for their labour and insightful recommendations.

At University of Toronto Press, many thanks to Mark Thompson, Bob Davidson, and all the behind-the-scenes staff for supporting this project. Thanks also to Sr. Project Manager Deborah Kopka, copy editor Elizabeth Ferguson, and indexer Virginia Ling.

I would not have gotten to this point were it not for the intellectual guidance I received from the faculty at UC Berkeley: Emilie Bergmann, Natalia Brizuela, Margaret Chowning, Dru Dougherty, Laura García-Moreno, Michael Iarocci, and Minoo Moallem. I am especially grateful for the mentorship of Juana María Rodríguez, who continues to model a different way to be in academia. My studies at Loyola Marymount University is what got me to graduate school in the first place. I am so thankful for the loving support of José Ignacio Badenes and Alicia Partnoy. Thank you for making the study of literature a kind of refuge for me.

I have benefited greatly from conversations with numerous colleagues at various stages of the project. Thanks to Diane Brown, Krista Brune, Timothy Campbell, Naminata Diabate, Jason Frank, Rosa María Medina Doménech, Tracy McNulty, Daniel Nemser, Jennifer Row, Bécquer Seguín, Jennifer Smith, Wan Tang, Irina Troconis, and Aurélie Vialette for lending their time and expertise. I want to recognize the collegiality of Gabrielle Miller and Erika Rodríguez. Our surreptitious encounter in the *Real Academia de Medicina* was the antidote to the usual loneliness of archival work, and our shared finds shaped the Coda for this book. I extend my deepest gratitude to Sa'ed Atshan, whose impromptu brainstorming session over dinner led me to blurt out the key phrase "blood novels." To Ashley Brock and Manuel R. Cuellar, especially, thank you for being brilliant interlocuters and for holding me up during some of the hardest days of pandemic writing.

I owe a debt of gratitude to those that did the meticulous, painstaking labour of finding sources, formatting, and proofreading. Thank you to my research assistants, Matías Oviedo and (especially) Kelly Moore, who read nearly every word of this manuscript twice. To Bill Piper, my copy editor, who is a generous and engaging interlocuter.

I have written the bulk of this book at Cornell University – situated on the traditional homelands of the Gayogo̱hó:nǫ' (the Cayuga Nation). The vibrant intellectual communities fomented by my colleagues in the Department of Romance Studies and the Program of Feminist, Gender, and Sexuality Studies are ones that I am lucky to be a part of. I extend special thanks to colleagues whose support and kindness helped me along the way. Thanks to Gerard Aching, Debra Castillo, María Antonia Garcés, Durba Ghosh, Kathleen Long, Kate McCullough, Simone Pinet, Edmundo Paz-Soldán, Irina Troconis, and Marie-Clare Vallois. I am grateful to our department administration and staff – especially Rob Van Brunt, Marcus May, and Carolyn Keller – for supporting me in various ways. Across campus, a special shoutout goes to Shannon Gleeson for our writing sessions, walks, Spanish lunches, and backup childcare. At Brown University, huge thanks to Laura Bass and Evelyn Hu-DeHart.

This project was made possible by financial support from the Humanities Research Grant and the Monograph Writing Group Award from the Society for the Humanities, the College of Arts and Sciences, the Hull Memorial Publication Fund, the Professional Development Grant from the Office of Faculty Diversity and Development at Cornell University, and the "Harriet S. Turner Beca" from the Asociación Internacional de Galdosistas.

Parts of chapter one have been derived from "'Aquellos neófitos indios, chinos o anamitas': Asia and the Imperial Imaginary in *Doña Luz*," *Asia in the Hispanic World: The Other Orientalism*, special issue of *Arizona Journal of Hispanic Cultural Studies*, vol. 18, no. 1, 2014, pp. 235–46. An earlier version of chapter two was published as "Blood, Purity, and Pleasure in Leopoldo Alas's *La Regenta*," *Hispanic Review*, vol. 84, no. 3, 2016, pp. 299–321. ©2016 University of Pennsylvania Press. Reprinted with permission of the University of Pennsylvania Press.

Note on Translations

Unless otherwise noted, passages from the novels that appear in translation have been quoted from published English language editions. All other translations are my own.

BLOOD NOVELS

Realism's Blood

Blood – as metaphor and matter – courses through the pages of some of Spanish realism's most canonical novels, infusing its plots and vivifying its aesthetic worlds. And yet, we have been largely unaware of blood's prominence as a structuring element of the realist novel. Some of Spain's most prominent literary men – Juan Valera, Leopoldo Alas, and Benito Pérez Galdós – were clearly captivated by blood: its symbolic valences, visceral materiality, and, crucially, its gendered inflections. Amid the shifting political landscape of Restoration Spain, these authors examined blood's multifarious significance and registered the fraught cultural politics of blood that reanimated the early modern discourse of *limpieza de sangre* (blood purity). Far from being anachronistic or historically defunct, as one might assume, the discourse of blood purity which stemmed from the ideology of *limpieza de sangre* persisted in the second half of the nineteenth century, when the realist novel flourished in Spain. Indeed, Spain's historical concern with blood purity found an afterlife in Spanish realism, profoundly impacting how the genre's most canonical novels took shape. Valera, Alas, and Galdós's shared fascination with blood and bloodlines comes into focus, fundamentally, through their beautiful but troubled women protagonists, whom we know well: Doña Luz, Ana Ozores, Isidora Rufete, and Fortunata. This book, in part, sets out to trace a dominant pattern across these novels: a markedly masculinist anxiety around (mostly) women's disruptive bleeding and corrupted bloodlines.

Blood, as we shall see, operates as a powerful analytic in realist fiction – one that elucidates the unique problematics of modern gendered subjectivity, which gender, race, class, and sexuality alone cannot adequately capture. This book invites readers to reconsider the iconic women of male-authored realist novels, treating blood as a conceptual framework through which to view them anew.

Consider, for instance, Ana Ozores, the protagonist of Leopoldo Alas's landmark novel *La Regenta* (1884–5). It is a work that has generated significant scholarship on its formal innovations and treatment of gender and sexuality. Blood, however, remains a peripheral element in the criticism. This is so despite the fact that the social importance of bloodlines and physical bleeding are evoked throughout (mentioned more than sixty times throughout the text) and undergird the novel's central conflict – adultery – treated as a sign of Ana Ozores's ignoble origins (her aristocratic father having married an Italian seamstress). In other words, Ana's tainted blood is the source of her inherited vice – her mother's supposed promiscuity. Even as a child, when it is falsely believed that Ana has compromised her honour after disappearing overnight with Germán, a childhood friend, her English governess Doña Camila traces the moral transgression back to her mother's blood: "– '¡Como su madre! -decía a las personas de confianza-. ¡improper! ¡improper! ¡Si ya lo decía yo! El instinto … *la sangre* … No basta la educación contra la naturaleza'" ("'Just like her mother!' she would say to acquaintances. 'Improper, improper!' she would add, in English. 'It is just as I said! Instinct – *blood* – there is little education can do in opposition to nature'"; *La Regenta I* 253, my emphasis; Rutherford 82, my emphasis). The original stain of blood cannot be sublimated, and chastity and moral education thus prove futile: "Desde entonces educó a la niña sin esperanzas de salvarla; como si cultivara una flor podrida ya por la mordedura de un gusano. No esperaba nada, pero cumplía su deber" ("Henceforward she educated the girl without any hope of saving her, as if she were cultivating a flower which was already rotting after a grub-bite. She had no hopes, but she did her duty"; 253–4; 82). And, as if to add further "proof" of her sexual deviance, an archpriest later reveals that Ana first menstruated around this time (*La Regenta I* 480–1; Rutherford 221). Thus, the novel correlates Ana's menstruation, her becoming a "mujercita" (little woman), with this childhood scandal.

Tropes of the impure female body are woven into the fabric of these iconic realist novels, harkening back to the mid-sixteenth-century conceptualization of *limpieza de sangre*, when, as Max S. Hering Torres has argued, "purity of blood was linked to the idea of the stain of 'race' [and] expanded the meaning of impurity to the body" ("Purity of Blood" 19). In line with the sixteenth-century discourse of blood purity, Ana's inherited vice is biologized as a racial stain, a "genealogical impurity" and "an imperfection that was like a hereditary disease" ("Purity of Blood" 19). Fittingly, the protagonist racializes her mother by imagining her as a Moor. This cursory consideration of blood in *La Regenta* demonstrates a claim that I develop over the course of the proceeding chapters: the woman of im/pure blood was a focal point of social preoccupations – at the core of which lies the gendered legacy of *limpieza de sangre*.

The works examined here fall under the rubric of what I term "blood novels," that is, they register a masculinist preoccupation with women's bloodlines and blood loss, haunted by an ideology of blood purity. The preoccupation of blood is a compelling narrative pattern that exceeds any one novel. Juan Valera's *Doña Luz* (1879), Leopoldo Alas's *La Regenta* (1884–5), and Benito Pérez Galdós's *La desheredada* (1881) and *Fortunata y Jacinta* (1886–7) all revolve around extraordinarily beautiful and (initially) chaste women whose social status remains stubbornly tethered to their bloodlines. The symbolic power attributed to bloodlines allows its determinism to remain a constant force in these novels' plots. All the while, representations of physical blood – its visceral, repulsive, uncontainable flow – register the novels' persistent return to the feminine body in flux. Thus, realism's bloodshed locates material authenticity in a fragile, and at times recalcitrant, body that can never be fully contained.

In examining the significance of blood in Spanish realism, I do not seek to isolate a singular meaning or function. Blood is a semantically dense concept that takes on diverse (and at times conflicting) meanings, operations, and valences. It manifests symbolically in terms of lineage drawing from the historical discourse of *limpieza de sangre*. It is also the ethereal stuff of moral character, proof of racial authenticity, a source of republican politics, and the symbolic fodder for social parasites, i.e., "sanguijuelas" "leeches" that drain the nation's vitality. Rather than weaken its relevance, the polysemic nature of blood attests to its discursive power and cultural reach. Blood, as we shall see in these novels, evokes notions of gender, race, caste, and sexuality – often joining more than one of these – and this is precisely what allows it to be so pervasive. Yet it is not merely a metonym for these categories. Blood is rendered physiological: a source of health and the hereditary matter of biological inheritance. It emerges in its crude material form, spilling from freshly butchered animals, hemorrhages, wounds, and menstruating bodies. And finally, it manifests aesthetically as bloody hues, ink, and hallucinatory visions – endowing realism with a notably visceral aesthetic amplitude. Ultimately, blood's proliferation reveals it to be "a peculiar, multifarious, and ubiquitous prism" (Anidjar 38) – one that allows for a renewed understanding of the formation of gendered and racialized embodiment in *fin-de-siglo* Spain.

Blood Novels uncovers such historically enduring and untidy narratives of blood that infuse realism's plots, gendered and racial imaginings, and narrative aesthetics. In so doing, it also probes the ways in which the blood paradigm – blood as both metaphor and matter – serves as a unique literary device, one that lends itself to explorations of realism's fictionality, what Harriet S. Turner has referred to as realism's "magic": how "these writers [Benito Pérez Galdós and Leopoldo Alas] induce us to believe that something fictional is palpably real, all the while flaunting the fact that the story is a self-consciously wrought fiction" ("Afterlives" 285). Blood's duality complicates this key relationship by exposing the tension between the "palpably real" versus those fictions – bloodlines – parading as truth. All the while, blood novels probe the discursive limits of realism through blood's dual nature: matter and metaphor.

Collectively, the proceeding chapters examine gendered subjectivity as emerging through a tension between the lasting ideology of blood purity on the one hand and a nascent bourgeois regime of sexuality on the other. Considering *limpieza de sangre*'s modern afterlife invites readers to put aside the belief that bloodlines no longer operated as social capital during the Restoration, an era we readily associate with the cultural hegemony of the bourgeoisie. Finally, and most broadly, it unsettles criticism's rigid commitment to the "administration of sexuality" (Foucault, *History of Sexuality*) and a visual racial schema, or what Irene Tucker has called "racial sight," as two hallmarks of European modernity, and instead posits a third possibility – blood-qua-caste – as a pervasive identificatory category inflected by race, sexuality, and gender.[1]

Periodicity

Blood Novels challenges the assumption that the tenets of modernity are entirely distinct from and in sequential relationship with the early modern period. An attention to the shadowy but persistent valorization of bloodlines evidences precisely this. Michel Foucault's oeuvre has certainly proven fundamental to how scholars have conceptualized the nineteenth century as an era invested in the technology of sex, while blood, accordingly, remains an issue of the *ancièn régime*. In *The History of Sexuality*, Foucault famously described the modern period as transitioning from sovereign power to biopower, or from *"a symbolics of blood to an analytic of sexuality"* (148; emphasis in original). As Gil Anidjar put it simply, sovereign power was "the supreme right to spill and draw blood" (46). For Foucault, while in premodern Europe power "spoke *through* blood," in a modern society of sex "the mechanisms of power are addressed to the body, life, to what causes it to proliferate, to what reinforces the species, its staminas, its ability to dominate, or its capacity for being used" (147; emphasis in original). In short, Foucault concludes, the "bourgeoisie's blood was its sex" (124). Quite often, this is thought to mean that in the nineteenth century blood simply vanished as a sign of social distinction – eclipsed by a bourgeois moral code in a world that was now largely concerned with sexuality.

This book contends that blood and sex remain entwined in late nineteenth-century Spain. And despite Foucault's provocative and sweeping periodizing claims, the difficulty in disentangling blood from sex is, in fact, apparent (though less frequently cited) in his writings on the matter: "the passage from one [blood] to the other [sex] did not come about ... without overlappings, interactions, and echoes ... [T]he preoccupation with blood and the law," he continues, "has for nearly two centuries haunted the administration of sexuality" (149). Undoing the rigid temporal armature in nineteenth-century criticism that links up the modern with "the 'now' of sex rather than the 'then' of blood" (Biddick 451) allows for a more nuanced understanding of how the discourse of blood continued to operate in a modern economy of sexuality. Thus, I am less interested in refuting the historical veracity of Foucault's periodizing moves than I am in looking more closely at these "overlappings, interactions, and echoes," which are mentioned in passing. Foucault's work provides a rather swift account of these particularly decisive and fascinating moments of overlap between blood and sex – in his case, the Victorian era, and for the purposes of this study, the early years of the Bourbon Restoration (1874–1931) in Spain. Indeed, this transition – in Restoration Spain in particular – was hardly linear and far messier than we typically imagine.

Presently, approaches to gender and sexuality in nineteenth-century Spain have largely focused on their intersections with class, and more recently race, while largely eliding questions of blood. As a result, little critical attention has been paid to the ways in which blood interacted with sex, despite the irrefutable, historical, and transatlantic impact of *limpieza de sangre*.[2] If we are to understand how, in the nineteenth century, sexuality functioned as a "dense transfer point for relations of power" (103), a serious consideration of the discourse of blood purity – its early modern history and modern afterlife – will be crucial.

The ideology of *limpieza de sangre* originates in mid-fifteenth-century Castile. Blood purity initially denoted those of Old Christian ancestry and legitimate birth in contrast to heretics, Jewish *conversos* (converts), and, subsequently, *moriscos* (Christian moors). Over time, *limpieza de sangre* led to the establishment of blood purity statutes that would allow only those of pure Christian ancestry to enter ecclesiastical offices, select professions, and universities, as well as to obtain honours. The Inquisition would play an important role in identifying heretics among those converts who were viewed with great suspicion. Central to this ideology was the notion that blood "encoded cultural characteristics," which, like elsewhere in Europe, were linked with the conception of nobility based on blood (Hering Torres et al., "Editorial" 2). In an introduction to a recent anthology entitled *Race and Blood in the Iberian World*, historians Max S. Hering Torres, María Elena Martínez, and David Nirenberg contend that the idea that "these discourses of blood were extended early to more and more registers of culture – religious, political, economic – and began to thicken into what we might with due caution consider a racial concept" (2) was a feature unique to the Iberian Peninsula. As the ideology of *limpieza de sangre* travelled to Iberian colonial territories and persisted over time, it acquired new connotations (2).

Gender, as María Elena Martínez has shown, would become a significant factor early on in the history of *limpieza de sangre*, ultimately leading to the "feminization of purity" (*Genealogical Fictions* 54). As Jewish and Islamic practices were eradicated from public life, the Holy Office shifted its inquisitional gaze to the home, targeting women as agents of pollution (55). This, in turn, "produced a sexual economy that lessened the desirability of *conversas* and *morsicas* as wives" while simultaneously heightening the need to police the sexuality of old Christian wives for fear they might secretly pollute their families' bloodlines (57). Blood purity operated as an elusive ideal. The imposition of control on women's bodies was a way to attempt to regulate and to maintain the illusion of caste purity since paternity could never be confirmed. Medieval and early modern concerns with female chastity, therefore, cannot be fully understood in isolation from the desire for blood purity.

Gendered preoccupations around blood and bloodlines often co-emerge through a discourse of purity (e.g., hygiene, cleanliness, chastity) that significantly shaped the literary and cultural landscape of the Bourbon Restoration. Blood, however, remains largely understudied in this period. This is evidenced by the fact that recent monographs on the cultural politics of blood in Iberian Studies exclusively concern early modern Iberia and colonial and post-independence Latin America, eliding nineteenth-century Spanish cultural production altogether – again, implicitly taking for granted the notion that in modern Spain blood (i.e., blood purity) was a thing of the past. Perhaps for this reason any discussion of blood purity in the nineteenth century has an anachronistic feel to it. Yet the mere facts that the Inquisition was not officially abolished until 1834 (by royal decree signed by regent María Cristina during the minority of Isabel II) and that blood purity requirements extended at least two decades following this. Noël Valis has encountered prescriptions for blood purity as late as 1853 (*Culture of Cursilería* 309, n22).[3]

In 1822, the Spanish-born English writer Joseph Blanco White comments on the longevity of blood purity in "Letters from Spain." He writes: "There exists another distinction of blood, which, I think, is peculiar to Spain, and to which the mass of the people are so blindly attached, that the meanest peasant looks upon the want of it as a source of misery and degradation, which he is doomed to transmit to his latest posterity. The least mixture of African, Indian, Moorish, or Jewish blood, taints a whole family to the most distant generation. *Nor does the knowledge of such a fact die away in the course of years*, or become unnoticed from the obscurity and humbleness of the parties" (29–30; my emphasis). This racialized notion of blood, moreover, overrode notions of social class. Blanco White observes: "in Spain we esteem a common person who is *limpio* (clean) more than a hidalgo who is not *limpio*" (322). Tellingly, *fin-de-siglo* conceptions of cleanliness still carry with them a residue of the blood purity statutes. In 1884, *Diccionario de la Real Academia Española* defined the term "limpio" "clean" as follows: "Limpio, pia. adj. Que no tiene mancha ó suciedad. Aplícase á las personas ó familias que no tiene mezlca ni raza de moros, judíos, herejes ó penitenciados" ("Clean, adj. Not stained or filthy. It is applied to persons or families that have no mixture nor race of Moors, Jews, heretics, or prisoners of the Inquisition.") Challenging the notion that *limpieza de sangre* is an ideology confined to earlier periods, this book explores how blood purity evolves and persists into the late nineteenth century, operating as an untimely modern identificatory category.

In the period in question, the upper stratum of society was steeped in profound and widespread disquietude. This sense of insecurity arose from its rapidly shifting social and economic terrain – precipitated by uneven processes of modernization, political instability, and cultural change. One of the consequences of these rapid changes was an increased sense of uncertainty about the capacity to guarantee legitimacy, authenticity, and originality – in a word, purity. Social hierarchies and alliances of blood were upset by the emergence and consolidation of a bourgeoisie who maintained financial and familial ties to both the upper and lower classes. Valis makes an important observation about this period in which "[p]rivilege did not disappear, but it was seriously undermined," noting that an "awareness of what was modern did not always produce the modern" (49). By this Valis means that members of the middle class looked to the aristocracy (i.e., the past) as cultural models, producing the effect of *lo cursí* (tackiness, aspirational distinction) since they lacked the "distinction that blood conferred on the nobility"

(50). This sense of distinction, moreover, "proved particularly strong in Spain and was exacerbated by a religious past in which 'la limpieza de sangre' (purity of blood) had created mutual suspicion and fear and a caste system of Old and New Christian" (50). Valis goes on to assert that "[w]hile the nineteenth century mostly rendered this kind of blood purity a moot issue, the structure of exclusions and divisions that shaped it persisted for a long time" (50). Here, I concur with Valis that *limpieza de sangre* clearly structured the blood-based hierarchy that we see in blood novels. In this sense, I depart from Leigh Mercer's argument that Spain's bourgeoisie remained "unhinged from pureblood lineage and surname" ("A primera sangre" 64). Instead, as the novels examined here reveal, the bourgeoisie exhibits a strong attachment to blood-based forms of distinction, even as they take to the visual, commercial trappings of class-based identity.

While there was an undeniable decline in the importance of noble and Christian origins, in the cultural landscape of the Restoration – and in the realist novel in particular – blood prevailed as a sign of distinction, even as the discourse of sex proliferated.[4] Indeed, *fin-de-siglo* Spain can still be characterized as a "society of blood" in which "the systems of alliance, the political form of the sovereign, the differentiation into orders and castes, and the value of descent lines were predominant for a society in which famine, epidemics, and violence made death imminent" (Foucault 147). At the same time, this very period exhibits some of the most salient qualities of a "society of 'sex,'" whereby "the mechanisms of power are addressed to the body, to life, to what causes it to proliferate, to what reinforces the species, its stamina, its ability to dominate, or its capacity for being used" (Foucault 147). Spain's emergent bourgeoisie, as elsewhere in Western Europe, readily sought to "regulat[e] sexuality, within a regime of health, as a counter to the aristocratic privilege of 'blood'" (Porter). The institutionalization of medical hygiene in the last third of the nineteenth century – coinciding with the rise of realist and naturalist novels – evidences this point.

To be clear, I do not want to argue that Spain was unmodern by sustaining the claim that Spain was "late" to transition away from a society of blood. Rather, my aim is to take seriously the notion of the Restoration period as one of tension and transition and, in turn, attend to the untimely convergence of cultural paradigms. Blood undergirds conceptions of caste all throughout the nineteenth century. This insistence on having pure bloodlines persisted, even as the discourse of sexuality permeated bourgeois society. Thus, the politics of blood that circulate in the realist novels of late nineteenth-century Spain evidences a persistent investment in maintaining distinction based on birth, alliance, and lineage. An analysis of blood in the realist novel reveals the hauntings of *limpieza de sangre* that underwrite gendered embodiment in *fin-de-siglo* Spain. In the chapters that follow, I demonstrate that an ideology of blood purity continued to circulate in significant yet diverse ways: at times, it supplemented modern norms of sexuality, while at others, it undermined the bourgeoisie's rubric of morality. In modern Spain, "blood" was therefore not wholly supplanted by "sex," as we had once assumed; rather, the *right* blood continued to operate as a form of social currency.

Catherine Jagoe has argued that Galdós "used the realist novel to explore, among other contradictions, the tension between the conflicting imperatives that constituted the bourgeoisie's ideal of womanhood" (*Ambiguous Angels* 42). One of the central contradictions that plague women protagonists of the realist novel (of Galdós and his contemporaries) is precisely the ideological clash between the bourgeois regime of sexuality (the imperative of chastity) and the persistent value of blood and lineage. Far from being historically defunct in the nineteenth century, blood, I assert, and despite the apparent clash, is the starting point for what I call the "chastity bind," whereby the ideological underpinnings of *limpieza de sangre* subtend a gendered economy of purity – chastity being its fullest expression. Chastity (*castidad*), stemming from the Latin term *castus* (clean, pure), animates sister conceptions of purity, including blood-based or caste identity (*casta*), the chaste woman (*la mujer casta*), and ethno-nationalist authenticity (*lo castizo, el casticismo*). The lexical twinning of *casta* (fem. adj. chaste) and *casta* (n. caste) reveals the inherently gendered semantic density of the chastity bind. As a polyvalent concept, then, *casta* not only undergirded individual identity but also breathed life into Castilian-centric expressions of modern Spanish nationalism.[5] Yet, as I will later demonstrate, the persistence of *limpieza* (based on blood) paradoxically threatens to undermine chastity's social value rooted in behaviour. Thus, I use the term "bind" in two senses: first, to denote the conjoining of diverse iterations of purity and, second, to capture the social bind in which female subjects in particular find themselves as a direct result of the competing regimes of blood and sex. Women caught in the chastity bind undergo a crisis that results from the jagged misalignment of blood purity and moral purity. Indeed, blood's deterministic force has the power to undermine the moral valorization of chastity; in other words, tainted blood renders chastity a moot point. Countering the tendency in the scholarship on nineteenth-century Spanish fiction to de-emphasize the importance of bloodlines, this book treats caste and chastity as splintered derivatives of the *blood paradigm*.

Crucially, bleeding in the nineteenth century was a thoroughly gendered affair. We see this claim powerfully illustrated in Benito Pérez Galdós's novel *Fortunata y Jacinta*, which, as I will later argue, depicts a social hierarchy ordered according to those who visibly bleed and those do not – i.e., members of the elite caste whose identity is determined through their (invisible) bloodlines. As such, physical blood marks socially peripheral bodies. The effeminate Maximiliano "Maxi" Rubín is a rare but particularly poignant example of this hierarchical ordering, as the only male character who visibly bleeds. His bleeding results from a failed attempt to attack his rival Juanito Santa Cruz. Maxi's resulting bloody wound signifies his effeminacy and the consequential precarity of his life. Juanito, by contrast, walks away unscathed. Maxi's gendered bleeding illustrates Akiko Tsuchiya's assertion in *Marginal Subjects* that "the construction of deviance [in the nineteenth century] was hardly gender-neutral" (15); rather, it was gendered feminine. The realist novel's marked fixation on gender deviants (e.g., its fallen women and emasculated men) certainly speaks to this claim.

The gendering of blood loss, however, is further complicated by the suspicion that Maximiliano is of Jewish *converso* origin. According to the narrator, Federico Ruiz (a "fecundo publicista" ["prolific publicist"]) believes the name Rubín was once Rubén and that "fue usado por algunos conversos que permanecieron aquí después de la expulsión" ("[it] had been used by certain converts who stayed here after the expulsion"; *FJ I* 572; Moncy Gullón 227). This is a rather tricky passage in the novel. The narrator takes the time to describe the work that Federico Ruiz has put into substantiating this claim only to then say:

No quisiera equivocarme; pero me parece que todo aquel judaísmo de mi amigo era pura fluxión de su acatarrado cerebro, el cual eliminaba aquellas enfadosas materias como otras muchas, según el tiempo y las circunstancias. Y me consta que D. Nicolás Rubín, último poseedor de la mencionada tienda, era cristiano viejo, y ni siquiera se le pasaba por la cabeza que sus antecesores hubieran sido fariseos con rabo o sayones narigudos de los que salen en los pasos de Semana Santa. (*FJ I* 572)

I wouldn't want to be wrong, but it seems to me that all my friend's Judaism was just a cold in the head or the brain, which eliminated those troublesome substances like so many others, depending on the weather and the circumstances. And I am sure that Don Nicolás Rubín, the late possessor of the aforementioned shop, was a Christian from way back, and that it had never crossed his mind that his ancestors might have been Pharisees with tails or big-nosed executioners like the ones in Holy Week processions. (227)

The reader is then left to adjudicate this blood fiction – which of two accounts of Maxi's origin story is true? The mere fact that the *converso* lineage is mentioned plants a sense of suspicion around Maxi, who already adheres to certain racial stereotypes of Jewishness, e.g., effeminacy, a misshapen nose. Maxi's blood loss, as a possible Jew and the only male character to bleed, reanimates Spain's thorny history of *limpieza de sangre*. Significantly, it conjures up early modern beliefs in the so-called menstruating Jewish male body. In her book *Perfect Wives, Other Women: Adultery and Inquisition in Early Modern Spain*, Georgina Dopico Black cites a 1632 memorandum written by court official Juan de Quiñones and addressed to Philip IV's confessor. It explains that Jewish men experience "a flowing of blood from their posterior parts, as a perpetual sign of infamy and fame ... every month they suffer a flow of blood like women" (3). Dopico Black remarks that Quiñones, "in order to make the body legible, specifically, legible as that of a culpable Other ... invest[s] it with an explicitly female physiology" (3). With this striking early modern correlate, we begin to see the ways in which *limpieza de sangre* underwrites modern conceptions of gendered and racially inscribed forms of non-normative embodiment.

This caste system, which activates a historical discourse of blood purity, clashes with the notion that the bourgeoise "staked its life and death on *sex* by making it responsible for its future welfare" (Foucault 124; my emphasis). For Foucault, this biopolitical preoccupation with sex and the body – its health, hygiene, and longevity – comprises a "dynamic racism, a racism of expansion" linked to the "establishment of bourgeois hegemony" (125). While Spanish novels, replete with medical doctors and hygienists, certainly register an investment in the body's health, the biopolitical also coincides with a powerful racism of *exclusion*, one that relies on a notion of blood-based distinction and the early modern ideologies from which it stems.[6] In certain instances – as we will see with *Doña Luz* and *Fortunata y Jacinta* – this blood-based racism of exclusion converges with the more familiar visual nineteenth-century schema of race that underwrites literary tropes of whiteness and blackness. In these cases, the coloniality of the novel (whether explicit in the case of Valera or latent in Galdós) allows for blood as a supervening category to find expressions in racist imagery even as it undermines the visual operations of colonial racial hierarchy. This is not surprising since *limpieza de sangre* expanded to Spanish colonial territories as it evolved to incorporate new racial logics.

Race and blood are the subject of historian Joshua Goode's recent influential book *The Impurity of Blood*, which has established the prominence of the discourse of blood within the scientific community of the

Restoration period through the Franco dictatorship. Departing from the notion of blood purity – Goode's overarching claim is that race was conceived of as a "fusionary process" across the political spectrum in Spain (9). Examining, primarily, the works of Spanish anthropologists and medical doctors, Goode contends that Spain embraced and valued the mixing of blood (and, in turn, miscegenation) in late nineteenth and twentieth centuries – something that would later, Goode argues, set Franco's vision of race as radically divergent from other European conceptualizations, most notably that of Nazi Germany (1). Goode acknowledges that "[c]laims of racial purity emerged in Spain" but maintains that they "were often asserted in reaction to the otherwise overwhelming acceptance of mixture" (9–10). While Goode's analysis has been hugely productive for my understanding of the history of "racial thinking," I am also reluctant to wholly accept the claim that "race *always* reflected a belief in mixture" (17; my emphasis). Why not take seriously historical "claims of racial purity" and give them due consideration? Goode references, for example, Sabina Arana Goiri, the nineteenth-century Basque politician who asserted the racial purity and superiority of the Basque people only to dismiss its significance by arguing that it was "counterbalanced by others who envisioned the Basque as a fused element of the Spanish race" (10).[7] While starting from a shared premise – the prominence of the discourse of blood in late nineteenth-century Spain – this book sets forth a different argument: At a time when a significant part of the scientific community would begin to embrace Spain's history of miscegenation, novelists gave voice to a marked preoccupation with precisely the thing that anthropologists apparently disavow: an ideology of blood purity.

Blood Novels

Novels played a crucial role in the production of national imaginaries through the aesthetic education of the nation's "reading classes" (Benedict Anderson 73).[8] The Spanish realist novel, as Jo Labanyi has demonstrated, emerged as both an agent of nation formation and a forum for its critique. Thus, while the genre "illustrate[s] the problems arising from modernity's homogenizing project, [it] nevertheless serve[s] this same project by constructing the reading public as an 'imagined community' united by common anxieties" (Labanyi, *Gender and Modernization* 6). These anxieties are undoubtedly gendered and tacitly, or often explicitly, racialized.

Before fully grasping the significance of blood and its gendered implications in Spanish realism, then, the studies presented here initially set out to probe the dynamics of what Labanyi, in the concluding lines of *Gender and Modernization*, aptly described as the realist novel's "urgent need to construct its gallery of female protagonists" (416). I was keen to examine the gendered dynamics of, to borrow Nancy Armstrong's formulation, "the mutually constitutive relationship between novelists and their protagonists" ("Introduction"). A significant thread in this debate turns on the notion of the novel as a regulatory genre, deploying methods of surveillance, discipline, and control vis-à-vis its women protagonists. D.A. Miller, in his well-known *The Novel and the Police*, has argued that the realist-naturalist novel enacts a policing function, exhibiting a desire to track the sexually deviant women – Zola's *Nana* being a prime example of this. One could certainly make a case for this in the Spanish context. Along these lines, Labanyi has asserted that novelists attempted to control the disorder these women unleashed (*Gender and Modernization* 77). Amanda Anderson, writing about the Victorian novel, has argued that male novelists needed to ward off these "fallen women" who remained diametrically opposed to "normative masculine identity seen to possess the capacity for autonomous action, enlightened rationality, and self-control" (13).

Realism's unremitting fascination with women owes in large part to the fact that under modernity women's new roles and behaviour symbolized the breakdown of gendered space. The nineteenth century saw women, once confined to the domestic sphere, enter the factory, the streets, and the department store. Rita Felski notes, for example, that working-class women's movement into mass production and industrial labour, as well as middle-class women's roles as consumers, threatened the ideology of gendered spheres (public vs. private) (19). More recently, Leigh Mercer has examined the ways in which Spanish bourgeois women in the nineteenth century *needed* to appear in public places, such as the promenade and the museum, to maintain their social identity, thus challenging the notion that women were always confined to the domestic sphere (*Urbanism and Urbanity*). Akiko Tsuchiya, deploying a critical feminist framework and drawing on the work of Michel de Certeau, finds in Spanish realism "conscious act[s] of deviation" (5). Viewed in this way, narrative space opens up sites of resistance and "redefines the limits of what the dominant culture takes for granted as 'reality'" (5) in its obsessive depiction of gender deviance.

Taking a cue from Tsuchiya and deploying a critical feminist lens, it becomes clear that such literary acts of deviation are not only about social space, but they also exhibit deep-seated ambivalence about the feminine body, its allure, agentic capacity, its boundaries, and its ever-changing materiality. Boundary crossings were no doubt met with intense anxiety. The prostitute in *fin-de-siècle* cultural production is the subject of numerous paranoid male fantasies about gendered boundaries. Felski aptly describes the female prostitute as a "disturbing example of the ambiguous boundaries separating economies and sexuality, the rational and irrational, the instrumental and the aesthetic" (19). We know from Mary Douglas that margins are a site of danger and "pollution"; thus, so too are the women who breach them. In this way, as Anne McClintock has posited, "boundary figures are female," marking margins in such a way that suggests "a profound ambivalence in the European male" (26). Women existed on the margins of civil society, and their bodies served as the vulnerable margins of the family, i.e., borders requiring patriarchal surveillance.[9] To counterbalance these fears of the pollution, in these ensanguined narratives, wives were bestowed with the responsibility of propagating bloodlines, making them boundary figures of their lineage. But often, their unruly blood signalled the body's recalcitrance.

As the first foray into blood and gender in nineteenth-century Spanish literature, my interest centres on the interrogation of a masculinist preoccupation with women's bloodlines and bleeding gendered feminine as presented in the realist novel. The authors studied here – Benito Pérez Galdós, Leopoldo Alas, and Juan Valera – erect their narrative fantasies around the moral dilemmas and ill-fated social trajectories of their enticingly beautiful women protagonists. These women are responsible for reproducing their lineage or inherit the stigma of stained bloodlines, often, ironically enough, the result of their fathers' boundary crossings. They become the focal point for patriarchal social anxieties around originality, purity, and authenticity. And in some cases, as we have already seen, the act of bleeding becomes an entirely gendered, if not feminizing, matter.

To be sure, there are other works beyond what is examined here that could certainly fall under a broader conceptualization of "blood novels" – for example, Leopoldo Alas's *Su único hijo*, which revolves around a father's anxiety to have a child of his own blood, and, later, Miguel de Unamuno's *El marqués de Lumbría*, which shows the decadence of noble bloodlines. One might also ponder Emilia Pardo Bazán's novelistic oeuvre, particularly from her naturalist period. The decision to exclude Pardo Bazán – an avowed feminist and the only woman author in the Spanish realist canon – may be a surprising one. Blood surfaces (at times obliquely) in *Los Pazos de Ulloa* and *La madre naturaleza* – registering precepts of naturalism: inheritance and the transmission of social ills. *Insolación*, on the other hand, deploys a more explicit language of blood as a metaphor for race (e.g., African blood) but ultimately relies on notions of racial phenotype and privileges racial mixture over blood purity, as in the case of Pacheco, Asis's (the novel's woman protagonist) object of desire.[10] Pardo Bazán's treatment of blood is both diverse and complex and should be a topic for a future study.[11] Ultimately, however, these works stray (in distinct ways) from the rubric of blood novels that I have delineated here. Most importantly for the purposes of the present study, they do not exhibit the masculinist fascination/anxiety with women's blood purity and the gendered problematics of blood loss.[12] Blood as a "site of difference" (Anidjar 19) does not cohere around a woman protagonist, troubled yet enticingly portrayed through a male gaze.

The male gaze of fiction finds its counterpart in the dominant criticism of the novel. In his well-known and oft-cited study *Galdós and the Art of the European Novel*, Stephan Gilman writes of Fortunata: "We know her from within, and we know her at length, from spiritual birth to physical death and believed-in resurrection. We know her in a way we can never know women of flesh and blood – our mothers, our sisters, and our wives" (320; my emphasis). For Gilman, this universal masculine "we" of literary criticism gains unique access to Fortunata because Galdós has mastered the "art of consciousness" so much so that "[he] enables us to be Fortunata" (345). Fortunata represents literary perfection – a feminine consciousness crafted by masculinist design – that Gilman juxtaposes against the ordinary flesh-and-blood women to whom this heteropatriarchal "we" claims ownership. For his part, John Sinnigen points out that Galdós's mother died shortly before he finished writing *Fortunata y Jacinta*, maintaing that: "Todo eso se manifiesta en los fuertes personajes femeninos ... que sustentan la tendencia feminocéntrica de la novelística galdosiana. Galdós utiliza la ficción para intentar penetrar, representar y apropriarse de lo femenino" ("All of this manifests in the strong female characters ... that sustain the woman-centered tendency in Galdosian novels. Galdós uses fiction to try to penetrate, represent, and appropriate the feminine"; 117). These blood novels reveal a masculinist positionality, one from which these novelists attempt to reconcile the women as discursively created but inhabiting a precarious (and sometimes delectable) flesh-and-blood materiality.

From Ana Ozores and Doña Luz, whose fates are determined by the (alleged) taint of their mothers' blood, to Fortunata, who dies from a post-partum hemorrhage, and Isidora's recalcitrant behaviour dictated by the so-called voice of true blood, the male-authored novels I examine afford aesthetic expression to historically gendered preoccupations around bloodlines, which complicate our understanding of bourgeois cultural hegemony in nineteenth-century Spain. The realist novel – "the preeminent form of modernity" (Brooks, *Realist Vision* 7) – reveals the failures, contradictions, and indeed the fictions that undergird the ideology of purity in and around which the discourse of blood and chastity swirl. In these blood novels, this vital fluid plays a decisive role in the ordering of social arrangements and the management of life in an era of hasty modernization and imperial failure. Bringing the study of gender, caste, and race into dialogue with the politics of blood in nineteenth-century Spain, this book provides an account for how the woman of im/pure bloodlines came to be the vanishing point of biopolitical pre-occupations undergirded by the history of *limpieza de sangre*.

Realism and Gendered Matter

Bloodlines thicken realist plots, and at the same time blood functions as a particularly apt literary device – one that allows for the exploration of timely questions of fictionality at the apex of Spanish literary realism: the function and limits of representation, the structure of metaphor, and the notion of truth. Such questions, no doubt, have early modern antecedents, namely, the works of Cervantes, without which the realist tradition in and beyond Spain would be unthinkable. As Mary L. Coffey and Margot Versteeg have recently asserted: "The works of Cervantes and other Golden Age masters provided the nineteenth-century Spanish realist authors with an exceptionally fertile ground for representing and questioning the nature of lived reality and for exploiting the metafictional phenomenon of self-reflexivity, giving Spanish realism what is probably its most distinctive feature" (12). Crucially, Cervantes's fictional oeuvre critically engaged with the social valorization of bloodlines, dealing with questions of nobility, honour, and *limpieza de sangre* in ways that allowed for self-reflexive meditations on fiction's function. In an essay on blood purity in *Don Quijote*, Rachel L. Burk examines how *limpieza de sangre* works through a "discourse of metamateriality," which attends to the "material existence and semantic content" of "objects that signify," especially blood (27). This, Burk contends, evidences the fact that "[e]arly modern Iberia insistently attempted to transform the conceptual and the metaphorical into concrete realities" (27). For Burk, *limpieza de sangre* is exemplary of what Margaret Greer terms "the materializing instinct" (27).[13] Cervantes's treatment of blood purity in *Don Quijote* instantiates a critique of this so-called materializing instinct. Through a self-conscious exploration of fiction and textual materiality, Burk concludes that: "Cervantes ironizes the urge to make the metaphysical physical. He uses the play of fictionality of his novel to underline that blood purity is a rhetorical rather than fleshly reality, one produced and maintained by documents, not bodies" (29). Making similar claims about "La fuerza de la sangre," Amy Sheeran argues that "Cervantes asks us to dismantle the fiction of *limpieza de sangre* by dismantling the fiction he presents to us" (34). Paradoxically, Sheeran contends that it is precisely the "fiction of blood purity [that] allows the *novela* to cohere," making the novella and blood purity "mutually constitutive fictions" (58). If these foundational blood fictions lay bare the rhetorical workings of blood purity – going against the prevailing desire to materialize discourse – fiction, then, plays the work of exposure and truth telling.

The blood novels of late nineteenth-century Spain must be situated and examined in their historical moment. To begin, Labanyi's incisive claim that in the Spanish realist novel "modernity is constructed *as* representation" (*Gender and Modernization* 385; my emphasis). The realist novel, moreover, allows for the self-reflexive critique of modernity as representation, and by "commenting on the representation process that 'constructs' the nation, the realist novel [comments] on its own procedures" (385). The novel finds a fascinating correlate in finance. As Peter Brooks has argued, money "comes to represent representation itself" (*Realist Vision* 14). This is quite distinct in the case of Spain since, as Labanyi explains, the national bank abandoned the gold standard several decades (1883) ahead of its Northern European counterparts (*Gender and Modernization* 162). Thus, while there is still, in late nineteenth-century Spain, a "residual belief that money has an inherent value (that of its metal content)," there is also "an escalating awareness that it is an arbitrary sign whose value is purely relative" (391). That is, as money becomes detached from the gold standard, its value lies in solely its representational power. Like paper bills, then, realism becomes a potent fiction – one that tends to cohere around bodies deemed impure and feminine.

The uneasiness produced by the arbitrary value of signs – empty signifiers – helps explain the renewed fascination with blood and bloodlines in the cultural production of the Restoration. Clinging to bloodlines as a form of essence – a kind of truth of one's character and inalterable hereditary attributes – proves more meaningful than class designation, which relies on malleable, outward signs of identity. Blood purity, however, as in the times of Cervantes, relies on a faulty logic; it parades itself as an immutable essence, but it has no inherent value beyond its discursive function. In this way, it exhibits itself as a form of social currency, and not unlike the bank notes of modern Spain, it had the trappings of a valuable sign that lacked an internal referent. As the editors of the *Cultural Politics of Blood: 1500–1900* write: "Blood is both vital to our lives and obscured from our sight, visible only at times of injury or death; yet its unseen course under the skin allows it to transport a host of meanings that we attach to it" (Coles et al. 18). The invisibility of bloodlines – its ghostly materiality – allows for it to operate as a kind of phantom signifier. The notion of blood purity is a powerful fiction. Paradoxically, this very emptiness allows for its symbolic function while making it impossible to authenticate – hence we come back to how it participates in the imposition of control over women's bodies, or women consigned to the realm of the material.

The vacancy of symbolic blood gives way to a desire for the material as such. Thus, the persistence of ideology of blood purity in the realist novel, I argue, exhibits a yearning for something tangible through which to construct the modern nation. Anidjar trenchantly argues that as blood "becomes the marker, ultimately the substance, of the community, blood redefines and internally refashions the community – and the difference between communities. It bounds and defines an inside as if autonomously, independently" (67). Blood then becomes the invisible substance around which communities are constructed internally and against one another. In this way, we might think of Benedict Anderson's "imagined community" as discursively constructed but haunted by an unrelenting desire for the materiality that blood promises.

If blood novels narrate the corruption of bloodlines, the reading of realist fiction is also potentially an impure act: readers accept the terms of the narrative, which may lead them towards an unexpected object of identification or disorderly desire. Brooks contends that the realist novel provides "the sense of a parallel reality that can almost supplant our own" (*Realist Vision* 2). Indeed, the novel produces a reality that resembles but is not quite identical to, the reader's material and social reality. In that interstitial space of difference, the reader can slip into imaginative moments in which they can see a world that is familiar but somehow new – a world in which prostitutes are honourable, romantic love for a priest is legitimate, and women's sexual desire is a life-affirming force. The novel, therefore, has the capacity to change the course of the reader's perceived reality by impressing a fiction upon the reading subject and leaving its mark. The novel, in this way, contains the dangerous capacity to not only critique the norms of society, particularly those of gender and sexuality, but to perhaps alter them, in ways both intentional and unintentional.

The thick and complex manifestations of narrative and readerly fantasies, those iterations that are drenched in feeling and roused by desire, are also the stuff of realism. The blood novels I have identified here collectively illuminate how realism probes the performative aspect of gendered subjectivity on unsteady social terrain, simultaneously drawing attention to the material body as its condition of possibility. *Blood Novels* narrates the gap between the ideal of chastity, the scientific type, the performative reality of the subject-in-process, and the limits of subjectivity bounded by the fluid body. The subversive potential of novels is not, of course, unfettered, but it remains clear, as many scholars have observed, that its self-reflexive capacity – the ability to acknowledge its limitations and instability – and its lack of singular narration leaves it open to the possibility of interpretation, unexpected identification, resistance, and critique.

Mostly notably, for the purposes of this study, the novel reveals the obvious paradox of the ideology of blood purity; that is, the emphasis and trust placed in blood itself as an abstract ideal, the metaphorical substance of the pure. As such, blood figures as a ghostly sign – ethereal and haunted by its early modern past – that is mistaken for a hidden and precious object that itself appears to have no origins at all; it simply *is*. This tension between appearance and essence figures as a motif of the realist novel and also produces a crisis in value. Despite the realist novel's perceptive critique of impossible ideals, there still seems to remain a persistent and frustrated desire for some essential truth, some reassurance that not everything is constituted by pure surface and representation. To repeat the words of Maximiliano Rubín: "¿Qué más da que estén las botas con o sin betún? La que debe tener lustre es el alma, no el calzado" ("What difference does it make whether or not my boots are polished? What should shine is my soul, not my boots"; *FJ* IV 313; Moncy Gullón 651). While realism perceptively displays the dangers of a world constituted through essential truth and value, Maxi's frustration registers the opposite – that a reality increasingly constituted by untrustworthy appearances creates a feeling of disillusionment, a vacancy that cries out to be filled with luster.

The book comprises four main chapters organized in loose chronological order, followed by a brief coda. Chapter one, "The Colour of Blood: Racializing Illegitimacy in *Doña Luz*," begins by linking Juan Valera's treatment of illegitimacy with the under-explored colonial and orientalist imagery that saturates the narrative. Doña Luz, the novel's eponymous protagonist, embodies the epitome of pure Aryan beauty – she is blonde, blue-eyed, and fair-skinned – and yet she becomes a symbol of imperial alterity, called an oriental pearl, a *houri*, and a neophyte Indian. This anxious oscillation between Doña Luz's imperfect, aristocratic whiteness (a result of her illegitimate birth) and her Orientalist and colonial attributes, I argue, recalls the racial anxiety circulating throughout Spain during the second half of the nineteenth century, prompting Spaniards to look for "proof" of their whiteness through their lineage – in essence their blood. The question of legitimacy in the novel, then, uncovers a broader concern with the purity and therefore the legitimacy of Spanish whiteness. In an urgently needed postcolonial reading of this novel, I seek to show how racial alterity – wedded to blood – repeatedly slips into the narrative through alluring colonial and orientalist tropes – exposing the ambivalence towards an uncanny racial difference that Spaniards both desired and disavowed.

Chapter two, "From Blood to Flesh: Avowing Material Pleasure in *La Regenta*," explores the conflictive relationship between blood's determinism and the regulation of female sexuality, in essence the chastity bind. If, in *Doña Luz*, blood animates colonial and orientalist designations of racial alterity, in *La Regenta* blood reaches back into its early modern history. I begin by questioning the early modern–modern divide – characterized by Foucault as a shift from blood to sexuality. The novel's protagonist, Ana Ozores, internalizes the racialized rhetoric of blood by visualizing her obscure mother as a Moorish queen, while other characters suspect she would be deemed a non-Christian if tried by the Inquisition. While Doña Luz's impurities led her to subscribe to the futile rituals of hygiene (unable to make her truly clean), here, the chastity bind, evoking the lasting legacy of *limpieza de sangre*, captures Spain's difficult transition to modernity, reluctant to part with its early modern ideals. The administration of sexuality, a hallmark of modernity, ultimately fails to supplant blood-based identification as Ana wrestles with the misalignment between her stained aristocratic lineage and her chaste behaviour. Blood renders Ana's chaste comportment futile, but upon realizing this, she embraces her predetermined damnation and claims her "right" to pleasures of the flesh, once forbidden by the code of chastity.

Galdós's *La desheredada*, the focus of chapter three, "Social Blood: The Aesthetics of the Crowd in *La desheredada*," inverts the *chastity bind* as the novel's protagonist has no noble lineage (corrupted or otherwise) to speak of. Instead, the narrative explores the psyche of the beautiful Isidora Rufete in her journey through mental illness – a disability she has inherited from her father who lives in Leganés, Madrid's modern insane asylum. Here, the attachment to blood-based identity (the aristocracy) becomes associated with madness – and its only cure, I argue, is precisely what Isidora tries to avoid: physical contact with ordinary people. While throughout the narrative the protagonist persistently asserts her right to aristocratic privilege, all is momentarily suspended in an erotic encounter with a crowd of Republican protestors. The "social blood" of Republicans appears to temporarily cure her delusions of grandeur, but not long enough to save her entirely. Her madness ironically leads her to become a "public" woman, consumed by the city of Madrid.

Chapter four, "Transfusions: Queering Kinship in *Fortunata y Jacinta*," presents a social world that is divided between those who excessively bleed (the socially marginal characters) and those whose blood remains subcutaneous (members of elite families). Here, Galdós unsettles the chastity bind by restructuring the traditional family unit upon which bourgeois modernity depends. The working-class Fortunata bears an extramarital son with her lover Juanito, who fails to produce an heir with his wife and first cousin Jacinta. Jacinta's sterility becomes an extreme iteration of blood purity. Ultimately, the novel reveals that blood purity becomes untenable, turning on itself as it produces sterility. The future of the nation rests on the formation of queer kinship ties and the reconfiguration of the fictions of blood purity upon which they persisted. As the novel comes to a close, Fortunata on her deathbed – suffering from a hemorrhage no less – "bequeaths" her son to Jacinta, rather than Juanito, entering into a traditionally male-dominated gift economy by giving her rival the gift of blood. The two women, as the title unconsciously suggests – two stories of "wives" – are united in a queer blood bond just moments before Fortunata's life is drained of its vital fluid.

The book closes with a coda that meditates on the realist novel's persistent return to fragile corporeality. While these fallen women's bodies stand as symbols of tainted or otherwise common bloodlines, the very materiality of their bodies – rendered hypervisible – points to a kind of realness that gets lost in the discursive regime of blood purity, which deploys blood as a phantom signifier. My final reflections in this coda contribute to theoretical interventions from new feminist materialists who seek to recover the materiality of the body and nature. This body of scholarship emerges in response to the discursive-linguistic turn in feminist and gender theory, which provides an inadequate account of the body's agentic capacity and material properties. While new feminist materialism, at times, risks treating the sexed body as a universal category, this book attends to the historical and cultural specificity of the bleeding body – looking at the ways it is rendered more or less precarious by gender, caste, and race. These blood novels, which emerge in a tumultuous period of modernization, imperial decline, and social upheaval, lay forth timely reflections on the discursive nature of identity and the cultural inscription of the body. They do this, moreover, while making apparent the material reality that exceeds representation and the linguistic devices that comprise it. Spanish realism, then, which presents a world of seemingly tangible things construed through mimesis, powerfully reflects on the limits of its world-making mechanisms in the face of life's socially determined precarity.

Chapter One

The Colour of Blood: Racializing Illegitimacy in *Doña Luz*

I am white, in other words,
I embody beauty and virtue,
which have never been black.
I am the color of day.

Franz Fanon, Black Skin, White Masks

Blood. Race. For some critics, these terms remain sequential to one another, the former indexing medieval and early modern notions of caste identity and the latter invoking modern, pseudo-scientific formulations of biologized (phenotypical, epidermal, etc.) difference. By examining the entwinement of colonial racial discourse and the ideology of blood purity, this chapter takes as its starting point the premise that "the history of blood ideologies in early modern Spain and the Iberian Atlantic world ... belongs as much to the global history of early modern colonialism as it does to that of race and racism" (Hering Torres et al. "Editorial" 2). In this sense, I also draw from Ann Laura Stoler's critical reading of *History of Sexuality*, in which she connects the preoccupation with blood purity in Europe to racial hierarchies in the colonies: "The myth of blood that pervades nineteenth-century racism may be traced, as Foucault does, from an aristocratic preoccupation with legitimacy, pure blood, and descent, but not through it alone. It was equally dependent on an imperial politics of exclusion that was worked out earlier and reworked later on colonial ground" (50). Rather than treat blood purity and racial hierarchy as disparate regimes of social ordering, the present chapter attends to their points of convergence.

In thinking about the specific historicity of "difference" in Spain, Joshua Goode warns of the pitfalls in connecting the "racial thinking" of the fifteenth and sixteenth centuries to that of the nineteenth and twentieth, likening this "Isabella to Franco" trajectory to what he considers the tautological "Luther to Hitler" model (11–12). Max S. Hering Torres takes a middle ground approach as he questions "racism as a linear process (from purity of blood to the Holocaust) without historical differentiations (the racism of modernism as equal to colonial racism)" and rejects the approaches of decolonial scholars Walter Mignolo and Aníbal Quijano (13). At the same time, Hering Torres sees the necessity to "revise the positions which deny any form of racialization before the rise of modernity" ("Purity of Blood" 35). To be clear, I do not mean to simply equate blood with race, nor to assume there is a teleological linearity from one regime to the other. Rather, what becomes clear in the cultural landscape of modern Spain, of which *Doña Luz* is one prime example, is that the discourse of blood melds with a colonial racial rhetoric in rather untidy ways, demonstrating that blood and race are less ideologically distinct than we would like them to be. In this way, my work is informed by Stoler, who, drawing on Foucault, contends that "[r]ace as a concept performs in a mobile field. It animates vacillating discourses with dynamic motility. Racial lexicons accumulate recursively, producing new racial truths as they requisition and reassemble old ones" ("Racial Regimes" 250). The methodological significance of looking at the domestic impact of Spanish colonialism remains at the heart of this chapter. In his essay "What Does the Black Legend Have to Do with Race?" Water Mignolo argues that race in the Spanish Empire is not an "invention" of the Enlightenment in Northern European countries, as is sometimes assumed. Instead "when the secular and scientific discourse on race (which covered up racism as ideology) was formed in the nineteenth century, the conceptual frame had already been in place since the Renaissance" (312). For his part, George Mariscal argues that racially inflected concepts of religious orthodoxy in pre- and early modern Spain already constituted what Michael Omi and Howard Winant famously term "racial formation," typically attributed to European colonization in the Americas.[1] In other words, for Mignolo and Mariscal, the racial classification of Spain's colonial enterprise, sprang, at least in part, from an earlier framework that originated in Europe.

Rather than insist on blood and race as hermetically sealed ideologies and sequential modes of social ordering, I am interested in how the language of blood purity persists even as it gets mottled, finding an altered afterlife in the nineteenth century when the so-called modern racial schema takes shape through the Spanish colonial enterprise.[2] Here, I diverge from Goode, who, in his otherwise illuminating monograph *Impurity of Blood*, problematically suggests that human variation in Spain's American colonies shaped the need for racial hierarchy, thereby naturalizing the arbitrary set of somatic signs that constitute racial categories. Goodes writes: "The Spanish used different racial rhetoric on the peninsula than in the overseas colonies, where obvious physical differences in appearance did exist and conditioned the unfolding of racial ideas … Clearly the ethnic mix of Spain did not warrant a racial classification system so reliant on physical differences in appearance" (13). Tending to, perhaps to a fault, the historical specificity of these different racial regimes, Goode marshals "obvious physical differences in appearance" to posit that intra-peninsular racial thinking was – by necessity – ideologically divorced from that of Spain's colonial enterprise.

What we see in Juan Valera's *Doña Luz* (1879), by contrast, is the striking convergence of the two. Pure origins and wealth are markers of aristocratic identity. But the vestiges of early modern blood-based hierarchies converge with the contemporary reality of a colonial racial order. Set in a fictional town in rural Andalusia in the aftermath of the Spanish–Moroccan War, the plot centres on the beautiful Doña Luz, the illegitimate daughter of a deceased marquis and an unknown mother who is believed to have been of humble origins. Luz lives her life accordingly – the shame she feels for her tainted blood leads her to disavow her maternal lineage. Such a disavowal often expresses itself as reverence towards her father's surname, a pronounced phobia of the poor, and a marked obsession with corporeal hygiene.

Befittingly, Doña Luz exhibits the typical traits of Aryan beauty: blonde hair, blue eyes, luminescent skin. Luz's whiteness, however, is far from stable. The rather unconventional but poignant twist Valera incorporates into the narrative aesthetic is Luz's subsequent racialization as non-white: she is likened to an American Indian, an Annamite, and the Queen of the Amazons. She is even referred to as an oriental pearl, the phrase commonly used to denote the Philippines. The inconsistencies in Doña Luz's identity create a suspicion about her whiteness, suggesting that it is only skin deep. That Luz's whiteness is not self-evident attests to the power of invisible bloodlines and the untrustworthiness of visual signs of racial identity. The novel deploys a colonial racial rhetoric precisely to discredit her whiteness and, by extension, her purity.

Commenting on the history of whiteness in the Iberian context, Hering Torres has noted that the concept was consolidated in the colonial context: "the 'non-white' turned into a synonym for impurity; the 'white' for purity and prestige" ("Purity of Blood" 25). Indeed, the tension between these two identificatory regimes – blood and race – hinges on a question of purity. The narrative employs a racial vocabulary and orientalist tropes to represent socially marginalized Spanish characters, especially those deemed impure in some way: Spaniards who either attempt to dangerously assimilate or are otherwise likened to the colonized subjects of the Indies. This inverted movement of racial discourse – that is, a Spanish author framing a white-presenting Spanish character through racialized colonial and orientalist tropes – may be best understood as, to borrow Parama Roy's formulation, the complex "traffic" of colonial identities. Homi Bhabha conceives of mimicry from the bottom up – the colonized subject as the mimic man who never fully inhabits European whiteness – while Roy, by contrast, complicates Bhabha's formulation of colonial mimicry by exploring a diverse range of colonial identities that take shape through the relationship between originality and impersonation.[3] For Roy, this includes, for example, the nineteenth-century English fascination with "going native." For Bhabha, the colonial mimic man is a split, ambivalent subject, *a subject of a difference that is almost the same, but not quite* (122; emphasis in original). Rethinking Roy and Bhabha's work in the context of Spain, we might say that these characters' dangerous affinities with colonial subjects render these Spaniards *almost white, but not quite.*

In examining the ties between blood, race, and illegitimacy, the focus of this chapter will be the illegitimate daughter – Doña Luz – and her relationship with two colonial authorities: a missionary priest and a military captain. The most troubled women in nineteenth-century Spanish novels are those of socially ambiguous position – of which illegitimacy is one illustrative example; their very existence is the product of a taboo boundary crossing. Paul Smith has demonstrated that illegitimacy works as a powerful and decisive motif in Juan Valera's novels. Smith argues that Spanish literature – citing Cervantes as a notable example – has long exhibited a preoccupation with illegitimacy, but nowhere is this more pronounced than in the corpus of Valera's novels in which its impacts "become for the first time an important key to character development and a basic structure of an author's novelistic world" (804). While Smith is right to assert the significance of illegitimacy in Valera's novels and makes important connections with Cervantes's oeuvre, he elides a significant feature of this socially stigmatized status: its historical linkage with *limpieza de sangre* (blood purity).

Blood purity statutes historically required both old Christian ancestry and legitimate birth. Cervantes's *El retablo de maravillas* serves as a particularly compelling illustration of their ideological entwinement. A riff on the familiar tale of the *Emperor's New Clothes*, *El retablo* tells the story of two swindlers who put on a show that only those of legitimate birth and free of Jewish *converso* blood ("sangre de confeso") will be able to see. To all others it will remain invisible. The status of the bastard and the Jewish *converso* therefore are located on the same plane of social marginality, both marked by the taint of their unclean blood. *El retablo de maravillas* exposes the collective performance that allows for *limpieza de sangre*'s discursive power to cohere as a powerful fiction, and the culture of constant vigilance and suspicion that it spurs.

In light of this powerful literary antecedent, it is fitting that we consider the ways in which legitimacy in *Doña Luz* engages with the history of *limpieza de sangre*. Through my analysis of the concept in the narrative, I argue that both race and sexuality hinge on a concept of legitimacy as a modern iteration of blood purity. What is more, the ideology of blood purity that haunts Luz's unrelenting obsession with the fictive story of her origin cannot be understood in isolation from the novel's colonial backdrop, which has long been ignored in the criticism.

Given Juan Valera's long career in politics and diplomacy, it is unsurprising that empire and colonialism prove central to the novel's depiction of illegitimacy. In *Doña Luz*, *limpieza* becomes gnarled with colonial and orientalist racial tropes as the protagonist develops illicit feelings for Padre Enrique, an ailing missionary priest repatriated from the Philippines, only to later marry Don Jaime, a dubious military hero from the Spanish–Moroccan War. This notable amorous trajectory imparts a powerful story of conquest (by religion and by military force), propelled by an anxiety around the purity of the Spanish race and the legitimacy of its diminished empire. Indeed, Luz's quest for identity – marred by her origins – becomes entwined with the history of Spanish Empire, its aspirations and failures alike.

In this light, it is imperative to attend to the colonial overtones of the narrative, which inflect the novel's treatment of illegitimacy. Akiko Tsuchiya has commented that: "[t]he Spanish nation's anxieties over imperial loss and its sense of belated progress toward 'modernity' vis-à-vis the rest of Western Europe were exacerbated by the destabilization of established notions of social identity, including gender identity, at the end of the century" (6). The colonial and orientalist discourses that operate in this novel will therefore be fundamental to our understanding of how blood merges with a narrative of sexual and racial purity. To this end, I will argue that legitimacy bespeaks a notion of whiteness rooted in blood purity, while illegitimacy is likened to the racialized alterity of the colonial other. More broadly, this linkage between blood and legitimacy provides key insights into the anxiety around Spain's own racial legitimacy as Europe's peripheral nation. The Black Legend – a widely disseminated Northern narrative that cast the Spanish Empire as excessively cruel and racially inferior – provides a necessary historical anchor to the undercurrent of racial anxiety in the novel. Thus, Doña Luz's stain, I argue, emblematizes Spain's historical reputation as "a figure of contamination from which other kingdoms were to protect themselves" (Anidjar 76). As Susan Martin-Márquez put it: "The Black Legend made it impossible for Spain to escape the association with uncivilized otherness. Spaniards' obsession with blood purity was obvious proof of their impurity" (41). The enticingly beautiful, white-presenting, illegitimate daughter of a marquis displaced to rural Andalusia allegorizes this problem: Spain's legitimacy writ large in the eyes of Northern Europe.

Placing Race

In recovering the traces of empire that inflect an ideology of blood purity in *Doña Luz*, my methodological approach draws from the influential work of Edward Said and Gayatri Spivak. Their postcolonial readings of Victorian literature expose the novelistic structures of feeling that buttress British imperial power. Spivak reminds us that "[i]t should not be possible to read nineteenth-century British literature without remembering that imperialism, understood as England's social mission, was a crucial part of the cultural representation of England to the English. The role of literature in the production of cultural representation should not be ignored" (243). Edward Said goes one step further with the following provocation: "Without empire, I would go so far as saying, there is no European novel as we know it, and indeed if we study the impulses giving rise to it, we shall see that far from accidental the convergence between the patterns of narrative authority constitutive of the novel on the one hand, and, on the other, a complex ideological configuration underlying the tendency to imperialism" (*Culture* 69–70). Together, these interventions have spurred critical inquiries into how colonialism undergirds the fictional worlds of the European novel and the politics that make the novel possible.

Iberian studies scholars have recently begun to examine the impact of colonialism in nineteenth-century cultural production. Two notable collective volumes have paved the way for such analyses. *Empire's End: Transnational Connections in the Hispanic World*, edited by Akiko Tsuchiya and William G. Acree Jr., has broken new ground by exploring the geographically wide-ranging and enduring cultural impact of Spanish imperialism in the long nineteenth century.[4] N. Michelle Murray and Akiko Tsuchiya's more recent edited volume *Unsettling Colonialism* has further expanded this field of inquiry by privileging the study of gender in modern Spanish colonial discourse, which has long been androcentric in its approach. Colonial geopolitics, as I have elsewhere argued, plays a crucial role in the structuring of narrative fiction from Cervantes to the realist novel of *fin-de-siglo* Spain. Indeed, the realist novel attempted to grapple with the cultural and political significance of Spain's colonies – the so-called "provincias de ultramar" (overseas provinces) – vis-à-vis the emergent nation (Chang "Between Intimacy and Enmity"). Presently, however, no such studies have advanced a critical examination of colonial discourse in *Doña Luz*.

Evangelization projects in Asia and the Spanish–Moroccan War loom in the background of the novel, said to be Valera's favourite among his own works (Bauer "Introduction" 13). In addition to these historical anchors, the novel registers the traffic of people and goods to and from the Philippines and North Africa, creating a form of symbolic proximity between these colonial spaces and the national periphery, i.e., rural Andalusia. This in turn challenges the assumption that the regional novel, growing out of *costumbrismo*, simply documents local customs. Alison Sinclair maintains that regional novels "communicate a type of cultural myopia that restricts the concept of viable life to regional boundaries" ("The Regional Novel" 53). However, the cosmopolitan aspect of the *patria chica* (home province) in Valera's novel paints a complex image of Spain as an imperial nation comprising multiple spatial and social alterities.

In the novel, Luz is a paradoxical figure. At first glance, she is depicted like so many other nineteenth-century Spanish heroines as "casta" (chaste), "limpia" (clean), and "pura" (pure). She is even purity incarnate: "Doña Luz era en todo la pulcritud personificada" ("Doña Luz was pulchritude personified in everything"; *Doña Luz* 56; Fedorchek 30). These various iterations of purity, make Luz – "the color of day" (Fanon 27) – the epitome of white femininity. Admittedly, talking about whiteness in nineteenth-century Spanish novels is tricky business. The category white (*blanco/a*), for one, is never explicitly named in Valera's novel. But as the epigraph from Fanon illustrates, whiteness can emerge obliquely, operating as a taken-for-granted quality inherent to other qualifiers, such as beautiful, chaste, and clean. Whiteness is both an essential and yet ethereal aspect in such markers of identity. In *The Mirage of an Unmarked Whiteness*, Ruth Frankenberg, in a different context, writes that "'whiteness' is positioned asymmetrically in relation to all other racial and cultural terms, again for reasons whose origins are colonial" (75). "This indeed is why," Frankenberg explains, "it becomes extraordinarily difficult for white people to name whiteness, and why whiteness has a habit – annoying for those who are trying to name it – of sliding into class and nationality all the time. Indeed, it is for the same reason that even words like 'humanity' and 'Man' (uppercase 'M') are very easily elided into whiteness, thus giving it the appearance of being unbounded" (75). Whiteness in *Doña Luz*, at first glance, appears to have this elusive quality – it is self-evident, remaining unnamed as it "slides" into other qualifiers, like "pulcritud" (cleanliness).

Valera's narrator goes to great lengths to paint Doña Luz as exhibiting qualities of a white, feminine ideal. In a passage that evokes the visual tropes of baroque verbal portraiture, the narrator describes the protagonist as a stunning blonde beauty, reflecting the pure, virtuous qualities symbolized by her name:

> Doña Luz era un sol que estaba en el cenit. Gallarda y esbelta, tenía toda la amplitud, robustez y majestad que son compatibles con la elegancia de formas de una doncella llena de distinción aristocrática. La salud brillaba en sus frescas y sonrosadas mejillas; la calma, en su cándida y tersa frente, coronada de rubios rizos; la serenidad del espíritu, en sus ojos azules, donde cierto fulgor apacible de caridad y de sentimientos piadosos suavizaba el ingénito orgullo. (57)

> Doña Luz was a sun that shone in magnificent splendor. Graceful and slender, she possessed all the fullness, strength, and majesty compatible with the elegance of a young woman imbued with aristocratic distinction. Health glowed on her fresh, rosy cheeks; calm distinguished her smooth, candid brow, which was crowned with blond curls; and a serenity of spirit radiated from her blue eyes, which softened an innate pride with gentle light and pious sentiments. (31)

The luminous Luz embodies a kind of Northern European fantasy, standing out with aristocratic distinction in this rustic southern town. Her "candid brow" ("cándida frente") is another example of how whiteness gets conflated with positive qualifiers. "Blanco" is the first definition listed for the term "cándido" ("candid") in an 1869 dictionary (*DRAE*), stemming from the Latin *candidus* ("bright white"). It also conveys a sense of simplicity and innocence. While physical features operate as the outward signs of white, feminine beauty, Doña Luz's stained bloodlines betray her appearance – making her imperfect, in a word, illegitimate. Thus, Luz's *apparent* whiteness becomes a complex site of racial anxiety and ambivalent desire, stirring suspicion vis-à-vis a reality constituted primarily by appearance or, to adopt Jo Labanyi's words, "women's conversion into representation" (415).

Almost White, but Not Quite

Doña Luz inherits the stigma of her parents' illicit affair. A pure and revered figure in terms of her comportment and beauty, Luz remains nonetheless stained by birth. Consequently, she finds herself caught in the chastity bind: considered *casta* (chaste) because she is morally pure and physically clean ("se complacía más en este que podemos llamar aseo moral y corpóreo" ["she always attended to and took pleasure in what we might call corporeal and moral purity"; *Doña Luz* 56; Fedorchek 30]) but not *castiza* (of good origin and without mixing). Her character is pulled by these conflicting iterations of purity, anxiously oscillating from one to the other throughout the narrative. Her humbled status as a *doña* (a lady) as opposed to a marchioness positions her in an unfixed in-between state, unwilling to completely forgo the class status of her father while never fully belonging to it. In her own words: "Casi estoy fuera de toda clase social" ("It is as though I didn't belong to any social class"; 90; 56). Doña Luz at first takes full advantage of this fluid space and her financial circumstances, choosing to remain single for much longer than is appropriate. But ultimately her tainted origin and illegitimacy become sources of anxiety that disturb her sense of self and confuse her rank in society.

Attempting to maintain a respectable life and reputation in her town, Luz works excessively to maintain her status as *casta* (chaste) precisely because she is not *castiza* (of good origin). The story of her origin functions as an obdurate social stain, a gnawing reminder that she cannot escape the shadow of her mother's class and the licentiousness of her unwed parents. Here, the polyvalent word *casta* operates as the social yardstick of which Doña Luz is always reminded. She engages in fetishistic cleansing rituals. Luz desires to be pure and clean to an extreme, the narrator explains:

> La misma impureza de su origen, el vicio de su nacimiento, la humilde condición de su desconocida madre, obraban por reacción en su ánimo y casi convertían su orgullo en fiereza. Para limpiar aquella mancha original, quería ser doña Luz mucho más limpia y mucho más pura. (60)

> The very taint of her lineage, the dishonor of her birth, the humble status of her unknown mother, effected a reaction in her spirit and nearly converted her pride into hauteur. To wipe away that original stain Doña Luz wanted to be that much more clean and pure. (33)

Cleansing her "stain," however, proves futile because her origin story cannot be altered by her desire to be pure; ignoble origins operate as a permanent defect.

The narrator construes Doña Luz's origin in terms of original sin, "aquella mancha original" ("that original stain"), suggesting that she is a fallen subject from birth – of which she ought not to be proud, pride being the original sin in biblical terms. This aligns Doña Luz with Eve, the first to commit the deadly sin of pride. And pride, the narrator tells us, will ultimately lead to her downfall. In fact, Luz's pride is described as a kind of "ferocity" (*fiereza*), one that evokes an animality that will later come into view.[5] Illegitimacy requires the performance of humility, yet such a performance is ironically the source of her pride. Framing her illegitimacy as an original stain, moreover, evokes the discourse of *limpieza de sangre*; her precarious social status is determined by her inalterable lineage and further amplified by her gender.

The irony at play here is the fact that the story of her origin is fabricated, which letters from her father will later expose. While Luz's status of illegitimacy remains unchanged, she discovers that her mother was an aristocrat (albeit an adulterer), and Luz the sole heir to her fortune. All along Luz had disavowed her mother's alleged social class, believing (and leading the reader to believe) that she was of humble origins. But ultimately, Luz's social stain stems from her unchanged status as the bastard daughter of a marquis. Luz's deceased mother – the Countess of Fajalauza – is a highly paradoxical figure herself; she is of noble origins but sullied by her licentious sexuality as an adulterer. We might view the countess as the inverse of Luz: legitimate but unchaste. Licentiousness begets illegitimacy. One social stain engenders another.

Crucially, before this news is revealed, the falsified story of Luz's origin, conjured by her father to protect her from money-hungry suitors, is treated as fact. It is not only that Doña Luz and all those who surround her are led to believe this story within the novel. The narrator is also implicated in this narrative deception – showing the powerful reach of the fiction of bloodlines. That Doña Luz's origin story reveals itself to be precisely that – a story – reveals the limits of blood's discursive power, and harking back to Cervantes, the powerful "juridical fictions" of *limpieza de sangre* from which it extends (Martínez 61). Even though the social construction of identity and status is produced through shared stories (gossip, oral histories, letters, memory, reputation) it is the written word – crucially, that of the patriarch (i.e., posthumous letters from her father) and of the law (i.e., her mother's will) – that remains binding, evidencing that not all forms of narrative carry the same weight.

Competing fictions throughout the novel produce material consequences that affect Luz's anxieties and life choices. In the first part of the novel, Doña Luz performs humility, painfully aware of her impure origin. Several wealthy relatives of her father invite her to come live at their estates in Madrid and Seville, but she rejects these offers, not wanting to incur any debts. Instead, she accepts her simpler, semi-independent life in rural Villafría: "Su plan era vivir y morir oscuramente en Villafría" ("Her intention was to live and die in obscurity in Villafría"; *Doña Luz* 60; Fedorchek 33). What is more, despite the fact that her father made legal arrangements to transfer his aristocratic title to her, thus making her a *marquesa* (marquise), the difficulties of truly embodying this social category by marrying an aristocrat lead her to refuse the title. The narrator presents these actions, not as motivated by humility but once again by excessive pride: "[E]l orgullo de doña Luz se velaba y envolvía en el más discreto disimulo, y esto no sólo por prudencia y por interés propio, sino por vivo sentimiento de caridad" ("Doña Luz's pride was cloaked in the most discreet reserve, and this was not only out of prudence and self-interest, but out of a keen sense of charity"; 71; 42).

Financially impoverished for her social status, Luz must decide between marrying for the sake of avoiding the dreaded status of *soltera* (an unmarried woman) or, in her view, remain single so as not to further sully her father's name. Luz would likely have to "marry down," assuming her lack of wealth and the perceived inferior social category of her mother. The narrator suspects that Luz's greatest fear is giving birth to a child of a lower social status, thus forever damaging her father's bloodlines:

> Alguien podría sospechar pero no probar su invencible repugnancia a todo lo vulgar y plebeyo, y el horror que de ella se apoderaba la sola idea de poder un día tener un hijo que llevase su ilustre apellido en pos de otro apellido oscuro y rústico de algún ricacho villano. (*Doña Luz* 59)

> Someone might suspect, but not be able to prove, her insuperable aversion to everything commonplace and plebeian, and the horror that gripped her at the mere thought of one day having a child who would bear her illustrious surname following the obscure, rustic one of some rich villager. (Fedorchek 32)

Luz reviles the idea of bearing the child of a peasant father – a displacement of the hatred for her own supposed mixed lineage and the seamstress whom she imagines to be her mother – fearing she may further mar the lustre of her father's good name: "Tenía talento, estaba obligada a cultivarle; era bella y fuerte, necesitaba conservar su fuerza y su hermosura; había recibido un nombre ilustre, y, ya que no acertase a ilustrarle más, no debía mancharle" ("She had talent and was obliged to develop it; she was beautiful and strong, and needed to preserve her strength and her beauty; she had inherited an illustrious name, and if she did not add more luster to it, then at the very least she should not sully it"; 71; 41). Luz's fear of contagion – as if her proximity to poverty might further bring out her mother's status she so wishes to suppress – is exemplified by the self-serving limits of her so-called philanthropy: "su filantropía no podía extenderse a más que a dar la mano a los que estuviesen en condiciones de trepar hasta donde estaba ella, y no a aquellos que estaban tan bajos o tan hundidos en el lodo, que en vez de alzarlos, se dejaría ella arrastrar cayendo en el lodo también" ("her altruism [philanthropy] could only consist of giving a helping hand to those who were in a position to climb where she was, and not to those who were so far down or mired in mud that instead of raising them up, she would be dragged down into the mud herself"; 71; 41–2).[6]

Caste differentiation remains at the heart of Luz's vision of social ordering. The narrator recounts Luz's odd interpretation of a democratic society:

> La democracia optimista y sana consiste, sin duda, en creer que la mayor educación desde la primera infancia, el buen ejemplo y nombre de padres y abuelos, la obligación de no deshonrar ni deslustrar este buen nombre, y el vivir en medio más urbano y culto, deben ser espuela de incentivo eficaz para ser virtuosos, o discretos, o seductores, o dignos, o todo a la vez. (70)

> A healthy and optimistic democratic spirit consists, undoubtedly, in believing that the best education from infancy, the good example and the good name of parents and grandparents, the obligation not to dishonor or tarnish this good name, and living in a more urbane, cultured milieu should be spur and incentive enough to be virtuous, or discreet, or charming, or worthy, or all these qualities at once. (40)

By Luz's own standards, she must behave differently from women of lower social status: "la hija de un marqués, por ejemplo, aun cuando sea bastarda, debe conducirse mejor que la hija de un pelafustán" ("the daughter of a marquis, for example, even when she is illegitimate, should conduct herself better than the daughter of a ne'er-do-well"; 70; 40). Viewed in this way, Doña Luz's illegitimacy operates as a social disease that crosses boundaries and reveals the porosity of these purportedly discrete categories. This disavowal of her perceived working-class heritage demonstrates Luz's unrelenting desire for the containment and the (impossible) erasure of her maternal social taint. Here, illegitimacy enacts a disciplinary function that is at times at odds with the gendered codes of domesticity that would value marriage and motherhood over the life of a *soltera*.

Interestingly, the narrator attempts to distance himself from Luz's political vision, defensively noting: "No es lo que escribo un tratado de filosofía política. No intento tampoco presentar a doña Luz como un dechado de excelencias, sino presentarla tal como ella fue" ("I am not writing a treatise on political philosophy, nor am I trying to present Doña Luz as a model of various kinds of excellence, just to present her as she really was"; 71; 41). But the fact that these views are mediated by the narrator, rather than presented as Luz's inner thoughts, reveals a fascinating conflation of the narrator's voice with Luz's world view and subsequently a kind of ambivalence towards her attachment to bloodlines. Indeed, if the fiction of the protagonist's origin dictates her behaviour and informs her sense of self, the narrator – far from immune – is also infected by this powerful fiction. As we shall see, the narrative descriptions of Luz are replete with colonial and orientalist imagery.

The imperial backdrop of the novel adds a layer of complexity to the novel's diverse expressions of purity – *castidad* (chastity), *casta* (caste), and *castizo/a* (origin) – that remain overlooked in the scholarship.[7] While the novel's narrator stays anchored in the peninsula, people, objects, and ideas from Asia and the Americas abound, forging a kind of intimacy between Spain, Asia, and Africa.[8] The colonial spaces that figure into the novel remain at the diegetic edge of the narrative, emanating a distant, unknowable quality and metonymically reproducing the idea of the colonies and of the Orient as strange, exploitable, and exotic yet available for consumption.

If Doña Luz's impure blood is a site of shame, it also operates as a source of racialized allure. While embodying all the visual characteristics of European whiteness, the narrator positions Doña Luz as an object of a masculine imperial gaze and paradoxically fashions Luz as a beautiful woman from a distant, exotic land. It is the combination of her illegitimate status and beauty, I argue, that easily align Doña Luz as the exotic other. The narrative fascination with female exoticism squares with Juan Valera's reputation as a diplomat, whose work evidently entailed amorous liaisons with foreign women. In 1925 – Juan Valera's centenary – the Marquis of Villarrutia delivered a commemorative speech in which he noted that:

El diplomático era, a su juicio, un hombre de mundo, enviado a recorrer lejanas tierras y a cultivar el trato de extrañas gentes, refinadas y cultas, entre las cuales merecían siempre preferente atención, por se las más dignas de estudio, las pertenecientes al sexo femenino. (146)

The diplomat was, in his view, a man of the world, sent to traverse distant lands and cultivate treaties with refined and cultured foreign peoples, among whom those that pertained to the female sex always deserved preferential attention for being the worthiest of study.

Doña Luz is an aristocratic "cultured" beauty even as qualities of animality, Greek mythology, coloniality, and otherworldliness betray her conspicuous whiteness: "Cuando quería, bailaba como una sílfide; en el andar airoso, semejaba a la divina cazadora de Delos, y montaba a caballo como reina de las amazonas" ("When she wanted to, she danced like a sylph; in her airy step she resembled the divine huntress of Delos; and she rode horseback like the queen of the Amazons"; *Doña Luz* 57; Fedorchek 31). This description exhibits a narrative dissonance between her Aryan appearance and her physical strength and agility, which, likened to that of Artemis, the Greek goddess of the hunt, or Hippolyta, queen of the Amazons, exceed the bounds of aristocratic whiteness. The young men in the town are completely enchanted by the mythologized Luz, and they too see her as an exotic creature: "Doña Luz parecía una garza real, una emperatriz, una heroína de leyendas y de cuentos fantásticos; algo de peregrino y de fuera de lo que se usa; el hada de Parabanú; la más egregia de las huríes" ("Doña Luz looked like a black-crested heron, an empress, a heroine of legends and fantastic tales, something strange and exotic, the fairy of Parabanú, the most illustrious of houris"; 58; 31). The motley assemblage of exotic animals alongside colonial and mythical figures finally crescendos with the references to Arab and Islamic icons.

The Fairy of Pari-Banou comes from the tale "Prince Ahmed and the Fairy Pari-Banou," translated by Antoine Galland from Arabic to French and appearing in *Les Milles et Une Nuits* in 1714.[9] In this story, the fairy of Pari-Banou is an exceptionally beautiful and powerful superbeing who marries Prince Ahmed and helps him overthrow his father's (the sultan) empire. Johnson, Maxwell, and Trumpener in their study of *The Nights* and European fiction observe that "[i]n its sexual explicitness and unfettered sensuality, its tableaux of lust and sexual coercion, *The Nights* shaped pornographic fantasies ... In a nominally Christian Europe ... men fantasize about Eastern-style domestic despotism, male sexual dominance, and female surrender" (256). Hence Valera, too, figures in this tradition of the European novelist who creates sexual fantasies with characters from *The Nights*. Ironically, however, from the northern European perspective (specifically in eighteenth-century French writing), *The Nights* were commonly linked with Spain, seen by the French as a southern land of exoticism and desire (Johnson et al. 258). The juxtaposition of these foreign (and yet not so foreign) images can, on one hand, show a lack of coherence in the narrative depiction of Doña Luz. Yet, as Hélène Gill contends: "Orientalist discourse, and the representations which derive from it, are never ... entirely coherent. Gaps and contradictions are, in any case, inherent discursive formations" (13).

Spain has a particularly contradictory history of representing the so-called Orient. Juan Torres-Pou, in his study on Valera's late novel *Morsamor* (1889), writes that the Orient for Spaniards symbolized a "distant but still very alive past ... the hidden other repressed by historical circumstance" ("The Exotic as Subversive" 254). The effect of this is that, in Spanish literature, "Oriental exoticism" figures as "simultaneously strange and familiar, new and ordinary" (254). The novel's characterization of Luz – she embodies white, aristocratic ideals of Northern Europe while she is simultaneously characterized by her seductive, Orientalized exoticism – exemplifies this contradictory stance. In a rather poignant moment in the novel, la Filigrana – a Romani woman (*gitana*) who fries *buñuelos* in front of Don Acisclo's house – describes Doña Luz as "una perla oriental" ("an Oriental pearl"; *Doña Luz* 181; Fedorchek 124). And "la perla" ("the pearl") she goes on to say "no repara en el pescador" ("takes no notice of the fisherman"; 181; 124) – a comment on Luz's refusal to marry a man of humble origins. In this highly ironic moment, it is the socially marginalized *gitana* who casts Luz as racially other by calling her "Oriental." The pearl, moreover, is an apt feminine metaphor; it represents a lustrous, commodified whiteness – too valuable for the lowly fisherman. But juxtaposed with the modifier "oriental," Luz the oriental pearl comes to signify at once the strange and the familiar that must be plucked from its conch and possessed. Notably, the Philippines, under Spanish colonial rule, was commonly referred to as "la perla del Oriente." In reflecting on this charged metaphor, it is useful to bring in Anne Cheng's theoretical framework of ornamentalism – a supplement to Edward Said's theory of Orientalism – which provides a brilliant account of how in the Western imagination Asiatic femininity underwrites aesthetic personhood.[10] "Since antiquity," Cheng writes, "the ornament has almost always been associated, even downright identified, with the Oriental and the Asiatic" (15). Simultaneously elevated and objectified, Luz as the Oriental pearl recalls what Cheng terms "the yellow woman" (14). She is "neither mere flesh nor mere thing" but a being who "[straddles] the person-thing divide" (14).

"As a figure of artistic investment and racial denigration," Cheng continues, "the yellow woman bears the privileges as well as the penalties for being an aesthetic being" (16). Luz, once again, becomes a site of ambivalence, likened to a pearl – an ornament – for her luminescent whiteness, and yet positioned as the racialized Orient.

The juxtaposition of whiteness and the Oriental is not an uncommon pairing, Susan Martin-Márquez observes: "[in] Orientalist pictorial conventions … curiously, the 'exotic' object of desire is nearly always figured as white" (134). While many scholars have argued that whiteness in the Orientalist tradition comes to represent passivity and submissiveness, Martin-Márquez adds that: "the construction of this figure [the odalisque] as white facilitates her metaphorical consumption by European viewers, since she is aligned with a 'safer' form of difference – only the superficial accoutrements of architecture, interior décor, jewelry, and when present costume signal her as other" (134). In the case of Doña Luz, we have no visual accoutrements that point to her otherness. She does not don, for example, Orientalist habiliment or appear against the ornate decor found in the paintings of the Catalan artist Mariano Fortuny. In fact, she does nothing to perform this identity. It is the narrator, exploiting the fiction of her origins, and other characters in the narrative that project this fantasy onto Doña Luz, grafting a seductive image of racial alterity onto the status of her "mixed" blood. Luz is not adorned with ornamental pearls; she *is* the ornamental/Oriental pearl. In this way, Luz's whiteness departs from that of the *odalisque*. She does not present a "safe" form of consumption for the Spanish reader. Instead, the juxtaposition of her Aryan beauty and orientalist metaphors points to an anxiety around this hidden other – the repressed, latent Orient inherent to Spain's imperial history. Like the pearl of the Orient, Luz's whiteness functions as a lustrous, tantalizing veneer that overlays but fails to whitewash her obdurate stain. As such, the narrator and other characters exoticize her aesthetic whiteness, revealing it to be fraudulent, bastardly, in a word, illegitimate.

We have seen, thus far, that Doña Luz's impurity takes on racialized dimensions, which roughly map onto Northern European ideals juxtaposed with largely Orientalist stereotypes. Both images are arguably foreign and simultaneously domestic. While the conflicting images of Aryan and Arab figures both appear from outside of Spain, they in fact also represent ethnicities and heritages that draw from longstanding internal histories. Doña Luz's hybrid identity – pure, chaste, aristocratic, illegitimate, stained, fierce, exotic, uncivilized, etc. – pushes us to nuance Said's conceptualization of Orientalism and his ironic omission of the case of Spain. For Said, Orientalism is "a style of thought based upon an ontological and epistemological distinction made between 'the Orient' and (most of the time) 'the Occident'" (*Orientalism* 2).[11] The history of Spanish empire complicates this geopolitical configuration because there simply is no hard and fast division between the so-called Orient and the Occident. Said's parenthetical gesture in the aforementioned quote points to the potential messiness of this opposition yet leaves it unexplained. As Martin-Márquez succinctly states: "Spain is a nation that is at once orientalized and orientalizing" (9). These lines of demarcation between the self and the other in Spain were precisely the subject of political and scientific debates in the nineteenth century, frequently evoking the discourse of the Black Legend, which casts Spaniards (from the perspective of the English) as a barbaric and uncivilized people. George Mariscal suggests the Black Legend is an example of how the English, early on, used Western racial discourse (rooted in the ideology of blood purity) against the Spanish for political purposes (19). Mignolo echoes this claim, commenting on the significance of the Black Legend for understanding the racialization of Spaniards as Europe's internal other. First, Spain, and before France and England, distinguished itself from Muslims in North Africa; the English then "distinguished itself from the Spaniards, who, the English said, had Moorish blood and acted as barbarians in the New World. About two centuries after the Black Legend was told and retold, Immanuel Kant stated as a fact that Spaniards had a non-European origin" (Mignolo 312). In Kant's words: "he [the Spaniard] displays in his taste an origin that is partly non-European" (231–2).

Doña Luz becomes the projection of the racial anxiety that reverberated across Spain in the nineteenth century. As Martin-Márquez has shown, scientists in the northern regions of Spain were attempting to prove their whiteness, in part, by tracing their ancestry (i.e., bloodlines) to the Celts (in the case of Galicia), Northern Europe (in the case of Catalonia) and Iberians (in the case of the Basque Country), while linking Andalusia to North Africa (39–50). While Joshua Goode has argued that racial thinking in this period overwhelmingly embraced mixture over purity, advancing a notion of *Hispanidad*, Martín-Márquez's study provides evidence of a more heterogeneous debate. In the novel, we see the persistence of a discourse of purity at the same time the narrative continually harkens back to the racialization and exoticization of its "white" protagonists. Nonetheless, the context of this racial anxiety that fractured the scientific community on regional lines is significant because it demonstrates that even modern, scientific conceptualizations of race did not rely solely on phenotype and skin colour but also turned to lineage – in other words, blood. Thus, looking white was not enough to be white. Just as in the case of Doña Luz's legitimacy, Spaniards had to continually prove their whiteness and Europeanness through a genealogical fiction, for the visible, outward markers of race could not reliably index one's inner essence.[12]

Domestication

If the first half of the novel sets out to allure the reader with enticing and exotic depictions of Luz, the latter half leads us to her sexual subjection. Padre Enrique's entry into the narrative signals a shift from the orientalist devices that frame Luz's grandeur as mythical and goddess-like, to a colonial racial discourse that positions her as savage and uncivilized, eliciting her admirers' desire for domination. It is worth noting that this contrast between exoticized allure and colonial debasement of Luz reflects Juan Valera's later writings on the Americas and the so-called Orient.[13] Valera viewed the Americas as a land of savagery prior to Spanish colonization, while the Orient evoked a kind of cultural grandeur.[14]

Luz summarily ignores the young men who admire her, denies all suitors, while Padre Enrique's presence awakens her erotic desires through religious practice. Padre Enrique's return from the Philippines introduces commodities from the Far East, an important structural influence on the novel that prompts a transformation in the reader's understanding of Luz's identity. It is important to make clear that Luz herself does not undergo a physical transformation, but rather the narrator shifts our perception of her. As we shall see, the narrator begins to deploy colonial stereotypes from the Oriental Indies to describe her character once Enrique comes into contact with Luz.

The reader is introduced to Padre Enrique first from the letters that he writes to announce his return from Manila due to poor health: "Mi querido tío: Mis males se agravaron hasta tal extremo en Manila, que los médicos decidieron que yo debía venir a Europa a pasar una larga temporada. Con los aires del país natal aseguraban que me repondría" ("My ills worsened to such a degree in Manila that the doctors decided I should come to Europe for an extended stay. They assured me that I would recover with the change of air in my native country"; *Doña Luz* 98; Fedorchek 62). Padre Enrique has fallen ill from his colonial surroundings and must return to breathe the restorative air of his homeland, a place he has seldom visited, after spending some twenty years in Manila. The doctor's response to Padre Enrique's illness was rooted in the theory of miasma, still prominent in nineteenth-century Spanish medicine, that held that diseases were transmitted through "bad" air (as opposed to germs), miasma meaning "pollution" in classical Greek.

The Philippines, and more specifically Manila, had become the noxious, miasmatic space to the missionary priest. But Padre Enrique is hardly at ease in Spain. A social oddity, he and Doña Luz mirror each other in a peculiar way through their parallel qualities of otherness: Enrique contaminated abroad and Luz purportedly stained by birth. Their spiritual exchanges eventually spark amorous tensions that threaten to exceed the bounds of religious practices and social mores. What is more, their interactions mirror that of a confessor and penitent in complex ways that remain entwined with the colonial discourse that undergirds the narrative.

Crucially, Padre Enrique's subject position as a missionary turned priest leads him to see life in the Peninsula in colonial terms.

> Para tratar, dirigir, ganar almas y someter voluntades, [el padre Enrique] había sido maravilloso allá en los pueblos del extremo Oriente; pero como había salido de España muy mozo, y apenas había vivido en esta sociedad artificiosa y algo refinada de nuestro siglo, cuya cultura y usos convencionales se extienden hasta las aldeas, lo veía y estimaba todo con cierta sencillez selvática, interpretando las palabras y las acciones de diverso modo que el vulgo. (*Doña Luz* 121)

> Administering, directing, and gaining souls and subjecting others to his will, he [Padre Enrique] had been marvellous with the peoples of the Far East; but as he had left Spain at a relatively young age and had scarcely lived in this artificial and somewhat baneful society of our time, whose culture and conventional customs extend even to the countryside, he saw and regarded everything with a certain rustic simplicity, interpreting words and actions differently than the common people. (Fedorchek 80)

Enrique's time spent in the Philippines has led to the constitution of his assuming a colonizing subjectivity that cannot be undone when he returns home. The ability to acclimate to the tropics was seen by Northern Europeans as a distinct Spanish ability. German ethnologist Fedor Jagor, for example, wrote in *Travels in the Philippines* (1875) that "the capacity of the Spaniards for acclimatisation [*sic*] in tropical countries [can be attributed to] the large admixture of Syrian and African blood which flows in their veins" (Jagor 36; see footnote). Such commentary demonstrates the "illegitimacy" of Spanish whiteness within modern Europe. Padre Enrique's impurity is acquired by acclimating to the Philippines, while Luz's impurity is inherited – both are tacitly racialized as not quite white.

Here is it useful to briefly discuss the project of evangelization in the Philippines during the nineteenth century. Spain's empire was considerably diminished by the second half of the nineteenth century, but, as Alda Blanco argues, that the Spanish liberal intelligentsia still understood colonialism to be a modern enterprise central to the project of nation-building during the period of the Restoration. To cite one example, Blanco refers to Antonio Cánovas de Castillos's *Discurso sobre la nación* (1882) in which the Christianization of colonies, the civilizing mission of the Spanish Empire, was considered central to the future of the Spanish nation. Blanco writes: "For Cánovas the Christian nation is fundamentally a colonizing entity that must use force in order to fulfill its Divine mission" ("Spain at the Crossroads" 9). Spain, in fact, continued its evangelizing efforts throughout the eighteenth and nineteenth centuries in the Philippine archipelago, where priests and missionaries blurred the boundaries between spiritual domination and colonial administration. As John Blanco has shown, the Philippines were a special colonial context in which very few lay figures of Spanish authority were present and most were concentrated in Manila. As a result, clergymen, who from the start of the conquest in the sixteenth century occupied both the role of spiritual authority and by default, took on a series of temporal responsibilities normally given exclusively to administrative authorities of the crown.

Blanco draws from Foucault's notion of pastoral power to show how through the implementation of accountability, obedience, individualized knowledge, and mortification between the pastor and parishioner, Spanish missionaries were able to successfully convert the Indigenous subjects to Christianity through what he terms a "manufactured form of consent." This pastoral power, in conjunction with administrative authority, positioned priests as the "proto-police force on the colonial frontier" (John Blanco 76). Priests and missionaries therefore exercised a great deal of power, one that was viewed at times as threatening to the Crown, because of their relative autonomy, dual authority, and powerful administrative function in colonial rule through the production and maintenance of the *Respublica Christiana*.[15] In contrast to this historical profile of the missionary as proto-police in the colonies, hence effectuating colonial governance through a successful process of evangelization, *Doña Luz* provides an image of a once successful but now weakened, dying priest incapable of surviving in the "infectious" space of the Philippines. This enervated image of the missionary priest bespeaks an underlying fear about the fragility of the so-called Christian Republic and, in turn, the fear concerning the loss of control and regulation in the colonies.

In one striking moment in the text, the narrator couches Padre Enrique's desire in colonial terms in the text that recalls religious conversion as a colonial project:

La afición de doña Luz no se diferenciaba a sus ojos de la que le tuvieron estos o aquellos neófitos indios, chinos o anamitas, salvo en ser la afición de doña Luz más de estimar por la excelencia de la persona que la sentía, en quien el padre hallaba un sinnúmero de brillantes calidades: un espíritu cultivadísimo y capaz de elevarse a las esferas más encumbradas del pensamiento, y un corazón lleno de afectos tiernos, nobles y puros. (121)

The fondness of Doña Luz was no different in his eyes than the regard expressed for him by numerous Annamese, Chinese, or Indian neophytes, except that Doña Luz's fondness was to be esteemed more highly because of the excellence of the person who felt it, a person in whom the priest found countless splendid qualities, such as an exceptionally well cultivated spirit capable of rising to the loftiest planes of thought and a heart full of tender, noble, and pure feelings. (80)

With this comparison, Doña Luz is likened to the colonial subject vis-à-vis Padre Enrique the missionary. This is a strange moment of doubling in which the "not quite" aristocratic white subject from the metropole is viewed through the stereotype of the colonial other. Instead of the colonial mimic man, who is almost but not quite white, Luz is similar to but not entirely like the other, i.e., the neophyte Indian, Chinese, and Annamite. This is an unusual inversion of colonial mimicry (Bhabha), whereby the troubled subject from the metropole is likened to a "savage" from the Oriental Indies. Bringing this metaphor "home" shows that Padre Enrique's comparison positions Luz, an illegitimate marchioness, as an internal colonial subject. Doña Luz's illegitimate status and bad origins are arguably what align her with that of a colonial subject and alienate her from the role of a proper aristocratic lady expected by her society. Her status as an orphaned bastard, with seemingly indomitable passions, positions the priest as the paternal figure expected to domesticate her and to discipline her unruliness, much as he did abroad. Yet what apparently differentiates Luz from "aquellos neófitos indios, chinos o anamitas" ("numerous Annamese, Chinese, or Indian neophytes") is her well-cultivated spirit. Therefore, it is arguably her innate "predisposition" for Christianity that distinguishes her from the colonized. Moreover, this moment of (mis)recognition, where Enrique sees Luz in the same light as one of the savages abroad, recalls the modern Christian mission of civilizing the so-called primitive world. Differentiating between Luz and the colonial subject by suggesting that the latter lacks the spirit of the civilized echoes the contemporary debates concerning the plausibility of true religious conversion in the colonies. This moment, which reiterates the story of Spanish imperialism via conversion, is precisely when Padre Enrique arguably begins to fall in love with Luz and desire her, suggesting that he *must* view her through the eyes of a colonial missionary to make those desires legible and acceptable to himself.

This is a significant shift from the earlier depictions where the narrator exoticizes Luz as an oriental princess. She is now, in the eyes of Enrique, relegated to the status of colonized subject of the Indies. From this point on the narrator deploys other colonial metaphors to talk about Padre Enrique. During the latter's first bout of illness, for example, the narrator explains that "El padre desde entonces cuidaba de su cuerpo como cuida el esclavo de una prenda, de una máquina que su señor le confía, a fin de que sirviéndose de ella haga que la hacienda prospere" ("From that point on, he cared for his body as a slave cares for a jewel, or for a mechanical apparatus that his master entrusts to him, so that with its use he can make the estate prosper"; *Doña Luz* 209; Fedorchek 45). By employing the metaphor of a slave to discuss Padre Enrique's practices of self-care, the narrator takes on the colonial vision full force. As the relationship between Luz and Enrique continues to intensify, the narrator even refers to Enrique as a "pajarraco exótico y raro" ("an exotic rara avis"; 126; 83) an image that recalls the earlier depiction of Luz as the black-crested heron. The reader, in turn, is encouraged to view the world of Villafría through a colonial paradigm. By describing Padre Enrique as a slave to his health in the above passage, the narrator not only paints the picture of a degenerate missionary but represents him through a colonial paradigm. Consequently, Enrique figures as a quasi-colonial subject himself, unable to re-assimilate to his homeland.

In this way, the narrator aligns Luz and Enrique as impure subjects of the nation. Together they find a forbidden intimacy as they lose themselves in conversation.

En medio de aquella agitación polítca, habían hallado retraimiento dulcísimo en la misma casa de quien la promovía; y allí [en casa de don Acisclo] las pláticas suaves y encumbradas, y las conversaciones amenas, en que siempre aprendía algo doña Luz, en que siempre hallaba nuevas excelencias en el entendimiento y el corazón del padre, y en que el padre, a su vez, no dejaba nunca de pasmarse del despejo, de la agudeza, de la notable discreción, de la fantasía poética y de la sensibilidad exquisita de su bella interlocutora. (*Doña Luz* 150)

In the midst of all that politicking they had found welcome seclusion in the very home of the man who had brought it about. It was in Don Acisclo's house that their quiet, lofty talks and pleasant conversations took place,

> conversations in which Doña Luz always learned something, in which she always discovered new qualities of excellence in the priest's heart and intellect, and in which the priest, for his part, could not help but marvel at the ease of manner, insight, remarkable discretion, poetic imagination, and exquisite sensitivity of his lovely interlocutor. (Fedorcheck 99–100)

Doña Luz is the only one capable of cultivating such fondness for Padre Enrique. Whereas for the rest of the town, he is nothing more than a degenerate missionary and an ultimate disaster of a priest in Villafría.

Rumours concerning Enrique's character and beliefs circulate, creating an image of him as a barbaric and monstrous figure: "no hubiera sido difícil que alguien le supusiese conspirando en favor del restablecimiento de la Inquisición y hasta comiéndose los niños crudos" ("it would not have been difficult to suppose that he was conspiring on behalf of the restoration of the Inquisition and even that he was eating children alive"; 126; 83). The narrator demonstrates here that certain townspeople maintain a critical view of the Inquisition while omitting any direct critique of Spain's imperial "Christianizing missions" abroad. The townspeople people do, however, attribute his poor performance and inability to relate to them to his being accustomed to living among the "savages" of the Indies: "no sabía aconsejar por lo fino, acostumbrado a vivir entre los salvajes allá en las Indias" ("he did not know how to advise with any polish, accustomed, as he had been, to living among savages off in the Indies"; *Doña Luz* 101; Fedorchek 64). Padre Enrique, in effect, has become less civilized after spending nearly all his adult life in the colonies. While living in the Philippines has a pernicious effect on his health, in the eyes of his countrymen, he has assimilated all too well and can no longer be at home in Spain. Enrique suffers from what the narrator calls the "sentencia evangélica" ("scriptural saying"): "*Nadie es profeta en su patria*; también por él, si es lícito comparar lo pequeño con lo grande, pudo decirse que *estuvo entre los suyos y los suyos no le conocieron*" ("'A prophet is not without honor, save in his own country, and in his own house.' Also with reference to him, if it is permissible to compare the high with the low, it could be said: 'He came unto his own, and his own received him not'"; 101, emphasis in original; 64). Padre Enrique's return to the motherland diminishes his status. His life in the colony had a different meaning and purpose, and at home he is no longer recognizable or legible. While at first glance Padre Enrique appears to be a representative of colonial religious authority, he proves to be a liminal subject himself. Doña Luz, the illegitimate daughter, finds her forbidden match in the failed missionary, the "illegitimate" priest. The source of his colonial desire is the very cause of his death, and the airs of his native land were not enough to remedy his illness.

In the novel, religious conversion become a site of racially inflected sexual desire that comes into conflict with the desire for purity. In the case of Doña Luz, sexual desire is also a desire to produce some form of impurity through "illicit" intimacy with a priest. Notions of purity in the novel are framed largely in terms of class and social standing (determined by birth) and chastity, embodied and expressed in terms of racial difference. While early on the narrator likens Luz to mythological and fantastical subjects, purity takes on different forms when Doña Luz comes into contact with Padre Enrique, whose return to Spain brings about a more explicit colonial discourse in the novel, both through the language of the narrative voice and through the circulation of commodities and bodies from abroad.

From this point forward, the narrator begins to represent the domestic imperialist culture of this southern town and the everyday relations that are determined by Spain's status as modern empire. References to colonial spaces can be found scattered throughout the narrative landscape. While colonized people and colonial artefacts may not immediately appear to be central to the novel, it is precisely these traces of empire, which are both naturalized and fetishized, that serve as the framework through which the narrative gives meaning to categories of identity. Upon Padre Enrique's return from the Philippines, he brings with him many gifts from different parts of Asia, including China, Japan, and India:

> Para todos los primos y las primas trajo regalos: para ellos puros filipinos en abundancia; para ellas, o pañolones bordados, que llaman en mi tierra de espumilla y Manila en Madrid, o abanicos chinescos de los más primorosos. Para don Acisclo armas japonesas, y para doña Luz un juego de ajedrez de marfil, prolijamente labrado. (*Doña Luz* 99)

> He brought gifts for all his cousins – for the men, Philippine cigars in abundance; for the women, either embroidered shawls, which in Andalusia are called "crepe" and in Madrid "manila," or the most exquisite Chinese fans. For Don Acisclo he brought Japanese arms, and for Doña Luz a set of meticulously carved ivory chess figures. (Fedorchek 63)

Historically speaking, this is a significant detail because Manila was established as the main point of trade between the New World and Asia. By the mid-nineteenth century, Manila was more important than ever for Spain, having lost almost all of its colonies in Spanish America.

Valera's novel presumes a certain colonial intimacy between Spain and Asia, constructing a world in which the circulation of objects, people, and ideas from overseas was commonplace in the national imperialist imaginary.

Along with all the goods he brings from the Philippines, Padre Enrique also returns with a Chinese servant, known only as Ramón. While performing a seemingly indispensable role as Padre Enrique's primary caretaker and trusted confidant, Ramón never speaks and is never spoken about by the other characters. Instead, his only mode of appearance is through the narrator's third-person description. He reappears near the end of the novel, when Padre Enrique is suffering from hysterical attacks. Ramón, at Padre Enrique's request, is the only one who knows of his illness, and he is the sole witness to the priest's diminishing health, directly correlated to his amorous desires for Luz. The inventory of the items brought from abroad, including Ramón, introduces the colonial subject as colonial object in equal value to the other gifts from abroad. Ramón's inclusion in the novel thus underscores his own inhumanity in the eyes of the narrator. While the colonial discourse of the novel remains palpable throughout – sliding into dazzling commodified objects or serving as metaphor and motif – Ramón, the only colonized person to enter the narrative, is given flat representation.

Reading the figure of Padre Enrique in the context of empire and nation reveals that categories of identity that fall under the rubric of *casta*, such as race, gender, and class, take on new meanings when examined within the broader geopolitical context. It is significant that objects from the Far East appear as things that are hand-carried by Padre Enrique himself. They become part of the domestic landscape after Enrique's arrival, as his presence changes the course of the narrative.

Illicit Inheritance

Doña Luz's unfortunate circumstances are attributed to a complex family inheritance, the first being the social *descuido* (carelessness) of her mother and the second being the impoverished financial condition of her father's estate. There is a third and much less explicit form of inheritance, and that is sexual deviance transmitted by her libertine father and careless mother, further complicated by the imperial subtext of the novel. The narrator explains that Doña Luz's only valuable possession, other than her father's house, is her father's black horse: "El único lujo, el único regalo de doña Luz, era una magnífico caballo negro" ("The only luxury, the only indulgence, that Doña Luz permitted herself was a magnificent black horse"; *Doña Luz* 61; Fedorchek 33). The use of the word "lujo" or luxury here is significant since, as scholars have noted, "lujo" and female "lujuria" ("lust") share an etymology "luxus" ("excess") and linking to the widespread fear that women's excessive consumption of luxury goods would lead to moral transgressions such as adultery and prostitution.[16]

Sexual tensions are not infrequently represented through the images of horses and horseback riding in nineteenth-century novels. In Valera's *Pepita Jiménez*, thought to have served as a blueprint for *Doña Luz*, the horseback riding adventure between Pepita and Padre Luis is representative of Pepita's sexual appetite and Luis's sexual clumsiness.[17] Likewise, Doña Luz's unfulfilled sexual desire is represented through instances of aggressive horseback riding – we might recall that the narrator compares Luz to Hippolyta, whose name in Greek means "letting horses loose." In the first instance of this, horseback riding is coupled with an eroticized form of religious practice. In a highly erotic rendition of false mysticism, the narrator voyeuristically describes Doña Luz's physical reactions as she contemplates the provocative image of a half-naked, crucified Christ "vertiendo sangre aún" ("still bleeding"; *Doña Luz* 81; Fedorchek 49). The mention of the sacrificial blood of Christ speaks to Gil Anidjar's concept of "Jesus's kin" – the idea that Christians "were the first to conceive of themselves as a community of blood" (38). Thus, blood becomes the substance of an exclusive community (for which *limpieza de sangre* becomes a mechanism of sorting and expulsion) – in this case the Christian Republic – and yet all this is corrupted by the erotic nature of this narrative moment.

This provocative portrait, painted by el Divino Morales, is capable of producing "convulsions," "ataques de nervios" ("nervous seizures"), and even "delirio" ("delirium"; 82; 50). I quote this lengthy passage to underscore the intensity and excess of this eroticized religious scene:

A casi nadie se le mostraba; pero ella, que tenía muy rara condición y muy contrarias propensiones en el espíritu activo e infatigable, tal vez después de trotar y galopar y dar saltos peligrosos en su caballo negro, durante dos o tres horas; tal vez después de haber limpiado, bañado y frotado con complacencia su hermoso cuerpo, que del valiente ejercicio había vuelto cubierto de sudor; rebosando ella salud, en todo el brío de la mocedad y en todo el florecimiento de la belleza plástica, se sentía llena de ímpetus ascéticos, y, abriendo su cuadro, le contemplaba largo tiempo, y las lágrimas acudían a sus ojos, y acudían a sus rojos labios plegarias inefables que ella murmuraba y apenas articulaba. (82)

She showed it to very few people, but she herself, who had a most peculiar nature and very contrary propensities in a tireless active spirit, perhaps after trotting and galloping and making dangerous jumps on her black horse for two or three hours; perhaps after having happily curried, sponged and rubbed its [her] magnificent body, which the strenuous exercise had covered with sweat; and brimming with health and the go of youth and the full bloom of her statuesque beauty, she Doña Luz would be overcome by ascetic impulses and, opening the painting, would contemplate it for long periods of time, and tears would well up in her eyes, and indescribable prayers would rise to her red lips, prayers that she murmured and barely articulated. (50)

Here, the narrator reveals to the reader Doña Luz's habit of privately viewing this image that is "horrible y bello a la vez" ("at once horrible and beautiful"; 81; 49), so much so that it must be covered up by another painting and viewed only under special circumstances. Based on this passage, we can gather that Doña Luz is inclined to view this painting only once she has completed her meticulous cleansing ritual; one that first involves vigorous exercising, followed by a three-fold purification process: washing, bathing, and rubbing. Herein lies a cycle of dirtying and cleansing which is infused with sexual desire. The act of riding, which is erotically charged throughout the novel, is paradoxically necessary to expunge impurities (through perspiration) so they can be wiped away clean.

If legitimacy is Luz's perceived lack, then other forms or conditions of purity, including beauty and hygiene, work as mechanisms of fetishistic compensation. Cleanliness thus becomes an obsession for Doña Luz: "[S]e miraba y se complacía en este que podemos llamar aseo moral y corpóreo, por lo mismo que se veía circundada de gente algo ruda y no muy limpia ni de cuerpo ni del alma y como si tuviese el temor de contaminarse" ("She always attended to and took pleasure in what we might call corporal and moral purity, for the very reason that she was surrounded by somewhat coarse people who were not very clean in body or soul, and as though she feared being contaminated"; 56–7; 30). That Doña Luz fears class "contagion" – as if it were a contractible disease – is a disavowal of her own repressed origins. Luz is motivated by the thought of her own inner corruption to maintain hyperbolic levels of corporeal cleanliness. Her dedication to hygiene and her rejection of male suitors reveals the fetishistic operations of origin in the narrative as she anxiously tries to mask her impurity through displaced, metonymic iterations of purification.

It is important to point out here that bathing was not a common daily ritual but was prescribed by nineteenth-century hygienists as both a method for cleaning the skin and as a medical treatment for various ailments. Pedro Felipe Monlau, considered to be the father of Spanish hygiene, acknowledges that the general population cleans and bathes their animals and yet neglects to wash and care for their own skin (*Higiene Privada* 79). In *Higiene Privada*, Monlau depicts bathing as a newly revived ancient practice and foreign import, referring to the bathing practices of the Romans, the Russians, the Finnish, and the Turks, even noting that Russian bathhouses had opened in Madrid (82–3, 87). In the context of the novel, then, bathing can be read as an exotic, albeit hygienic, practice.

There were strict procedures for bathing, which are reflected in this passage. While a cool bath is recommended after perspiring or if skin is warm, one should not enter the bath water with sweat still on the skin (81, 85). Monlau also prescribes "friction," or rubbing of the skin, to complete the bathing process (91). This bathing process not only aided in purifying the skin but also produced "una satisfacción indefinible" ("an undefinable satisfaction"; 83). Monlau also acknowledges that "las fricciones practicadas por personas de sexo diferente, pueden disponer a los placeres de la reproducción" ("Frictions practised by people of different sexes could incite the pleasures of reproduction"; 91). The excessive cleansing ritual appears as the compulsory but also pleasurable hygienic preparation for Doña Luz to contemplate this painting. She must present herself in the purest material state before the image of Christ, which in turn sparks her erotic excesses, leaving her in an ecstatic, if not orgasmic, and speechless state.

This rather peculiar purification process demonstrates the ways in which purity and impurity are intricately interwoven. All the while, the narrator invites the reader to take pleasure from this scene. The repeated use of the expression "tal vez" "perhaps" introduces some uncertainty into the passage. Rather than provide an exact account of Luz's actions, this "perhaps" seems to reflect a certain amount of guesswork – the narrator pleasurably filling in the schematic gaps of a habitual act with his own imagination. The fact that the act of purification is also a site of symbolic dirt and desire complicates the relationship between chastity (*castidad*) and its opposite, sensuality. The infusion of the erotic with religious practice and imagery blurs the boundaries between pure and impure, sacred and profane, a confusion that permeates the entire novel. The Christ image simultaneously recalls the blood of Christendom and Luz's repressed desire for Enrique. Joined with the act of horseback riding, we see the perversity – from the position of empire – of the sexual tension that builds between Luz and Padre Enrique. Moreover, the image she contemplates is that of Christ's bloody corpse, linking death with Doña Luz's desire for Padre Enrique, a harbinger of his eventual death in direct connection with his own forbidden desires. (Upon the pronouncement of Enrique's death, Luz retrospectively acknowledges the connection between her contemplation of the dead Christ image and her desires for the priest.) This is curious, however, not only because of what it foretells in the novel but because these activities (horseback riding, cleansing, and ascetic contemplation) are eroticized in tandem with one another. In these back-to-back scenes, it is not only Luz who takes pleasure from these activities, but it is also the reader who is invited by the narrator to consume these sexualized representations. These illicit forms of desire deviate from what Stoler has identified as "those sexual practices that were nation-building and race-affirming," marking "'unproductive eroticism,' as Doris Sommer has well shown, 'not only [as] immoral, [but as] unpatriotic'" (135).

The black horse is a powerful image in the novel and adds further complexity to such "unproductive eroticism" when considered in the context of empire. Lisa Surwillo, for example, has examined how the trope of the horse in *Don Álvaro* (1835) ushers in "modern racial terminology" (namely, colour-based) that applies zoological principles of taxonomy to humans ("*Speaking of Race*" 59). In *Doña Luz*, the black horse elicits a kind of racialized eroticism that we come to associate with Luz's savagery. I would like to recall that the horse is one of the few objects Luz's father bequeathed to her, marking again the importance of inheritance, material or otherwise, in connection to sexuality. There is a curious chain of signification here that operates through the semantic evolution of the word *casta* as origin and purity but also as caste or breed. Before proceeding with the analysis, it is worth repeating some of the key terms outlined in the introduction. One of the earliest definitions of *raza* (race) in Covarrubias's *Tesoro de la lengua castellana o española* (1611) refers to "castes" of purebred horses (Mignolo 77). The idea of race in the following century would later be extended to humans and be used not to refer to good, legitimate lineage but rather to bad lineage, that is, Muslim or Jewish, rendering Catholics a racially unmarked group. In the eighteenth century, *casta*, as defined by the *Real Academia Española*, would take on the meaning of both "generation" and "lineage" in terms of humans and "breed" in terms of animals, most notably horses.[18] The emphases in both explanations rest on the affirmation of known progenitors, something Doña Luz struggles with for the majority of the novel.

The indomitable black horse symbolizes the hypersexuality of an impure white woman without explicitly stating it as such. This rhetorical shorthand in fiction illustrates the semantic density of chromatic blackness – akin to what Toni Morrison calls Africanism. Morrison writes that Africanism is a "term for the denotative and connotative blackness that African peoples have come to signify as well as the entire range of views, assumptions, readings, and misreadings that accompany Eurocentric learning about these people" (6). While Morrison is ultimately interested in the "Africanist persona," her analyses extend to ambient descriptions of blackness and whiteness, such as snow, shadow, and darkness. Morrison succinctly explains how such a chain of signification works through a reification of blackness: "the simple expedient of demonizing and reifying the range of color on a palette … [makes] it possible to say and not say, to inscribe and erase" (7). Sander L. Gilman makes a parallel argument in his analysis of Black figures in nineteenth-century visual art in *Black Bodies, White Bodies*. Gilman maintains that Black women emblematized the taboo sexuality of white women when the two were coupled together, as in Manet's *Olympia*. Crucially, in later portraits of licentious white women (e.g., Manet's *Nana*) the figure of the Black woman disappears. Instead, the artist draws on a "vocabulary of signs" to represent "the black hidden within" (232). The black horse, I argue, figures among these signs that implicitly stand in for a white woman's illicit sexuality. With the ambiguous use of the possessive "su" ("its/her") in the aforementioned passage ("su hermoso cuerpo" ["its/her beautiful body"]), the narrative conflates Doña Luz's body with that of her black horse. The signification of chromatic blackness operates metonymically to evoke a sense of Doña Luz's animalistic-racialized desire that contaminates the entire scene.

This trope reappears in a later moment in the novel, when Padre Enrique and Doña Luz meet by chance on horseback. Enrique, who is an experienced rider from travelling on horseback in Asia, directs Luz's horse with the crack of his whip:

> Doña Luz se aventuró demasiado y estuvo a punto de dar una peligrosa caída al saltar una zanja. Su caballo no llevaba ímpetu bastante y hubiera caído en ella, si el Padre, conociéndolo, no hubiera llegado en sazón, excitando el caballo con el látigo, y con el ejemplo, porque saltó primero. (*Doña Luz* 107)

> Doña Luz ventured too much and very nearly took a nasty spill on jumping a ditch. Her horse did not have enough momentum and would have fallen in it if the priest, who realized what was happening, had not reached them in time, driving the horse with his whip, and with his example, because he jumped first. (Fedorchek 69)

Rather than taming Doña Luz's horse, Padre Enrique further "excites" it with his whip. Morever, Luz is an aggressive rider: "montaba a caballo como la reina de las amazonas" ("she rode horseback like the queen of the Amazons"; 57; 31). The horse's violent movements metonymically signifiy her (inherited) unbridled passions and her seemingly indomitable "fiereza."

That Padre Enrique is tasked with chastening (*castigar*) Doña Luz, highlights the disciplinary force of the discourse of *casta*. The cracking of Enrique's whip has a dual significance here, for while the use of whips is commonplace in riding, lashing was also a common form of punishment used in the Philippines by the missionaries during the conversion to Christianity (John Blanco 68). Thus, through the icon of the black horse Luz is framed as a wild indomitable subject whose impurity derives from the lasciviousness of her parents and the caste of her unknown mother. This colonial image that further racializes Luz's illegitimacy serves as a reminder that "[i]n this age of empire, the question of who would be a 'subject' and who was a 'citizen' converged on the sexual politics of race" (Stoler 133).

Legitimate Love: From Priest to Soldier

Padre Enrique's entry into the narration signals a change in the narrator's perception of Doña Luz. Her very relationship with a priest as a single laywoman is considered morally suspicious, as she is not properly regulated by a patriarchal supervisor; that is, she is an orphan who wants neither to marry nor take the veil of Christ. Even for married women in this period, frequent contact with a priest in confession posed a real threat to the patriarchal order of the family. In a chapter entitled "Crisis," Doña Luz tries to reckon with the fact that her dearest friend Doña Manolita has surmised that Padre Enrique's fondness for Doña Luz is becoming more than just spiritual. While Doña Luz defends the moral sanctity of their relationship, it is clear she feels embarrassed and ashamed that their secret desires have become apparent to Manolita. It is then that Doña Luz decides to remedy this situation and "poner su descuido en reparo" ("[patch] up her carelessness"; *Doña Luz* 159; Fedorchek 108). Doña Luz's decision to correct her unchaste feelings coincides with the arrival of former war hero from the Spanish–Moroccan War and aspiring politician Don Jaime Pimentel y Moncada, who in the following chapter, "Solución de la crisis" ("The Solution of the Crisis"), will profess his love for her and propose marriage. After much doubt and resistance Luz, who had once declared to her confidant Manolita that she would remain single forever, decides to marry Don

Jaime. Her decision is motivated in part by Don Jaime's alleged "disinterested" love; that is, he loves her for who she is and cares not that she is impoverished or illegitimate. They maintain similar socio-economic positions, as Don Jaime is also considered to be financially "poor" for his social rank.

This marriage presents two moral conveniences for Doña Luz: first, she is able to divert her "unclean" desires from Padre Enrique to Don Jaime:

> El mismo amor de ella hacia D. Jaime aclararía lo que en su inclinación hacia el Padre podía haber de ocasionado a dudosas interpretaciones. Esto la impulsaba a creerse y a sentirse enamorada de D. Jaime. Amando a D. Jaime desaparecería a sus ojos todo lo que hubiera podido tener de raro su amistad con el misionero. (*Doña Luz* 173)

> Her very love for Don Jaime would clarify what could have given rise to dubious interpretations regarding her inclination towards the priest. This made her believe and feel that she was in love with Don Jaime. Everything that could have seemed odd or peculiar in her friendship with the missionary would disappear in her eyes by loving the representative. (Fedorchek 119)

Secondly, she can also remedy the troubles of her class and social positioning by fostering what the narrator calls a "legitimate" form of love: "su amor a don Jaime era legítimo, correcto, conforme a la clase y posición de ella, y fundado, por último, en causas no menos poéticas que el amor por el padre Enrique, si hubiese sido lícito, hubiera ella podido sentir" ("her love for Don Jaime was legitimate, proper, in accordance with her class and position, and founded, lastly, on motives no less poetic than ones she would have been able to feel for Father Enrique, had such love been permissible"; 219; 153). Marriage between two individuals of similar social standing, therefore, presents itself as the best solution for correcting Doña Luz's unstable position and sullied reputation. It will allow her to produce a legitimate heir/offspring, something Valera's other illegitimate women (Juanita La Larga and Pepita Jiménez) could not do. "Licit" love, in this scenario, shows that affect is also bound to the terms of social legitimacy, sanctioning normative and intra-class relations while forbidding others. Doña Luz's surrender or repression of her feelings thus depends on how they are received by the outside world. The conditional clause "si hubiese sido lícito, hubiera ella podido sentir" ("had such love been permissible") establishes the ability to feel love as contingent upon the state of social legitimacy of the relationship itself. The desire for legitimacy permeates Doña Luz's world.

While Doña Luz appeared before Padre Enrique as an indomitable "colonial" subject, responsible in part for his death, Don Jaime, a soldier and aspiring politician, proves to be a more appropriate match. That Doña Luz's only two love affairs involve a missionary priest and a colonial war hero is no insignificant detail. Don Jaime appears to be all that Padre Enrique was lacking; he is well regarded, physically fit, eloquent, and sociable. His masculinity and patriotism are reinforced by his accomplishments abroad, and he is a womanizer (like Luz's father) who, unlike Padre Enrique, was not weakened by his time spent abroad, but rather strengthened. Don Jaime is ushered into the narrative (in 1861) by Don Acisclo, who, much to the surprise of his friends, has decided to enter the world of politics. Noticing a change in his behaviour, they suspect he might be getting prepared to leave town on an evangelizing mission, having once been an "hermano de cruz" ("brother of the cross"; 65; 37), a member of a confraternity. Doña Manolita asks if he plans to "ir a la China o a la India a convertir infieles" ("go to China or India to convert infidels"), to which Don Acisclo replies: "Infieles voy a convertir, pero sin salir por ahora de Villafría" ("I am indeed going to convert infidels, but for now without leaving Villafría"; 129; 85). This is the second instance in which the metaphor of colonization through conversion is applied to subjects in Spain. It is in this moment that Don Acisclo announces his plans to enter regional politics as a *cacique*: "Quiero ser hombre político, personaje influyente, dueño de este distrito electoral, derrotando al cacique de la cabeza del distrito, que hoy lo puede aquí todo" ("I want to be a politician, an influential man, master of this electoral district, and defeat the capital boss, who these days has everything under his thumb"; 130; 86). He successfully replaces the existing political boss in town by backing Don Jaime the "candidato ilustre, un sujeto de inmenso porvenir, un héroe de la guerra de África" ("an illustrious candidate, a man with a bright future, a hero of the war in Africa"; 132; 88) in the election.

That the concept of religious conversion is applied to the politicization of the countryside implies that this provincial southern town is an uncivilized part of Spain and that the cacique is its governmental colonizer. The representation of *caciquisimo* in the novel echoes what Labanyi calls (in reference to *Pepita Jiménez*) a "new brand of cacique with a moralizing mission" (*Gender* 274). While the case of Luis's Don Acisclo's political machinations differ from those of *Pepita Jiménez*'s Luis, from his perspective, he falls back on missionary metaphors – converting infidels – a reference to the election as part of a larger project of nation formation and modernization. Valera, who supported Catholicism as an effective extension of the central government, blends *caciquisimo* with the idea of religious conversion abroad, thereby treating the rural south as an internal colony.

With the arrival of Don Jaime, the controversial Spanish–Moroccan War forms part of the backdrop of the novel, which takes place during 1860 and 1861. At a time when morale was low, the initial success of the Spanish–Moroccan War helped boost Spain's national sentiment, creating a false hope that Spain had secured its place in Africa, thereby regaining a position among the imperial powers of Europe. Here, it is useful to further explore the brief reference to the Spanish–Moroccan War precisely because it spurred much debate around the topic of Spanish racial identity. Martin-Márquez demonstrates how the prospect of colonization in Africa provoked a reformulation of Spanish racial identity. As Spain struggled to secure itself as an imperial power, it saw colonization in Africa as a means through which this could be done. Whereas a discourse of purity prevailed among debates around Spanish racial identity, insisting that Spaniards had no common roots with North Africans, once Britain and France had taken root in Africa, intellectuals (including liberal Arabists) and politicians sought to legitimize their imperial endeavours in Africa by claiming that their historical affinity with North Africans, a risky claim given the rise of scientific debates on race in the late nineteenth century.[19] So while it is typically assumed that Spaniards sought to eradicate possible ties with the "Moors," Martin-Márquez argues that the process of constructing a (racialized) Spanish national identity was actually more complex than is traditionally thought, "leading to the formulation of hegemonic as well as alternative conceptualizations of the nation which recognized an incorporation of the other within the self" (28).[20] This concept of the nation as having the other within the self – "the hidden black within" (to return to Sander Gilman's formulation) – can help account for the pervasive ambivalence regarding different forms of purity articulated through race and sexuality.

When Don Jaime arrives in Villafría for the first time (after having won the election) Don Acisclo lets him ride Doña Luz's black horse. It is then that Doña Manolita, Doña Luz's only female confidant, feels inspired to pull a prank on Doña Luz (an unconscious presentiment) by telling her that Don Jaime has fallen in love with her and wishes to marry her. At this point in the novel, Doña Luz is tormented with shame because of her feelings for Padre Enrique and is on the brink of losing the only thing she has some control over, her chastity: "Si el padre la hubiera inspirado otro más vivo sentimiento, ella hubiera pecado contra Dios, contra el mundo, contra su honra y contra su decoro" ("If the priest had inspired her with another more intense feeling she would have sinned against God, against the world, against her honor, and against her decency"; *Doña Luz* 219; Fedorchek 153). Don Jaime's timing could not have been more auspicious. Soon after Manolita's prank, he begins courting Doña Luz, and after much resistance she decides that her crisis can be resolved through marriage with Don Jaime, a man of her father's class. The official succession from Padre Enrique to Don Jaime (both colonialists) then takes place at their wedding when Padre Enrique, serving as one of the few witnesses at the church, presents Don Jaime with a gift: a bronze statue of Shiva collected during his travels in India:

> [C]onservaba aún, a pesar del regalo hecho a don Acisclo cuando vino de Filipinas, varias armas japonesas, chinescas, e indias, con las cuales se podía forma una bella panoplia, y un extraño ídolo de bronce que representaba al dios Siva. Este fue el presente que hizo el padre Enrique a don Jaime para que adornase su despacho. (200)

> He still retained, notwithstanding the gift he had given to Don Acisclo when he came from the Philippines, various Indian, Chinese, and Japanese weapons, with which a fine panoply could be formed, and a strange bronze idol that represented the god Shiva. The latter was the present that Father Enrique gave to Don Jaime as a decoration for his study. (138)

The bronze statue of Shiva, the Hindu deity whose name is etymologically linked to purity (Apte 919), symbolizes transference of colonial power. Enrique passes the torch of the civilizing/purifying mission to Don Jaime. The irony here, of course, is that the statue itself is a representation of a Hindu god and is thus itself a form of religious impurity, so to speak. With this newfound power, "[s]u don Jaime parecíale un dios" ("her Don Jaime seemed like a god"; 204; 140), extending the metaphor of the civilizing process via religious conversion.

Now legally joined with Don Jaime through marriage, she is free from the gossiping tongues of Villafría and has contained the problem of her illegitimacy. Like Luz's father, however, Don Jaime's record is far from pristine, having had many lovers in Madrid. Rather than see this as a strike against him, Doña Luz paradoxically views this as her own civilizing mission. While understanding that this correct and proper form of love, marriage, will save her from committing a carnal sin with Padre Enrique, she also believes she is cleaning up Don Jaime's past with her own chastity and with the legitimacy of their relationship:

Doña Luz sabía que don Jaime había sido adorado en Madrid, y, al verle tan prendado, tan rendido y tan amoroso y humilde, se llenaba de orgullosa complacencia, juzgándose mil veces más amada que todas sus antiguas rivales. Para completar su satisfacción, hacía además doña luz un deslinda crítico, acerca de este negocio, que rara vez dejan de hacer las mujeres de su condición y en sus circunstancias. El amor de don Jaime por las otras mujeres había sido profano y pecaminoso: el que a ella tenía era virtuoso y santo; para las otras había nacido de capricho, de vanidad, de extravío juvenil o de otras pasiones ilegítimas; para ella nacía el amor de don Jaime del manantial más elevado y puro del alma, el cual, con su benéfica corriente, iba purificando el corazón de su amigo, borrando de él toda huella y toda mancha de las pasadas culpas y dejándole más limpio que el oro. Toda esta santificación y limpieza íntima era obra poco menos que milagrosa y sobre humana del amor de doña Luz y del fuego purificante de sus ojos. (*Doña Luz* 202–3)

Doña Luz knew that Don Jaime had been adored in Madrid, and on seeing him so captivated and so enamored, so tender and so humble, she swelled with dignified pleasure, considering herself infinitely more loved than all her former rivals. In order to complete assessing her situation, Doña Luz made, in addition, a critical distinction as regards this matter, one that women of her social class and her circumstances rarely fail to make. Don Jaime's love for the other women had been profane and sinful, whereas the love he had for her was virtuous and holy; for the others it had stemmed from caprice, from vanity, from youthful misconduct or other illicit passions. Don Jaime's love for her was born of the soul's purest and most exalted fountainhead, which, with its beneficent current, gradually cleansed his heart, erasing from it every trace and every stain of past offenses and leaving it spotless. All this sanctification and inner cleansing was nothing less than the miraculous and superhuman work of Doña Luz's love and the purifying fire of her eyes. (Fedorchek 140)

The passage above evidences an obvious gendered double standard. While Doña Luz's stain is viewed as permanent (though contained), the product of her unchaste mother, Don Jaime's lasciviousness is framed as easily effaceable through the chastity of another woman. Doña Luz feels great pride in extending her obsession for purity to her marriage, a contract of social purification. Much to her dismay, however, Doña Luz is unable to purify Don Jaime's heart. Through a series of secret letters written by her father, Doña Luz later discovers the truth of her origin: her mother was not a seamstress, but rather the Countess of Fajalauza who bequeathed to Luz her ample wealth. Luz then discovers that she was merely an instrument for Don Jaime's political and financial triumph in Villafría – he was privy to her pending inheritance – and that his love for her is counterfeit. The Spanish war hero becomes the novel's deceitful villain.

Doña Luz's trajectory from priest to soldier has the allegorical trappings of the collective dilemma of Spanish imperial dilemmas and dreams alike. Padre Enrique's defeated return to Spain and failure "to conquer" Luz duplicates the failed colonial missions abroad. Doña Luz's struggle as the bastard daughter of a marquis from the capital living in a backwards rural town reflects a larger national anxiety over how to reform or expel impure subjects – whether from in the countryside or the colony – from the body of the nation. But while Doña Luz as an illegitimate daughter can be reformed through the patriarchal institution of marriage, Padre Enrique has no chance at salvation. He can neither survive the Philippines nor assimilate at home. His death is therefore construed as the only solution for the priest who has been contaminated by the colonies; Enrique's enfeebled body must be expunged from the "imperial nation" (Alda Blanco). While Don Jaime is robust and healthy, he represents the urban elite that resides in the capital while maintaining his political and financial exploits in rural Spain. A military captain who fought in the controversial Spanish–Moroccan War, Don Jaime represents the imperial aspirations of an ailing empire, signalling the false hopes of a newly secured position of power alongside Britain and France. (It may be worth noting that Valera began writing this novel during the early years of the Restoration, at which point it was clear that Spain's imperial hold in Morocco had been superseded by the British.) Just as O'Donnell's war against Morocco proved to be a national sham war, so too does Don Jaime reveal himself to be a crook.

Upon discovering the truth of Don Jaime's motives, Doña Luz is overcome by a hysterical attack and subsequently shuts herself in her home for four months before she tells anyone the truth of her deception. In solitude, she mourns the death of Enrique, whom she finally recognizes as her true love and condemns herself for having foolishly rushed into marriage with Don Jaime. The story of deceit ends with the newly married couple living separate lives. Don Jaime collects his handsome inheritance and pursues a career of politics in the capital. Doña Luz upholds the gendered codes of chastity and caste by marrying a man of her father's social status and bearing a legitimate heir, but she remains secluded in a life of relative obscurity in rural Spain. The narrator's succinct final words bring the novel to an abrupt and rather cynical close: "Mientras su marido brilla sobremanera en la corte, ella cuida de un hijo muy hermoso y muy inteligente que Dios le ha dado, y cuyo nombre de pila es Enrique" ("While her husband cuts a glittering figure in the aristocratic circles of Madrid, she is raising a lovely and bright little boy given to her by God, a little boy whose first name is Enrique"; *Doña Luz* 245; Fedorchek 173).

Conclusion

In *Doña Luz*, the problems of the illegitimate daughter of a marquis come to stand in for those of the imperial nation. Spain had not escaped its shadowy reputation, as what Edmund Spenser in the sixteenth century called the "most mingled, most uncertain, and most *bastardly* nation" (44). In 1897, an aging Juan Valera would publish an essay in which he virulently refuted a contemporary critique of Spain's imperial wreckage. Likely reproducing the discourse of the Black Legend, the English-born American intellectual John William Draper had apparently attributed the destruction of "oriental" and "occidental" civilization to Spanish colonization. In response to the latter, Valera exclaims:

> ¡Qué diantre de civilización había en América antes de su descubrimiento! Por casi todas partes era completo el salvajismo … Si hubieran sido aventureros ingleses, franceses ó alemanes los que á fines del siglo xv hubieran ido á América, ¿se hubieran conducido con más humanidad que los españoles? ("Sobre dos acusaciones tremendas contra España" 120–2)

> What god-forsaken civilization was there in America before its discovery? It was complete savagery nearly everywhere. If the explorers had been English, French, or German, the ones that had come to America at the end of the fifteenth century, would they have behaved with greater humanity than the Spanish?

The essay reads as a rather unsympathetic and staunch defence of Spain's imperial legacy as a civilizing mission. Published just a year before the so-called Disaster of 1898, the essay by the former under secretary of state, unapologetic for the destruction of colonialism, would desperately cling to the memory of an empire that once was in the face of immanent collapse and the rise of American empire.

Throughout the narrative, illegitimacy conjures up such historical anxiety around the Spaniards' impure blood and by extension its uncertain whiteness spurred by the discourse of the Black Legend. Spain's tarnished imperial legacy causes the narrative to vacillate ambivalently between a desire for the alluring white beauty that is Doña Luz, and the danger, fear, and ultimately hysteria that is unleashed by her status as an illegitimate marquis, "the black within." For much of the novel, Luz's deceased mother casts a dark shadow even as her identity remains unknown ("desconocida"), a rarity in narrative fiction. Her anonymity contradicts the oft-cited refrain *pater semper incertu est* ("the father is always uncertain") and *mater semper certa est* ("the mother is always certain").[21] That the novel closes with Luz as a single mother relegated to rural obscurity is notable. And even with the ironic discovery that Luz's unknown ("desconocida") mother was in fact an Andalusian countess, her status of legitimacy and her mother's licentiousness remain unchanged – failing to undo the taint on Luz's birth. But ultimately, it is the licit marriage of the illegitimate daughter and her transition into motherhood that allows her to remain – however tenuously – a member of this "community of blood."

Luz is the sole character who is made to embody whiteness along with conflicting stereotypes of oriental allure and colonial savageness, representing the diverse identities Spaniards struggled to negotiate in this period: from one moment to the next, she is an Aryan beauty, an Arab Fairy, the pearl of the Orient, and an uncivilized savage of the Indies. Simultaneously representing all that is pure and impure, Doña Luz breaks down the boundaries between these categories, demonstrating that they are intricately intertwined, perhaps always already contaminated. But this is not, I argue, a form of "subversive orientalism" that Joan Torres-Pou attributes to Valera, leading him to problematically name the diplomat of an imperial state a "predecessor" of Edward Said ("The Exotic as Subversive" 255).[22] Instead, when we scrutinize Valera's Orient/ornament, we uncover "the intersection of beauty and terror" (Cheng 17). Or, to appropriate the words of the narrator, "[lo] horrible y bello a la vez" ("that which is at once horrible and beautiful"; *Doña Luz* 81; 49). Valera's is a novel that unveils, but it is not one that subverts. It exposes, in all its ambivalence, the impossibility of purity (*limpieza de sangre*), perhaps Juan Valera's own nostalgia for imperial glory, and an increasing suspicion of identity construed by appearance. In a modernizing world in which representation is everything, competing fictions of identity come to the fore. Apparent whiteness betrays an oral history of blood, only to be upended by the written word.

Chapter Two

From Blood to Flesh: Avowing Material Pleasure in *La Regenta*

> *The rallying point for the counterattack*
> *against the deployment of sexuality*
> *ought not to be sex-desire,*
> *but bodies and pleasures.*
>
> Michel Foucault, *History of Sexuality I*

Leopoldo Alas's *La Regenta* (1884–5) has become iconic for its depiction of gendered and sexual perversions. Its cast of wayward characters includes an adulterer (Ana), a lecherous priest (Fermín de Pas), an effeminate acolyte (Celedonio), and a donjuanesque libertine (Álvaro Mesía). More often than not, it is a work we remember as teeming with forbidden desires rather than marred by blood. *La Regenta* is also, however, a novel about blighted origins. Like Doña Luz, the beautiful protagonist Ana Ozores is marked by the taint of her deceased mother's blood. But distinct from Valera's novel, *La Regenta* – Alas's debut work of fiction – is neither a tale of illegitimacy nor mistaken identities. Absent are the Cervantine ironies that underwrite the fictive tale of origin. The social status of Ana's deceased mother is well known: an Italian seamstress who brought public shame to the illustrious family name when she wed its primogenitor Don Carlos. This stain on her lineage, the narrative suggests, is the origin of Ana's future licentiousness. That is, her ill-fated destiny as an adulterer, a fallen woman, and a hysteric are predetermined by her mother's blood. Among the aristocracy, this marriage "representaba una alianza nefasta en que la sangre, a todas luces azul de los Ozores, se mezcló en mal hora con *sangre* plebeya; y lo que es peor … según todos sabemos, representa esa niña la poca meticulosa moralidad de su madre" ("stands for an ill-starred alliance in which the manifestly blue blood of the Ozoreses was mixed, in an evil hour, with plebeian *blood*. And, what is even worse, as we all know, the girl stands for the negligence in matters of morality of her mother"; *La Regenta I* 281, my emphasis; Rutherford 96, my emphasis). Correlating class and morality, sexual deviance becomes an "expression" of her mother's plebeian blood. That is, Ana's sexuality becomes proof of this taint.

This chapter explores the significance of Ana's blood in the novel's sexual economy: the symbolic power of blood, how blood materializes around sexuality, and ultimately how the deterministic force of bloodlines leads Ana to reject the social expectation of chastity and avow the material pleasures of the flesh. In *La Regenta*, the blood paradigm comes into sharp view when the young Ana racializes her marginalized mother as a moor and obliquely, with the town's hypocritical investment in Ana's purity – both in terms of caste and chastity – as her adultery is seen as a consequence of her bloodlines. "Blood," as Alison Sinclair writes of *La Regenta*, "thus appears as a substance not simply thicker than water, but one which marks indelibly" (*Dislocations of Desire* 25).

Indeed, the narrative enfolds a social world in oscillation: it moves between competing regimes of what Michel Foucault terms "'sanguinity' and 'sexuality.'" And while Foucault largely focuses on the latter supplanting the former, Alas lays bare the tumultuous, non-linear transition from "a symbolics of blood to an analytic of sexuality," from the pre-modern to the modern. Indeed, *La Regenta* is a temporally complex narrative that exposes, through Ana, a belated society of sexuality in which power still "spoke *through* blood" (147). Vetusta – meaning ancient or antiquated – is the provincial metropolis in which *La Regenta* takes place. The fictional town – likely modelled on Oviedo – remains enchanted by Spain's pre-modern heritage – the legend of the Spanish *godo* (Goths) ossified in the town's gothic cathedral tower. The men in Ana's life emblematize early modern masculine stereotypes. Her husband Don Víctor is an avid hunter obsessed with Calderón de la Barca's so-called wife-murder plays in which cuckolded men cleanse their honour through the spectacular bloodletting of their dishonoured wives. Víctor's obsession with honour killings only further compounds the irony of his death: slain in a duel by Ana's seducer Don Álvaro, the contemporary Don Juan who openly boasts of his sexual adventures. In a moment that foreshadows his death, Víctor's blood takes on phatansmagorical properties. At a staging of *Don Juan Tenorio*, Ana has a hallucinatory vision of her ill-fated future as a widower: "Ana vio de repente como a la luz de un relámpago, a don Víctor vestido de terciopelo negro, con jubón y ferreruelo, bañado en sangre, boca arriba, y a don Álvaro con una pistola en la mano enfrente de cadáver" ("As in a flash of lightning, Ana saw Don Victor in jerkin and tippet of black velvet lying face upwards bathed in blood, and Don Alvaro standing over the corpse with a pistol in his hand"; *La Regenta II* 122; Rutherford 375). (Blood novels by and large tend to depict women's physical bloodshed, but in this case the novel affords aesthetic space to the [imagined] bloody death of the feminized celibate Don Víctor.) Finally, we have Fermín de Pas, the lecherous priest, who likens himself to Pizarro in his conquest of women's bodies and souls. In short, Alas nostalgically animates supposedly antiquated gender codes that allow for the symbolic force of blood, and by extension *limpieza de sangre*, to persist.

The Chastity Bind in *La Regenta*

La Regenta serves as an exemplary blood novel that lays bare the vicious, interstitial moments of transition in which the preoccupation with bloodlines comes into conflict with a nascent bourgeois moral order that expects women to be chaste wives and mothers. The ideology of blood purity requires female chastity: women of notable origins must remain chaste to ensure the purity of the caste. Yet for women of illegitimate, cross-class, or humble origins, their "sullied" blood renders chastity futile, upending the incipient bourgeois moral code through which social identity is determined by behaviour and not by birth.[1] In this expansive moment of social transition, women like Ana find themselves caught in the *chastity bind* – compelled to be chaste by virtue of their gender and yet deemed impure and unsalvageable by their unclean blood. Beyond the symbolic force of bloodlines, physical blood materializes in punctuated moments of the narrative: Ana's oft-overlooked menstruation and, befittingly, a duel – sanguinary justice – that leaves her Calderón-obsessed husband Víctor tragically slain. This unsteady transition from "a symbolics of blood to an analytic of sexuality" serves as a point of departure for examining the relationship between origins and sexuality in *La Regenta* – a novel whose central conflict hinges on the knotted ties that bind blood with sex. Yes, blood "marks indelibly" (Sinclair *Dislocations* 25), yet in Vetusta sex is a pervasive concern, "an object of fear and excitement at the same time" (Foucault 148). In such a world, Ana Ozores figures as "victim, scapegoat, the necessary focalization of that aspect of Vetustan life – its idealism fused with sexuality – which has to be castigated" (*Dislocations* 28).

In what follows, I trace the conflicts that arise from the disjunctive *simultaneity* of blood and sex in *La Regenta* that have heretofore been neglected. To this end, I examine how Alas represents a blood-based hierarchy in contention with the administration of sexuality. As Ana finds herself at the crossroads of these two regimes, I argue that the path to her adulterous "fall" – as she transits from husband to confessor to medical hygienist and seducer – becomes the sole avenue through which she attempts self-actualization – a process that occurs in accord with her impure lineage and against the prohibitions of religion and medical hygiene. In other words, Ana, already believed to be lascivious as a result of her bloodlines, realizes the futility of her chastity and avows the material pleasures of the flesh.

Born of patriarchy and inflected by gender, chastity and blood purity have been historically channelled through women (as is the case with Ana and her mother). As anthropologist Mary Douglas has observed, "The mother is the decisive parent for establishing caste members. Through women the blood and purity of the caste is perpetuated" (178). Thus, women are either polluters of the caste (e.g., Ana's mother), or what Anne McClintock calls "threshold figures" (24), marking its penetrable boundaries. The disproportionate scrutiny applied to women's bodies and matrilineal inheritance, and what Foucault termed the "hysterization" (104) of women's bodies, is not entirely new to the nineteenth century. Instead, it finds a compelling correlation with the early modern discourse of *limpieza de sangre*, which, in the sixteenth century, "shifted the focus of the 'heresy problem' to the family and helped to construe women as main sources of impurity" (Martínez 55). Affirming Douglas's claim, this change subsequently produced widespread anxiety around sexual relations (56).

In the nineteenth century, women's health became a prevailing concern within the male-dominated medical–legal community, eventually cohering into the study of modern gynecology. Examining the gendered nature of medical discourse, Catherine Jagoe argues, "En el siglo XIX la salud tiene un género, el masculino … Todo indica que la mujer normal, tal y como se la construía, es una figura liminal cuya fisiología linda con la enfermedad" ("In the nineteenth century health is gendered masculine … Everything indicates that the normal woman, as she was then construed, is a liminal figure whose physiology borders on illness"; "Sexo" 307). For hygienist Pedro Felipe Monlau, women had a natural predilection for virtue, but their hypersensitive nerves meant they were also easily excitable. Women's bodies, especially, warranted medical attention since, it was believed, a mother could physically transmit her hysteria to her children:

La propiedad hereditaria, al parecer, respecto a esta enfermedad, no procede sino de la madre, hecho que se comprende fácilmente, si se reflexiona que casi solamente la mujer goza de aquella impresionabilidad del sistema

> nervioso, de aquella disposicion afectiva, de la cual el histerismo no es
> mas que un modo particular, una especie de exageracion especial. (*Higiene
> del matrimonio* 550; diacritics missing in original)

> It seems that the hereditary property, with respect to this illness, proceeds
> from none other than the mother, a fact that can be easily understood, if
> one considered that it is almost exclusively women that have an impres-
> sionable nervous system, an affective disposition, of which hysteria is just
> one particular mode, a type of special exaggeration.

While seemingly disparate historical examples, in both cases women
figure as easily contaminated and uncontainable bodies posing a threat
to their future offspring.

In *La Regenta*, the persistence of early modern gender norms in the
nineteenth century cannot be underestimated. Bridget Aldaraca, in her
landmark study *El ángel del hogar: Galdós and the Ideology of the Domesticity in Spain*, demonstrated the longevity of Fray Luis de Leon's *La perfecta
casada* (1583) and its influence on modern norms of female domesticity.
Aldaraca's work makes clear that the tenets of bourgeois femininity figured as modern iterations of sixteenth- and seventeenth-century gender ideals. Indeed, Alas's narrator evokes Fray Luis de Leon's iconic
image of early modern femininity: "En Vetusta, decir la Regenta era
decir la perfecta casada" ("In Vetusta, to say the judge's wife was to say
the perfect wife"; *La Regenta I* 237; Rutherford 74). Along these same
lines, I contend that throughout the nineteenth century, the ideological
underpinnings of blood purity continued to "haunt" – to use Foucault's
term – the deployment of sexuality, particularly in the case of female
subjectivity.

Crucially, both blood and chastity hinge on a gendered conceptualization of purity, rooted in the Hispanic notion of caste. The semantic
ambiguity inherent in the feminine, adjectival form of *casta* as chaste
and the noun form of *casta* as caste illustrates the semantic inseparabil-
ity of blood and sexuality. In this way, the collectivized social value
placed on chastity is implicitly tethered to a desire for the collective
purity of the caste and vice versa. These semantic linkages between
caste and chastity underscore the ways in which gendered identity is
often inflected by (even as it conflicts with) other categories of identity –
in this case, blood.

In Vetusta, sex does not simply supplant blood, as Foucault would
have it. Instead, Alas depicts a morally deficient world in which the
deep-rooted value attributed to pure, noble lineage clashes with modern sexual norms, particularly chastity – the ubiquitous ideal that

underwrites female subjectivity. The chaste woman achieves iconographic status in the nineteenth century as the *ángel del hogar* ("angel of the hearth"), yet as Jagoe has demonstrated (see *Ambiguous Angels*), realist novels unveil the ambiguous, and at times conflictive, iterations of this gender ideal. In the case of *La Regenta*, Ana's chastity – a rare and enviable quality in the decadent Vetusta – becomes even more remarkable because of her inherited filth. Described as "casta por vigor de temperamento" ("[one] whose chastity depended upon her strength of character"; *La Regenta I* 298; Rutherford 108). Ana perfectly embodies the chastity bind: she is at once impure by birth and yet chastity incarnate. What is more, as the narrative gaze continually eroticizes Ana, even her chastity appears to be an ambivalent, erotically charged designation. Stephanie Anne Sieburth observes that these "conflicting scenes of promiscuity and virtue attached to Ana make for perpetual controversy among the Vetustans as to whether Ana is exceptional or just like other Vetustan women, that is, lascivious" (15). For Sieburth, "[the townspeople's] belief in biological determinism means that their heroine will be more likely to sin if her mother was promiscuous" (15). We cannot know for certain, however, whether Ana's mother was ever truly "promiscuous" to begin with since she figures as a narrative void, overlayed with the townspeople's ever-evolving rumours and Ana's own imagination, making her life story even less accessible. Indeed, the aristocracy grafts their fantasy of lasciviousness onto the story of her mother's humble origins, thereby knitting together sexuality and class. Read in this way, the controversy is not predicated on becoming like other Vetustan women, but rather "como su madre" ("like her mother"; *La Regenta I* 253; Rutherford 82). Thus, as Joan Ramon Resina explains: "Nymphomania is the unspoken name of the perversion [Ana] is suspected of inoculating into the Ozores's blood" (245). "That assumption," he continues, "underlies the accusations of precocity brought against Ana and resurfaces when the scandal of her adultery breaks out" (235). Ana's tainted blood determines by and large how others predict and interpret her comportment.[2]

Even as Ana emblematizes the Ozores family's sexual shame, the aristocracy eventually – though reluctantly at first – admits her into her father's "class."[3] Ana's virginal beauty earns her the admiration of well-to-do members of society. For the time being, female attractiveness trumps origin. The narrator recounts:

Su belleza salvó a la huérfana. Se la admitió sin reparo en *la clase*, en la intimidad de la clase por su hermosura. Nadie se acordaba de la modista italiana. Tampoco Ana debía mentarla siquiera, según orden expresa de las tías. Se había olvidado todo … era un perdón general. Ana era de la clase; la honraba con su hermosura, como un caballo de sangre y de piel de seda honra la caballeriza y hasta la casa de un potentado. (*La Regenta I* 293)

The orphan girl's beauty was her salvation. She was admitted without reserve into the ranks of *persons of quality*, into the fellowship of the *classes*, on the grounds of her beauty. Nobody remembered the Italian dressmaker. Nor must Ana even mention her, by express command of the aunts. Everything had been forgotten … it was a general pardon. Ana was *of quality*; she honoured the classes with her beauty as a pure-blooded, silk-skinned horse honours the stables and even the house of a potentate. (Rutherford 104)

Masking the pernicious stain of her mother's blood, Ana's singular beauty creates a luminous veneer of oblivion. Her transitory acceptance into *la clase* reveals how beauty may temporarily obfuscate origins. To help facilitate this "perdón general" ("general pardon"), Ana's aunts forbid her from speaking of her mother. The pact of silence helps engender a new fiction that papers over her past.

Yet, the fact that the narrator likens Ana to "un caballo de *sangre*" ("a pure-blooded horse") is no innocent detail. This loaded image recalls the intertwinement of chastity and caste identity.[4] As Nina Auerbach has observed, the image of the horse in nineteenth-century literature has been linked to fallen women (as in the case of Zola's *Nana* and Tolstoy's *Anna Karenina*) (178–9). In the Hispanic context, the pairing of women and horses in narrative fiction – most notably in the works of Juan Valera – metonymically connotes a sense of unbridled female passion or deviant desires, as we saw in the case of *Doña Luz*. In *La Regenta*, however, the narrator goes one step further than Valera – heavy handedly comparing Ana to a horse rather than depicting her as rider. This move explicitly consigns Ana to the realm of animality and as feudal property.

Keri Weil, writing about nineteenth-century French literature, argues that "the horse increasingly functioned as a kind of 'transitional object' for talking not only about aesthetics, but also about gender, race, and sexuality (or breeding) in French society" (3). Likewise, in the case of Spain, there are profound connections between the figure of the horse and issues pertaining to sexuality, caste, and race. Historically, the usage of the term *casta* ("caste") intersects within a semantic genealogy that links animal breeds with lineage and race. With the mention of the horse's pure blood (*sangre*), we are reminded of the blood-based exclusivity that defines the aristocracy even as Ana is allowed to pass into their caste. The equine analogy is, therefore, a conflictive, if not ironic, designation. It evokes the racially inflected history of blood *qua* caste, evidencing the way origin undergirds sexual norms and categories of deviance.

In *La Regenta*, the discourse of blood intersects with modern sexual norms; it reanimates these early modern conceptions of race and caste through the trope of cleanliness that repeatedly surfaces in the novel. As Ana is depicted as pure and impregnable, figurative forms of filth (*lodo*, *cieno*, and *tierra*) ("mud," "silt," and "earth") abound in the narrative landscape. The whole of Vetusta is dubbed a *lodazal* ("mire") to which Ana attempts to remain pure and immune. But those closest to her, including her friend Visita, "[q]uería ver aquel armiño [Ana] en el lodo" ("wanted to see that little ermine [Ana] sunk in mud"; *La Regenta* I 410; Rutherford 173). Alison Sinclair, analysing Alas's iconography of dirt, remarks that "[t]he quality of cleanliness ... has particular connotations in the Hispanic context of *limpieza*: cleanliness with regard to lineage and blood, and cleanliness that is understood as freedom from shame" (*Dislocations* 53). Here, it is crucial to recall that the 1884 definition of *limpio/a* (clean) still denoted a sense of religious-racial purity: "Aplícase a las personas o familias que no tienen mezcla ni raza de moros, judíos, herejes o penitenciados" ("It is applied to persons or families that have no mixture nor race of moors, Jews, heretics, or Inquisition prisoners"; *DRAE* "limpio/a").

Tellingly, as a young child, Ana racializes her mother: she imagines her as a "reina mora" ("Queen of the Moors"; *La Regenta* I 258; 80), a designation that activates the notion of *limpieza* as the absence of Moorish blood. Not fully comprehending the racialized rhetoric used to describe her mother, the young Ana with her "lógica poética" ("poetic logic"; 251; 80) believes all doves with black stains on their heads must be mothers. Here, is it important to recall that Vetusta is a fictionalized Oviedo, which, Eric Pennington reminds us, was the capital of "the reduced Visigoth Empire when Muslims held the rest of the peninsula" (170). That Ana imagines her mother as a moor in the historic land of the Visigoths whose heritage is evoked in the late nineteenth century to signify whiteness effectively couches her origin story in a narrative of imperial failure and racial decline.[5] Like *Doña Luz*, the cultural force of *limpieza de sangre* intertwines with a racial discourse. But whereas Juan Valera focuses more squarely on the illegitimacy of his protagonist's physical whiteness, Alas racializes Ana's sexuality as the product of her mother's "bad" blood.

Just as the blood purity statutes focused on matrilineal heritage, Ana's stain is couched as a hereditary, matrilineal disease – a designation that profoundly affects her social status. But blood does not merely take on the metaphorical trappings of race. Rather, the narrator relays the suspicion that Ana might actually be of non-Christian lineage. In a seldom remembered passage of the novel, the narrator remarks, "Ripamilán, que sabía tratar en serio los asuntos serios, nunca había hablado al Magistral de lo que podía ser la Regenta, juzgada desde el tribunal sagrado" ("Don Cayetano [Ripamilán], who could be serious when dealing with serious subjects, had never spoken to the canon theologian about the judge's wife from the point of view of one judging her from that sacred tribunal"; *La Regenta I* 203; Rutherford 53). Refusing to even say the name of Ana's suspected taint – as though uttering might make it real – the narrator leaves it to the reader to imagine "lo que podía ser" ("what she could be"). At once admired for her chastity and desired for her beauty, Ana's shadowy origin makes her inscrutable from the outset as she comes into representation under an inquisitive gaze. Thus, as Ana faces the social consequences produced by the jagged misalignment of her enviable virginal qualities and her stained lineage, it becomes clear that beauty and chastity cannot cleanse her blood.

Ana's Blood

Ana's unclean blood is not merely symbolic. It is markedly a material reality. In a seldom remarked passage of the novel, Ana's early onset of menstruation coincides with the start of her quasi-mystic experiences that are associated with nervous or hysterical attacks.[6] The archpriest of Vetusta goes as far as to link the two:

> – Ella ha visto visiones … pseudo-místicas … allá en Loreto … al llegar la edad … *cosa de la sangre* … al ser mujercita, cuando tuvo aquella fiebre y fuimos a buscarla su tía doña Anuncia y yo. Después … pasó aquello y se hizo literata … En fin, usted verá. No es una señora como estas de por aquí. Tiene mucho tesón; parece una malva, pero otra le queda; quiero decir, que se somete a todo, pero por dentro siempre protesta. Ella misma se me ha acusado de esto, que conocía que era orgullo. Aprensiones. No es orgullo; pero resulta de estas cosas que es desgraciada, aunque nadie lo sospeche. (*La Regenta I* 480–81; my emphasis)

> She saw visions, pseudo-mystical visions, in Loreto – at that critical age – *something to do with the blood* – when she was turning into a woman and suffered that fever, and her aunt Doña Anuncia and I went to fetch her. Then she recovered from all that, and became a bluestocking. You'll soon see what she's like. She isn't just another fine Vetustan lady. She is a tenacious woman. She may seem as meek as a lamb, but under all that she's a

different person altogether. What I mean to say is that she consents to everything, but in her heart of hearts she is always objecting. In confession she has spoken of this, saying she realizes that it is all pride. Empty fears. It is not pride, but the outcome of it all is that she is feeling wretched, although nobody suspects it. (Rutherford 221)

Here, the volatile periodicity of the female body – premature menstruation – correlates with religious fanaticism and, crucially, hysteria. The archpriest views Ana's precocious entry into womanhood as the source of her untrustworthy docility and veiled tenacity.

This pivotal moment coincides with Ana's unusual and pernicious penchant for reading. In her examination of the gendered implications of literacy, Catherine Jaffe has rightly noted that *"La Regenta* insistently links female hysteria and reading" (3). Jaffe goes on to examine the unconventional way in which Alas collapses two types of women in his depiction of Ana: "the transported, erotic novel reader and the impassioned religious reader" (10). Yet despite this, Jaffe explains, "Ana exhibits a seriousness of intent in adult reading that is completely different from the commonly portrayed frivolous woman reader" (12). Hygienists like Pedro Felipe Monlau wrote of the dangers of young girls reading, noting that "lascivious" texts could lead to premature menstruation (*Elementos de obstetricia* 93). This fear of the sexually precocious child – a threat to society – aligns with what Foucault termed the "pedagogization of children's sex," the second of four unities (the first being the "hysterization of women's bodies") that comprise the "deployment of sex."

It bears mentioning that as an adult Ana suffers from anemia, perhaps as a result of her menstruation. As Álvaro, her soon to be seducer, pines after her, he fantasizes about a possible blood transfusion to cure her anemia: "'hubiera dado sangre de un brazo por verla correr por aquellas venas que se figuraba exhaustas. ¡La vida, la fuerza a todo trance, para aquella mujer!' Hasta habló un día don Álvaro de transfusiones. 'La ciencia había adelantado mucho en esta materia'" ("'he would have given blood from one of his arms to see it running through those veins which he imagined to be exhausted. Life, strength at any cost for that woman!' Don Alvaro even spoke one day about transfusions. 'Science had made much progress in this matter'"; *La Regenta II* 226; Rutherford 450).

With these examples, we see how blood – both symbolic and material – manifests in decisive moments of Clarín's narrative, determining the social castigation of its young heroine and simultaneously fuelling her menacing willfulness. All the while Ana's ill-advised reading impels menstrual blood, draining her of this vital fluid which Álvaro dreams of replenishing. Moreover, Ana's premature menstruation subsequently unleashes the gendered maladies that spill forth from this pivotal moment. True to the medical beliefs contemporary to the novel, Ana's pathological bleeding appears to body forth the symbolic valences of her impure bloodlines. In the end, the hereditary logic of blood purity that underlies female sexuality triumphs, and impure blood is thought to elicit impure actions. Thus, the townspeople "saboreaba por adelantado la lujuria de lo porvenir" ("savour[ed] a foretaste of future lechery"; *La Regenta I* 254; Rutherford 82).

Confession: A Ritual of Pleasure and Deceit

Stigmatized from the outset, Ana knows to be vigilant about her chastity and public comportment, unlike the other aristocratic women in Vetusta. Her caution illustrates the nineteenth-century saying "Ya que no seas casto, sé cauto" ("casto/a") ("Since you are not chaste, be cautious") (*DRAE* "chaste"). As a child she learns firsthand about the power of public scandal when she and her friend Germán play out their escape fantasies to watch the moonlit night and end up falling asleep together on a boat. Once discovered, their nocturnal disappearance is cruelly misrepresented by Ana's English governess, Doña Camila. The narrator invites us to empathize with Ana by exposing Camila's ill intentions. But regardless of Ana's innocence, her reputation has already been coloured by the original sin that flows through her veins. This early experience with public scandal enacts a pedagogic function: Ana learns about the mechanisms of the production of truth. Following this event, she is forced into her first confession – "la hicieron confesar" ("made her confess") – after which the priest concludes "por ignorancia o por malicia, ocultaba su pecadillos" ("out of either ignorance or artfulness she made a secret of her transgressions"; *La Regenta I* 225; Rutherford 67). The townspeople of Loreto subsequently construe Ana's silence as proof of her moral transgression rather than as a sign of her innocence. If confession is, as Foucault contended, "one of the West's most highly valued techniques for producing truth" (59), Alas's text exposes the hermeneutic shortcomings of confession by showing how fiction via the confessional can achieve the status of truth.[7] The seeds of this formative moment have yet to bear their fruit, but the narrator remarks that henceforth Ana "vivió en perpetua escuela de disimulo" ("turned her life into a perpetual schooling in dissimulation"; 256; 83). Learning the art of "disimulo," or concealment, as we shall see, is a shield for Ana. Indeed, throughout the novel, the narrator deftly moves between that which is public versus concealed, spoken versus thought and felt to show us Ana's inner truth, and the ways in which it clashes with public opinion, surveillance, and scrutiny.

As an adult, Ana actively seeks religious guidance and confession. Purity and cleanliness initially undergird her engagement with Catholicism. Under the tutelage of her confessor Fermín de Pas, Ana reflects on his definition of virtue:

La virtud era la belleza del alma, la pulcritud, la cosa más fácil para los espíritus nobles y limpios. Para un perezoso enemigo de la ropa limpia y del agua, la pulcritud es un tormento, un imposible; para una persona decente (así había dicho) una necesidad de las más imperiosas de la vida. (*La Regenta* I 424)

"Virtue was the beauty of the soul, its cleanliness – the easiest thing in the world for noble, pure souls. For people who are indolent, and have an aversion to water and to freshly laundered clothes, cleanliness is a torture, an impossibility; yet for a respectable person" (yes those had been his words) "it is one of the most imperious necessities in life." (Rutherford 184–5)

In Ana's words, virtue mirrors hygienic conceptions of cleanliness (*limpieza*), which, as we have seen, evokes the religious-racial connation of *limpieza de sangre*. Yet vis-à-vis the obdurate stain of Ana's origin, confession becomes an iterative but futile ritual of moral cleansing. Moreover, as Ana – much like Doña Luz with bathing – seeks out this purifying modality as a "fetishistic compensation" (Chang "Aquellos neófitos"), the confessional itself becomes a locus of contamination as her relationship with de Pas blurs the boundaries between religious and erotic passion.

Indeed, confession provokes Ana's earliest erotic experiences. In an oft-cited passage, Ana undergoes an examination of conscience (in preparation for confession) in which she cultivates an autoerotic sense of pleasure:

Después de abandonar todas las prendas que no habían de acompañarla en el lecho, quedó sobre la piel de tigre, hundiendo los pies desnudos, pequeños y rollizos en la espesura de las manchas pardas. Un brazo desnudo se apoyaba en la cabeza algo inclinada, y el otro pendía a lo largo del cuerpo, siguiendo la curva graciosa de la robusta cadera. Parecía una impúdica modelo olvidada de sí misma en una postura académica impuesta por el artista. Jamás el arcipreste, ni confesor alguno, había prohibido a la

Regenta esta voluptuosidad de contacto del aire fresco por todo el cuerpo a la hora de acostarse. Nunca había creído ella que tal abandono fuese materia de confesión ... abrió el lecho. Sin mover los pies, dejóse caer de bruces sobre aquella blandura suave con los brazos tendidos. Apoyaba la mejilla en la sábana y tenía los ojos muy abiertos. La deleitaba aquel placer del tacto que corría desde la cintura a las sienes ... ¡Confesión general! (*La Regenta I* 217)

After leaving aside the garments which she did not wear in bed [*sic*] she stood upon the tiger-skin, burying her bare feet, small and plump, in the fur with its brown markings. One naked arm rested on her head, which was slightly tilted, the other hung alongside her body, following the strong hip's graceful curve. She looked like some immodest model, transported by the sensuousness of the academic pose which an artist had told her to strike. Neither the archpriest nor any of her other confessors had ever prohibited the delight of stretching her torpid limbs, or of feeling the touch of cool air over her body, alone at bedtime. She had never thought such relaxation to be a matter for confession. Ana drew back the bedclothes. Without moving her feet, she let herself fall face downwards, arms outspread, upon the silky softness of the sheets. She rested her cheek on the bed, keeping her eyes wide open. She took great delight in that tactile pleasure, which ran from her waist to her temples. "General confession!" (Rutherford 62)

For Ana, the anticipation of confession allows her to discover, in solitude, self-pleasure through touch. Confession as a purifying ritual only further compounds Ana's sins by figuring as a source of erotic inspiration.

Indeed, de Pas hails Ana as a lascivious subject and, in turn, her lasciviousness becomes the requisite condition for confession. For Ana, the ritual of self-narration during confession, whether based on truth or fabrication, provides an intoxicating sense of pleasure: "las confesiones emborrachaban [a Anita]" ("Anita was intoxicated by confessions"; *La Regenta II* 130; Rutherford 387). Through the eroticization of confession, *La Regenta* lays bare the corruptibility of pastoral power, illustrating Noël Valis's observation that, for Alas, "the sacred and the profane are never far apart. Sometimes they are confused, sometimes the sacred is profane" (*Sacred Realism* 155). Indeed, confession ultimately fails to discipline Ana – fanning the flames of erotic excess instead of quelling the fire.

Despite the fact that confession permeates the narrative as a whole, the reader rarely witnesses characters speaking frankly about desire.

Indeed, readers of *La Regenta* will note that "the direct representation of confession is oddly missing" (Valis, *Sacred Realism* 178). At the same time, Alas's narrator slips into the characters' interior "confessional," revealing their thoughts and feelings. In fact, these private narratives, particularly Ana's, comprise a staggering portion of Alas's tome. For Valis, Ana's internal narrative becomes a kind of confession unto itself, a text that Ana produces in an attempt to "construct a self out of damaged, imperfect parts" – her imperfection being her origin (*Sacred Realism* 167). The prevailing theme in Ana's inner confessional narrative is erotic yearning. Indeed, pleasures of the flesh prove tantamount to matters of confession, particularly for the lecherous de Pas, who derives both power and pleasure from extracting narratives of a lascivious nature. Yet as Ana begins to evade the truth in confession, it becomes the reader (and narrator) who alone bears witness to unspoken desires.

Throughout *La Regenta*, the truth is often obfuscated by omission and silence. In this way, concealment (*disimulo*) stems from the "perpetual spirals of power and pleasure" that structure confessional speech in the novel (Foucault 45). De Pas exercises an extraordinary amount of power over women (potential lovers), if and only if they speak the truth: "Habla, habla así" "Speak, speak on," commands de Pas, "bendita sea tu boca" ("blessed be thy lips!"; *La Regenta II* 130; Rutherford 387). Ana eventually intuits the value of withholding information when de Pas probes her to confess her attraction to his rival Álvaro. The previous night, during a clandestine ball in the town casino, Álvaro cajoles Ana into accepting his invitation to a dance. Previously, Ana could be satisfied with the mere feeling of temptation: "[l]a tentación era suya, su único placer. ¡Bastante hacía con no dejarse vencer, pero quería dejarse tentar!" ("Temptation belonged to her – it was her only pleasure. She was doing quite enough if she avoided being conquered; but she did want to be tempted!"; *La Regenta I* 446; Rutherford 198). But this night she capitulates at the sound of music. The narrator remarks, "Cuando Ana tuvo fuerza para separar todo su cuerpo de aquel placer del roce ligero con don Álvaro, otro peligro mayor se presentó en seguida: se oía a lo lejos la música de salón. – ¡A bailar, a bailar!" ("As soon as Ana found the strength to separate her body from the pleasure of brushing against Don Alvaro, another greater peril loomed: the ballroom music could be heard in the distance. 'Let's dance, let's dance!'"; *La Regenta II* 381; Rutherford 552). Dancing with Alvaro ignites "un placer que parecía fuego; aquel gozo intenso; irresistible: la espantaba" ("a pleasure which was like fire; this intense irresistible delight terrified her"; *La Regenta II* 381; Rutherford 552). Soon after, Ana faints in his arms, and the following day she rushes off to confession. Horrified by the intensity of her own feelings, she declares, "estuve loca" ("I was mad"; *La Regenta II* 388; Rutherford 556). De Pas impatiently attempts to elicit Ana's confession: "Eso quiero saber yo, Ana; saber ..., saberlo todo. Yo también padezco" ("That is what I want, Ana. To know – to know everything. I am suffering too"; *La Regenta II* 388; Rutherford 557).

Ana, who hoped to confess and be absolved of her sins, alters her story when she realizes how the truth, if made public, might put her at risk. De Pas's desire to peg her as guilty of betraying him becomes apparent to her. She realizes that withholding the truth can be a form of power, and, conversely, sharing it could be a form of self-endangerment – a lesson that harkens back to her publicized childhood "scandal" with Germán. The narrator explains, "Ana recogió sus fuerzas, atendió a la realidad, a lo que le preguntaba, con intensidad, luchando con el confesor, batiéndose por su interés que era ocultar lo más hondo de su pensamiento" ("Ana gathered her strength and concentrated on reality, on what she was being asked; now she was struggling with her confessor, fighting to protect her own interest, which was to hide her deepest thoughts"; 389; 557–8). De Pas the inquisitor repeatedly questions her, but Ana feigns amnesia: "Yo no recuerdo ... tal vez" ("I can't remember, perhaps ..."; 389; 558). Disavowing the deed in confession, Ana somewhat clumsily takes control of her own narrative, for, as Judith Butler contends, speaking of the deed in question "presumes and solicits recognition and constitutes the first act as public, as known, as having truly happened" (*Undoing Gender* 165). Here, Ana's childhood lessons come full circle, and she adopts the ethic of *disimulo* ("concealment") as a mode of protection and learns to manipulate the production of truth. And while silence may not save the protagonist, it momentarily detracts power from her inquisitor. De Pas, dumbfounded by Ana's lie, loses his composure, and it is in this moment that Ana's gut tells her the priest longs to be her lover, a realization that "la hizo sonreír a ella misma con amargura que llegó hasta la boca desde las entrañas" ("made her smile to herself with a bitterness which came to her mouth from deep in her body"; *La Regenta II* 392; Rutherford 559). In this surprising reversal of roles, confessor confesses, revealing that he too suffers ("Yo también padezco" ["I am suffering too"]) from moral illness. He and Ana become aligned with one another as "sick" patients, stricken with the maladies of stilted pleasures. But while de Pas needs the truth to heal, Ana withholds it to survive. Far from a sanctified space, then, the confessional itself becomes a conduit for the traffic of desire and deceit. In this way, confession awakens Ana's erotic pleasure and drives the impulse for self-narration. While Ana cannot alter her fate – predetermined by the taint of her blood – this internal transformation evidences a willfulness that allows her to defy the restrictive norms of chastity.

On the Limits of Hygiene

Under the guidance of de Pas, Ana's religious devotion culminates in the spectacular barefoot procession during Holy Week that constitutes her first public "fall" in Vetusta. As readers of *La Regenta* know quite well, Ana "venía guapísima, pálida, como la virgen" ("was looking very very pretty and pale, just like the Virgin") and becomes the object of multiple and simultaneous desirous gazes: "se la devoraba con los ojos" ("[they] devoured her with their eyes"; *La Regenta II* 428; Rutherford 584). As Ana's image becomes pure visual delight for others, shame impairs her own vision: "Sus ojos no veían" ("her eyes could not see"; *La Regenta II* 433; Rutherford 589). Yet even as her senses begin to decline, Ana realizes this theatrical performance of religious devotion has become "una especie de prostitución singular" ("a singular kind of prostitution"; *La Regenta II* 433; Rutherford 589), and rightly so. Drawing from Auguste Rabutaux's typology of prostitution, Nuria Godón has argued that Ana's spectacle would have fallen under the category of what was known as religious prostitution, "fundamentada en una tradición religiosa pervertida y transformada" ("founded in a perverted and transformed religious tradition"; 253). For Víctor, Ana's performance is much worse than prostitution, as he ironically declares, "¡Primero seducida que fanatizada!" ("Sooner seduced than fanaticized!"; *La Regenta II* 437; Rutherford 593). Viewing herself through the eyes of other Vetustans, Ana imagines all the titles for deviant women she has accrued in this single moment: "Allí iba la tonta, la literata, Jorge Sandio, la mística, la fatua, la loca, la loca sin vergüenza" ("Here was the foolish girl, the bluestocking, George Sand, the mystic, the prig, the madwoman, the shameless madwoman"; *La Regenta II* 433; Rutherford 589). Finally, she recalls passages from Fray Luis de León's *Perfecta casada* and thinks to herself, "condenaban lo que estaba haciendo" ("they condemned what she was doing"; *La Regenta II* 433; Rutherford 589).

Ana subsequently renounces her religious practices in an attempt to cure herself of nervous attacks that followed. Acquiescing to a new regime of self-discipline under the direction of her new doctor, Benítez, Ana declares, "Seré esclava de la higiene" ("I shall be a slave to hygiene"; *La Regenta II* 444; Rutherford 596). Initially she finds "salvation" in medical hygiene and enjoys the pleasures of living with "sangre pura y corriente en medio de la atmósfera saludable" ("in a healthy atmosphere, with pure blood coursing through me"; *La Regenta II* 444;

Rutherford 596). United with nature, Ana no longer suffers from anemia. In this rare instance, blood symbolizes health and vitality rather than lasciviousness and pollution. Of course, one cannot help but note the cognitive dissonance that underlies the ironic allusion to pure blood in Ana's declaration. Hygiene, then, figures as a markedly modern mode of purification and replaces religious confession as yet another practice intended to eradicate Ana's proverbial filth. Moreover, that the medical hygienist takes over the religious confessor's role illustrates the Foucauldian transition from Christian pastoral power to secular biopower. But this shift, too, did not occur without conceptual overlap. On multiple occasions, the narrator portrays de Pas as a doctor of the soul, and confession is equated to the ingestion of medicine: "tomar la medicina" ("take the medicine"; *La Regenta II* 127; Rutherford 384). Couching religious confession in medical terms, Alas depicts a swiftly modernizing world in which religion must re-establish its legitimacy by appropriating medical discourse.[8]

Ironically, Ana's pledge to this new regime of health may actually be a harbinger of her future adultery. Eduardo López Bago used the phrase "esclavas de la higiene" ("slaves to hygiene"; 125) to describe the prostitutes in his medical-social novel *La prostituta*, published in 1884, the year before Alas would release part two of *La Regenta*. Bago's use of the term "slave" evokes sympathy towards sex workers, who were subjected to routine medical examinations in accordance with the law. In *La Regenta*, we might argue that Alas, too, invokes a sense of compassion for Ana, who is subjected to yet another patriarchal figure: she has transitioned from religious prostitution to so-called hygienic slavery. The phrase "esclava de la higiene" certainly takes an ironic turn as Ana's subscription to hygiene precedes her total submission to illicit pleasure – Ana's second and final fall. Thus, just as confession proved to be a futile mode of purification, so, too, does hygiene fail as a cleansing mechanism.

Surprisingly, hygiene plays a crucial role in Ana's seduction: Álvaro Mesía prepares to seduce Ana by reading hygiene manuals. The narrator recounts, "[C]uanto más lejos estaba una mujer del vicio, más exagerada era cuando llegaba a caer. La Regenta, si caía, iba a ser exageradísima. Y se preparaba Mesía. Leyó libros de higiene, hizo gimnasia de salón, paseó mucho a caballo" ("the further the woman was from vice, the more excessive she was when she fell. If the judge's wife fell she was going to be very excessive indeed. And Mesía prepared himself. He read books about hygiene, he did physical exercises, he went for frequent rides"; *La Regenta II* 398; Rutherford 562). Here, our attention is drawn not only to hygiene but also to the act of reading: we read about Álvaro reading. This self-reflexive moment reveals the linkages between hygiene, reading practices, and self-discipline.[9] But as Álvaro takes the lessons of the manuals against the logic of hygiene, that is, to preserve his sexual energies for a future sexual conquest, we learn that prescriptions and prohibitions are always susceptible to subversion. Ultimately, Alas's narrative makes clear that hygienic practices fail to discipline their subjects.

Monlau, the aforementioned hygienist, was well aware of the unruly potentiality in reading hygiene literature. In the preface to his famous manual *Higiene de matrimonio* (the first to explicitly treat the topic of sex in Spain), he condemned the deviant reading practices associated with illicit medical literature published abroad:

> Mi higiene del matrimonio … *no* se parece en *nada* á [*sic*] *ninguna* de las várias [sic] obras que acerca de la materia, aunque con fines poco loables, se han publicado con sobrada libertad en el extranjero, *no* mucho menos tiene punto alguno contacto con aquellos librejos inmundos en cuyas groseras páginas y obscenas estampas va á [*sic*] buscar inspiraciones eróticas la inexperta juventud. *No* es una obrilla de esas que han de leerse en secreto, como quien comete una mala acción, *no*: mi libro es una verdadera HIGIENE DEL MATRIMONIO, es una obra séria [*sic*], es una obra filosófica y médica, que puede leerse sin empacho *ni* escrúpulo de conciencia, porque se propone un fin moral, útil y saludable. (vii–viii; my emphasis)

> My hygiene of marriage … does *not* in *any* way resemble *any* of the various works that approach this topic, though with ends that are far from praiseworthy, which have been published with excessive liberty abroad, *nor* does it share *anything* in common with those filthy books whose vulgar pages and obscene pictures are sought after by an inexperienced youth in search of erotic inspiration. It is *not* one of these works that one ought to read in secret, as if one were doing something wrong, *no*: my book is a true HYGIENE OF MARRIAGE, it is a serious work, it is a philosophical and medical work that one can read without shame or scruples of conscience because it proposes a moral, practical, and healthy end.

This preface gives the reader moral licence to freely read the *rationalized* literature on sex. But reading, as Monlau apparently understood, risks becoming titillating and thus subversive, precisely due to the corporeal consciousness that hygiene at once seeks to cultivate and control. With the addition of each negation, Monlau's own anxiety escalates, and it becomes clear that his authorial control remains precariously contingent on the reader's acquiescence.

While not made explicit here, in the nineteenth century, the fear of undisciplined reading was tethered to the woman reader.[10] As Kate Flint put it, "No body was perceived as being more vulnerable to impure mental foods as that of the young woman" (53). Male doctors and intellectuals alike feared women's self-empowerment through literacy, as well as the stimulation of women's delicate nerves. According to Monlau "[l]a mujer tiene por lo común una sensibilidad mayor: sus sentidos son mas delicados. En la mujer predominan las facultades afectivas, así como en el hombre las intelectuales" ("woman generally have heightened sensitivity: their senses are more delicate. The affective faculties are more dominant in woman, as the intellectual ones are in man"; *Elementos* 500). Highly susceptible to moral corruption and erotic excess, women were thus deemed less capable of detached, intellectual reading. Perhaps not surprisingly, the fear of the lettered woman and the fear of the nervous woman co-emerged alongside a culture of sensibility. Fittingly, then, Monlau deemed aesthetics a kind of hygiene:

"Las facultades del alma humana (sentir, pensar y querer) tienen también su disciplina o higiene: *Estética* se llama la higiene de la *sensibilidad*" ("The faculties of the human soul (feeling, thinking, wanting) also have their discipline or hygiene: *Aesthetic* is the hygiene of *sensibility*"; *Elementos* 310; emphasis in original).

Historian G.J. Barker-Benfield traces the gendering of the nervous system and its impact on the perception of women's agentic capacity. Sensibility "connoted the operation of the nervous system ... The flexibility of a word synonymous with consciousness, with feeling, and eventually identifiable with sexual characteristics, permitted a continuous struggle over its meanings and values ... [N]ot only were women's nerves interpreted as more delicate and more susceptible than men's, but women's ability to operate their nerves by acts of will ... was seriously questioned" (xvii–xviii). There is certainly a tendency to read Ana in this way, as succumbing to her nerves, eventually leading to her nervous fits. Crucially, Joan Ramon Resina asserts that in the 1860s and 1870s, "neurosis overruled the reproductive organs in the etiology of hysteria" (239). Citing Alain Corbin, Resina explains that this shift in the etiology meant that women with refined sensibilities were seen as more susceptible to hysteria. Thus, "Ana's elevated thoughts and literary inclination (and thus to some extent her class extraction) were warranted by medical speculation" (239).

Ana, according to this view, is the victim of her nerves, unable to achieve self-possession or show any agentic capacity.[11] The senses, eroticism, pleasure – all are opposed to any notion of intellect and knowledge. In what follows, I show that, against all odds, Ana gains a heightened sense of clarity precisely as her erotic sensations reach a fever pitch. That Ana achieves self-knowledge through erotic channels suggests that the aesthetics of the novel run counter to Monlau's "hygiene of sensibility." This raises important questions about how *La Regenta* might intervene in the aesthetic cultivation of the senses, the female nervous system, and pleasure.

Reading Pleasures

If blood/purity is the premise for narration in *La Regenta*, then pleasure is the additive that thickens the plot. In tracing desire in *La Regenta*, Sinclair has argued that the novel "presents all forms of desire as forbidden and outlawed" and "at every turn desire is formulated in terms of disgust" (*Dislocation* 64). While I largely agree, I would further nuance this idea by adding that, by contrast, forms of self-pleasure – which remain shielded and thus permissible throughout the novel – run parallel to the pervasive norms of prohibition and stilted desires. That is, in accordance with the town's imposition of "disimulo" ("concealment"), pleasure surfaces in private, sensorial forms that elude public scrutiny. Randolph Pope has recently noted that Ana's solitary forms of pleasure are characterized by "a striking observational internal distance that insulates Ana from any responsibility for this enjoyment" (242).

The sensuousness of Alas's prose is undeniable. As Germán Gullón observes, "Clarín dota a su texto de una corporalidad, de una sensualidad que el lector experimenta en toda su vileza, porque la palabra viene impregnada de una fuerte contaminación y nos urge a sentir" ("Clarín endows his text with corporeality, with a sensuality that the reader experiences in all of its vileness because that Word comes impregnated with a strong contamination that urges us to feel"; n.p.). In Gullón's view, Clarín's words are contaminated with a kind of vile sensibility that is transmitted to the reader. But this is not the only affect that infuses the text. Voluptuous pleasure swells from the "corporeality" of Alas's prose. These at once disorderly and pleasurable feelings appear to escape language and instead figure in an internal visual register. As Valis remarks: "Disorder – unacceptable desire, passion – comes from deep within, bursting through to visibility in a serious of fragmented, distorted shapes of unconsciousness. Unseen, disorder is also unspoken" (*Sacred Realism* 167).

This is a protective narrative strategy that fences off desire from Vetustan scrutiny while making such knowledge available to the reader. It allows the text to subvert the prohibitive discourse that hygiene and religion represent. But rather than remain inchoate in the realm of the unconscious, Ana achieves a sense of clarity and purposiveness vis-à-vis her illicit desires and the pleasures they entail. Strikingly, her self-knowledge begins with a corporeal or, more precisely, visceral sensation that collapses the Cartesian division of the mind and body: "Sentía en las entrañas gritos de *protesta*, que le parecía que *reclamaban* con suprema elocuencia, inspirados por *la justicia, derechos* de la carne, *derechos* de la hermosura" ("She felt cries of *protest* in her very bowels, cries which seemed to call upon her with supreme eloquence, cries inspired by *justice*, by the *rights* of her flesh, by the *rights* of her beauty"; *La Regenta I* 461, my emphasis; Rutherford 207; my emphasis). In eloquent "silence," Ana bodies forth and reclaims her rights of the flesh and of beauty.

In contrast to traditional confession, where speech etches out the contours of sin, the unspoken desires remain shielded from the administration of sexuality that would render them disorderly. Stilted speech and silence permeate the novel, but while voluptuous feelings remain unarticulated, they surface at the novel's diegetic edges: in the intimate spaces of mental reflection and corporeal consciousness. Gonzalo Sobejano has noted several instances in the novel in which characters, namely Ana and de Pas, grapple with their "sentimientos sin nombre" ("nameless feelings"), characterized by new, indefinable qualities (1). The elusive and slippery quality of such desire reflects Alas's own scepticism around language's ability to capture affect – he firmly believed "[e]l diccionario tiene la culpa de muchas grandes injusticias" ("the dictionary is guilty of many grave injustices"); and in a similar vein, he pondered, "¿quién sabe si hay sentimientos que todavía no tienen nombre?" ("who knows if there are feelings that do not yet have names?"; García Sarría 271–2; qtd. in Sobejano 6). Nevertheless, unspoken feelings precipitate as "oral fixations" whereby the narrator mutes speech and instead rivets the narrative gaze on characters' mouths.

To cite one example, early in the novel Ana sees Álvaro on horseback – an image that arouses her desires. Unable to speak them, "casi lo decía con los ojos. Se le secaba la boca y pasaba la lengua por los labios" ("she almost said as much with her eyes. Her mouth was dry and she ran her tongue over her lips"; *La Regenta II* 80; Rutherford 357). The descriptions of Ana's silenced feelings towards Álvaro frequently draw attention to facial orifices: the eyes and the mouth. Consider the following sexually charged scene in which Ana, while experiencing a surge of "voluptuous" feelings towards Álvaro, kisses and bites cherries that Petra picks for him:

Ana sintió que su mano temblaba sobre las cerezas y aquel contacto le pareció de repente más dulce y voluptuoso. Y cuando nadie veía, a

hurtadillas, sin pensar lo que hacía, sin poder contenerse, como una cole-
giala enamorada, besó con fuego la paja blanca del canastillo. Besó las cerezas
también … y hasta mordió una que dejó allí, señalada apenas por la huella
de dos dientes. (*La Regenta II* 461)

Ana felt her hand trembling on the cherries. Their touch was even smoother
and more sensual now. And when nobody was looking, not thinking what
she was doing, unable to help herself, like a schoolgirl in love, she kissed
the white straw of the basket with a kiss of fire. And she kissed the cherries, and bit one of them, which she replaced, bearing the faint marks of
two teeth, in the hand-basket. (Rutherford 608)

Unable to articulate her erotic feelings towards Álvaro, Ana momentarily indulges in this sensorial pleasure. What is more, she leaves the
half-eaten cherry that bears the imprint of her teeth – a sign of her
voluptuous delight left for others to "read." Alas's narrative continually displays desires and pleasures that evade orality, all the while
eroticizing those body parts that together create speech: lips, teeth,
and tongue.

Ana's speech, and more precisely her confessions, prove central to
both spiritual and physical health. De Pas sees himself as a spiritual
hygienist, and in her new hygienic regimen, Ana observes, "Benítez
cuando se decide a hablar parece también un confesor" ("When Benítez
makes up his mind to talk he is like a confessor, too"; *La Regenta II* 449;
Rutherford 600). Doctor and priest seem to have little distinction, and in
this way *La Regenta* anticipates Foucault's theorization of the proliferation of pastoral power under Western modernity – the mechanism by
which the modern subject becomes a "confessing animal" (59). But as
Ana continues to narrate her own desires in this silent journey of self-
exploration, medicine presents the prime opportunity for Ana to once
again revel in pleasure. Benítez suggests that Ana and Víctor retreat
to the countryside, in hopes that recreation and fresh air will revive
Ana's vitality. Álvaro, supporting Víctor, joins them as they journey
to the country estate of the Marqués de Vegallana. Ana brings along
books from her childhood and finds, between the pages of a mythology book, a sketch she made of Germán as a marine. This token of that
moonlit night with her childhood friend is a reminder of Ana's desire to
escape to the sea – a longing that remains tethered to her fantasies of her
mother as a Moorish Queen in the land of the Visigoths. Crucially, Germán's image recalls Ana's "originary scene of culpability" in which she
did no wrong but was publicly condemned nonetheless (Valis, *Sacred
Realism* 183).

At the Vegallana estate, while the others play a childhood game of *cachipote* – akin to a game of hot and cold – a thunderstorm rages, and Ana and Álvaro conveniently find themselves alone. In this instance, Ana remembers her childhood self and "sentía las emociones de los quince años al frisar con los treinta" ("this woman of nearly thirty years of age who was experiencing the emotions of a fifteen-year-old girl"; *La Regenta II* 491; Rutherford 628). In this moment, we are told that Álvaro breaks his silence and declares his love for Ana, who "oía por la primera vez de su vida una declaración de amor apasionada" ("listened, for the first time in her life, to a declaration of love"; *La Regenta II* 491; Rutherford 628). It is crucial that in this moment the narrator mutes Álvaro's speech and instead makes space for Ana's internal thoughts: "No, no, que no calle, que hable toda la vida" ("'No, no, I don't want him to stop, I want him to talk for ever'"; *La Regenta II* 491; Rutherford 628). On the brink of adultery, Ana resignifies her seduction as a fall into heaven. Deploying *el estilo latente*, the narrator remarks: "Se sentía caer en un abismo de flores. Aquello era caer, sí, pero *caer al cielo*" ("She could feel herself falling into an abyss of flowers. She was falling, yes indeed – but she was falling into heaven"; *La Regenta II* 491; Rutherford 628). Privileging, once again, thought and feelings over speech, it is Ana's inner voice, through free indirect style, that fills this void:

> Para lo único que le quedaba un poco de conciencia, fuera de lo presente, era para comparar las delicias que estaba gozando con las que había encontrado en la meditación religiosa. En esta última había un esfuerzo doloroso, una frialdad abstracta, y en rigor algo enfermizo, una exaltación malsana; y en lo que estaba pasando ahora ella era pasiva, *no* había esfuerzo, *no* había frialdad, *no* había más que placer, salud, fuerza, *nada* de abstracción, *nada* de tener que figurarse algo ausente, delicia positiva, tangible, inmediata, dicha sin reserva, sin trascender a *nada* más que a la esperanza de que durase eternamente. "*No*, por allí *no* se iba a locura." (*La Regenta II* 492; my emphasis)

> The only matter for which she still had any thoughts, apart from what was happening to her, was the comparison between the delight which she was enjoying and the pleasure afforded by religious mediation. The latter involved painful effort, cold abstraction and something which one had to admit was unhealthy, a morbid exaltation; in what was happening now she was passive, there was *no* effort, there was *no* coldness, there was *nothing* but pleasure, health, strength, *no* abstraction, *no* need to imagine something absent, just positive, tangible, immediate delight, joy without

reservation, giving rise only to the hope that it would last forever. "*No*, this was *not* the path to madness." (Rutherford 628; my emphasis)

Deploying the very rhetorical strategy used in Monlau's prologue to *Higiene del matrimonio* – a series of negations – Ana claims her right to pleasure. It is profound that Alas – the master of free indirect discourse – would allow for a suspension of Ana's objectification to make way for such a subversive reclamation. This moment of Ana's defiance and self-definition, necessarily prompts us to reconsider the trenchant consignment of Ana to the realm of things. She is not uniformly, in my view, the "non-thinking object" who "laps[es] into a feminine silence which we know to expect from the heroine of the pornographic novel" (Charnon-Deutsch 93–4). Indeed, Alas's frequent and masterful use of free indirect style shifts the focus from Ana as visual object to Ana as thinking-feeling subject with whom the reader is compelled to identify. In the case of the latter, the narration cultivates the reader's empathy. It is not always clear, therefore, if we are to desire Ana or identify with her as a desirous subject.

Sinclair rightfully notes that Ana displays "an ultimate lack of attraction or bonding" to Álvaro, thereby "denoting her seduction, typical of the hysteric, by the *ideal* of sexuality and sexual enjoyment" (*Dislocations* 28). This leads Sinclair to conclude – along the same lines of Charnon-Deutsch – that Ana "holds back from the incorporation of such elements into a relationship, except in the form of a packaged and submissive object, whose contours are defined by others" (*Dislocations* 29). The lack of attraction or bond to Ana's seducer does not preclude, I argue, her own physical pleasure. Such a claim infers that women do not experience sexual pleasure in the absence of men. Ana's mindful attention to and explicit naming of the material sensations she identifies as pleasure (*gozo*) attest to the fact that it exceeds the mere "idea" of it. Alas, moreover, excises Álvaro's speech. It is significant that the narrator makes space for Ana's authorial voice (e.g., "no," "nada") – her right to say "no" – guiding the reader to affirm her erotic self-knowledge and refute attempts to label her as a lascivious "half-breed" or hysterical woman. Indeed, in this sexually subversive moment, Álvaro, the agent provocateur, fades from view as Ana wilfully challenges the blood-based determinism that has plagued her social status. While there is no question that Álvaro seduces Ana, he too falls victim to his own unrelenting desires. Just as confessor momentarily became sinner, so too does the seducer become seduced. Ana's delayed speech itself becomes a source of desire for Álvaro: "Anita sentía seca la boca; para hablar necesitaba humedecer con la lengua los labios. Lo vio Mesía que adoraba este gesto de la Regenta, y sin poder contenerse, fuera de su plan, *natura naturans*, exclamó: ¡Qué monísima! ¡qué monísima!" ("Anita's mouth was dry, in order to speak she had to moisten her lips with her tongue. Mesía noticed this action, one which he adored, and, unable to restrain himself, departing from his plan, *natura naturans*, he exclaimed: 'How lovely! how lovely!'"; *La Regenta I* 447; Rutherford 199). Ana's halted speech proves to be an explosive that undermines Álvaro's calculated self-restraint. Desire's ambiguity and inability to remain fixed or named elicits pleasure and unintended consequences throughout the narrative. Álvaro's confidence in his ability to conquer Ana, without reflecting on his own submission to attraction, shows eroticism's precarious potentiality and its ability to destabilize power relations.

If Ana is destined to be a fallen woman because of her tainted lineage, then purification via religious confession and hygienic discipline prove to be fruitless undertakings. Her open embrace of self-pleasure emerges in excess of her origins that predetermine her "fall." This act brings into focus the failure of the administration of sexuality to completely supplant the symbolic force of blood. As Ana is *always already* doomed by her blood, then her efforts to maintain her chastity are rendered meaningless. Rather than simply resign herself to this predetermined fate, however, Ana (if only momentarily) finds freedom and vitality in this reclamation of forbidden pleasure.

Complicating James Mandrell's assertion that "*all* desire in the novel is masculine," the narrator, I argue, silences masculine desire in favour of Ana's *pleasure* for which Álvaro becomes a mere prop (20). Ana's use of the word "placer" ("pleasure") is crucial here and significantly contrasts with desire, which, following Mandrell, is construed as predominantly masculine. Men like Álvaro and de Pas seem to suffer from their desire, while Ana's pleasure is a life-affirming force that explodes the control of hygiene. To this end, Ana's reclamation of pleasure affirms Foucault's differentiation between desire and pleasure: "We must not think that by saying yes to sex, one says no to power; on the contrary, one tracks along the course laid out by the general deployment of sexuality. It is the agency of sex that we must break away from, if we aim – through a tactical reversal of the various mechanisms of sexuality – to counter the grips of power with the claims of bodies, pleasures, and knowledges, in their multiplicity and their possibility of resistance. The rallying point for the counterattack against the deployment of sexuality ought not to be sex-desire, but bodies and pleasures" (157). While Ana is unable to change the deterministic force of her tainted bloodlines, at the very least she is able to make her inevitable fall pleasurable. Ultimately,

Ana undoes the chastity bind produced by the misalignment between her unchaste origins (blood) and her chaste behaviour (sexuality) by positively affirming her rights of the flesh.

That Alas narrates this scene from Ana's subject position is significant – it brings the reader into proximity to the protagonist's corporeal desires. We are invited to feel *her* sensations, rather than take pleasure in her objectification. Thus, in this instance, it is not only that we (as readers) must "confront the fundamental relationship between reading and voyeurism" as Lou Charnon-Deutsch has posited ("Voyeurism, Pornography and 'La Regenta'" 94) – though the novel certainly plays with the voyeuristic complicity of the reader. Instead, it is through the narration of Ana's interior – her thoughts, her feelings, her sensations – we are invited to feel *with* Ana and not only desire her:

> Ana sentía un placer *puramente material,* pensaba ella, en aquel sito de sus entrañas que no era el vientre ni el corazón, sino en el medio. Sí, el placer era *puramente material,* pero su intensidad le hacía grandioso, sublime. "Cuando se gozaba tanto, debía de haber derecho a gozar." (*La Regenta II* 493)

> Ana felt a purely physical [material] pleasure in that place deep inside her which was neither her stomach nor her heart, but something between the two. Yes, her pleasure was purely physical, but its intensity made it magnificent, sublime. "When one's joy [pleasure] was so great one must have a right to it." (Rutherford 630)

For Brais Outes-León, this is a false notion of the sublime: "Ana abandonará ... la búsqueda trascendental que articula su visión de lo sublime para abrazar la materialidad de su propio cuerpo – la carnalidad falsamente sublime que le brinda Álvaro Mesía" ("Ana abandons ... the transcendental search that articulates her vision of the sublime to embrace the materiality of her own body – the falsely sublime carnality that Álvaro Mesía offers"; 77). Rather than dismiss this turn to the material as a false notion of sublime, I offer a different reading that casts the scene in a feminist light. The narrator construes this as a sublime, enthralling moment – we are not pushed to question this – and in turn, Ana realizes an embodied understanding of a feminist sexual politics, boldly defying hygiene's prescriptions at the risk of confirming blood's determinism. If Doña Luz – tainted by her mother's licentiousness – sought out futile modes of purification, and ultimately containment, in the form of marriage, Ana does just the opposite: she fully delights in and claims the pleasures of her pre-determined fall.

Of course, this subversion is not completely unfettered. Just as Monlau's preface revealed the limits of his authorial control, so too does Ana's "advertencia" ("warning") remain contingent on the reader's interpretation. As Catherine Jaffe succinctly puts, Ana is a "text to be read and … a reader of texts" (4). What remains indisputable, of course, is that Vetusta collectively punishes Ana at the end of the novel – she is chastised, isolated, and finally denied the opportunity to confess. The ideology of *limpieza de sangre* that haunted Ana all along comes full circle, thoroughly saturating the discourse around her punishment. The narrator notes, for example, that "los Orgaz echaban lodo con las dos manos sobre la honra difunta de aquella pobre viuda encerrada entre cuatro paredes" ("Orgaz senior and Orgaz junior scooped up mud with both hands and poured it upon the dead honour of the poor widow, buried between four walls"; *La Regenta II* 585; Rutherford 702). Vetustan aristocrats quickly overturn the collective forgetting or "perdón general" ("general pardon"; *La Regenta I* 293; Rutherford 104) that allowed for Ana's temporary admittance into their caste. Suddenly all of Vetusta seems to recall her origins, and they cordon her off from the world to sanitize the town of her moral filth: "Y se la castigó rompiendo con ella toda clase de relaciones. No fue a verle nadie … La fórmula de aquel rompimiento, de aquel cordón sanitario fue ésta: – ¡Es necesario aislarla …! ¡Nada, nada de trato con la *hija de la bailarina italiania!*" ("Vetusta punished her by breaking off all relations. Nobody went to see her … The formula for the rupture, for the *cordon sanitaire*, was: 'She must be isolated! Have absolutely nothing to do with the Italian dancer's daughter!'"; *La Regenta II* 586; Rutherford 704).

But it is not the adultery alone that calls for Ana's damnation – for nearly everyone in Vetusta commits sins of the flesh. Instead, what leads to Ana's castigation is the *exposure* of her moral misstep. Breaking the code of *disimulo* (disguise), it is described as "un adulterio descubierto," "*aquel gran escándalo que era como una novela*" ("adultery, discovered," "that great scandal, just like a novel"; *La Regenta II* 584; Rutherford 702). But rather than represent this as a warning against the publicizing of erotic scandals, the very structure of the novel – by making a woman's private pleasure public – suggests that pleasure cannot always be contained. Indeed, the erotic persistently threatens to exceed diegetic boundaries. "The realist novel," Randolph Pope writes of *La Regenta*, "can be read as an example of how one can live beyond the pages of the book" (236). That Ana's erotic confession goes public *como una novela* ("like a novel") reveals the text's extradiegetic, aesthetic potential: to incite unruly feelings in the desirous reader – connecting reading pleasures to the body, much in the way that Ana's reading practices impelled her premature bleeding. In closing, I turn to the words of Lisa Gerrard, who noted that: "In the context of Alas' career … *La Regenta* represents a brief moment when, sensitive to the struggles of a talented woman living in a sexist society, Alas has written what, in many ways, is a feminist novel" (97). And as if provoking the reader to seize upon the eruption of such feelings, Ana – the precocious reader – daringly exclaims: "Las novelas era mejor vivirlas" ("Novels were better lived"; *La Regenta II* 272; Rutherford 479).

Chapter Three

Social Blood: The Aesthetics of the Crowd in *La desheredada*

Ya no hay protagonistas: solo hay coro.
There are no longer protagonists: only choruses.

José Ortega y Gasset

Until now, the issue of blood purity has been focalized through the daughters of socially taboo couplings who are subsequently burdened with the stigma of their inheritance. In *La desheredada*, Benito Pérez Galdós's work that initiates the *novelas contemporáneas* ("contemporary novels") series, Isidora Rufete is the quixotic and irresistibly beautiful protagonist that sets out to prove her imagined aristocratic birthright. Her disdain for the poor is palpable – though she herself lives in strained economic conditions – and her love of luxury goods to which she believes herself entitled, paradoxically leads her to a socially degraded life in a brothel.[1]

Isidora's unremitting attachment to her fabricated birthright bears the cultural imprint of the *antiguo regimen*, in which power "spoke through blood" (Foucault 147). Not surprisingly, this quest to prove her aristocratic lineage parallels the political struggles around blood and sovereign power contemporary to the novel's historical setting: the tumultuous transition from Revolution to Republic to Restoration frames the narrative. It is against this political backdrop that I wish to explore Isidora's fantasy of blood-based distinction and the novel's notable treatment of a Republican crowd.

The narrative conflicts take shape around Isidora's delusions of grandeur, which are, significantly, couched in terms of blood. As Leopoldo Alas put it in his review of the novel, *La desheredada* tells "la historia de una muchacha que, por culpa suya, de su mala educación y del mundo, llega a la degradación última en vez de subir a la nobleza la que se creyó llamada por voces de sangre" ("the story of a girl who, of her own wrongdoing, her poor upbringing and that of the world, ends up at the lowliest point of degradation instead of rising to the nobility, she who believed herself to be summoned by voices of blood"; *La desheredada* 236). In one decisive moment of the novel, Isidora treats blood as a transcendent entity that speaks to her: "La voz de la sangre me ha llamado hace tiempo; la voz de la sangre me pone ahora a los pies de la madre de mi madre" ("the voice of my true blood has called me for many years; the voice of my true blood places me now at the feet of my mother's mother"; *La desheredada* 265; Clark 210). This voice leads her to the Marquesa de Aransis, whom she believes to be her true maternal grandmother. Here, Galdós presents aristocratic birthright as a mental illness of sorts – the voice in Isidora's head is what she terms the "voice true of blood." Isidora personifies blood, vesting it with the power to determine her actions. Isidora's mental instability is given further credence by the fact that the novel opens rather provocatively from inside the psychiatric institution in which Isidora's biological father, Tomás Rufete (whom she disavows), is permanently housed.

Blood metaphors abound. In a novel where imagination threatens to overcome truth, the narrative of bloodlines occupies the realm of fiction, whereas physical bloodshed grounds us, rather viscerally, in an irrefutable material reality. Mariano, Isidora's younger brother, for example, partakes in a playful reenactment of a battle scene. This instance of imaginative play crosses over into reality when Mariano ends up stabbing one of the other boys – Zarapicos. His bloodshed makes their play suddenly criminal, fatal, and chillingly real:

> Aquello de que estaba manchado *Zarapicos* no era el almagre de que se pintaban alguna vez para jugar; era sangre, ¡sangre! *Zarapicos* no jugaba al muerto; no hacía gestos para hacer reír a sus compañeros; no decía con voz doliente ¡madre! para representar una comedia; era que se moría realmente. (*La desheredada* 161; emphasis in original)

> Zarapicos was not stained with the red clay they daub themselves with during games: that was blood, blood! Zarapicos was not feigning death; he was not making gestures to amuse his companions; he was not saying "Mother!" in a mournful voice imitating a play; he was really dying. (Clark 99)

Physical bloodshed draws our attention to the precarity of the material body – an anchor of the real that puts imaginative play to hault. Bloodshed signals the body's vulnerability and the physical limits of discursivity.

Physical blood is also associated with a precious medical commodity: the leech. Encarnación Guillen, Isidora's healthy and robust great aunt "de buena sangre" ("full blooded"; 99; 38) is known as *la Sanguijuelera* ("the leech lady") for being in the lucrative business of selling leeches. While actual leeches are curative, removing the bad blood of the infirm body, symbolic leeches refer to the blood-sucking aristocracy and the ruling class that feed off the working poor. Isidora is thus playfully called a "sanguijuela" ("blood sucker [leech]"; 126; 65) by Augusto Miquis – one of her suitors and, notably, a medical student – to describe her aristocratic aspirations that make her a social parasite. Isidora's younger brother Mariano – convinced of their shared aristocratic birthright – bears an "ardiente anhelo de ser sanguijuela" ("longing to be a leech"; 334; 280), and Juan Bou, the anarchic Catalan lithographer who proposes to Isidora, refers to them as pertaining to the "casta de sanguijuela" ("race [caste] of leeches"; 329; 275). (This contrast between symbolic bloodlines and physical blood is a tension that Galdós, as I demonstrate in chapter four, will further develop in *Fortunata y Jacinta*.) While physical blood abruptly interrupts the world of fiction, Galdós explores in *La desheredada* the symbolic force of fiction through bloodlines. Indeed, the references to symbolic blood – rather than physical blood – lies at the heart of Isidora's unending quest for social distinction as well as the cure for her aristocratic delusions.[2]

Crucially, Isidora's identity quest comprises two opposing types: the incipient bourgeois woman (haunted by the spectre of the prostitute) and the aristocrat. The former is determined through consumption and comportment, while the latter is reliant on bloodlines. Isidora as a consumer and prostitute has generated much scholarly debate, but less critical space has been afforded to how her sense of self emerges in relation to a force that challenges the very basis of individual identity and distinction: the amorphous and anonymous crowd. In *La desheredada*, crowds are the conduit of what the narrator terms social blood (*la sangre social*), which, I want to suggest, figures as the vital matter of Republicanism and the antidote to Isidora's delusions of grandeur.[3]

Crowds occupy a central place in nineteenth-century cultural imaginaries, and Galdós's *novelas contemporáneas*, of which *La desheredada* is the first, are no exception. This comes as no surprise since industrialization led to the influx of people from rural communities and provinces to the capital. Over the course of the nineteenth century, Madrid nearly doubled in population, reaching half a million inhabitants (Valdivia "Introduction" 16). In the latter half of the century, it tripled in geographic size (from 1,920 acres to 5,668 acres) as part of the *Ensanche de Madrid* or *Plan Castro*, an urbanization project which sought to develop new neighbourhoods at the city's periphery to accommodate the growing population (Valdivia "Introduction" 17).

But crowds do not only present challenges to the urban planner. The basis of political assembly and popular uprisings, the crowd conjured up images of a raucous horde characterized by irrationality, violence, and collective excitation.[4] For European elites and conservatives, the Paris Commune figures as the most notorious example of the anarchic power that crowds can wield. While in the case of Spain, *La Noche de San Daniel* and *La Gloriosa* serve as local touchstones. In addition to their collective political power, crowds are anathema to bourgeois social order, as they threaten hierarchies and modes of social distinction (including caste and class). The anonymous aggregation of bodies is significant precisely because it signifies the erasure of individuality, confounding notions of agency and autonomy. And finally, as the novel shows, when read from the vantage point of gender, crowds represent the opposite of domesticity and the private sphere – two concepts upon which notions of feminine social decorum rely. They necessarily entail public and anonymous forms of touch and allow for collective excitation, rendering meaningless the notion of the couple and even the discrete, individual body.

While crowds figure as a source of anxiety throughout the nineteenth century, with *La desheredada*, Galdós, I argue, offers a more nuanced and less paranoid account of crowds than some of his contemporaries. This noteworthy depiction of crowds provides rich fodder for understanding the complexity of Isidora's desire for distinction and the social forces that threaten it. Attending to the depiction and function of crowds in *La desheredada*, I hope, will prove key to advancing a more nuanced understanding of Isidora's attachment to aristocratic birthright, as well as renewed discussion on Galdós's treatment of gendered subjectivity. In what follows, I will focus on the narrative rupture instantiated by Isidora's encounter with a crowd comprising a mix of *carnaval* participants and Republican protestors. Central to this rupture is the circulation of "la sangre social" – the collective, indiscriminate blood of the crowd, flowing freely in contradistinction to the closed circuit of blue blood. This is a rare example in realist fiction in which symbolic blood takes a form other than noble or pure bloodlines. Rather than expose the tension between symbolic blood (bloodlines) and material blood, in *La desheredada* Galdós posits another possibility. *Sangre social* recasts symbolic blood outside of the heteropatriarchy and maternal inheritance and instead reconceives it as a democratic circulatory system. Moreover, social blood holds the potential to derail Isidora's quest for blood-based distinction; it is the antidote to her delusionary behaviour.

Before examining this scene, however, let us briefly consider Isidora as an incipient bourgeois subject.

The Shopper

La desheredada bemuses and befuddles its reader. The disorienting novel unfolds from the interior of an insane asylum, moves into spaces of cultural refinement, and thrusts the reader into the bustle of the city's whirling centre. As the narrator maps out the modern capital, he lingers on a glass display that reflects Isidora's rapacious, consumerist gaze:

> Al punto empezó a ver escaparates, solicitud de tanto objeto bonito, rico, suntuoso. Esta era su delicia mayor cuando a la calle salía, y origen de vivísimos apetitos que conmovían su alma, dándole juntamente ardiente gozo y punzante martirio. Sin dejar de contemplar su faz en el vidrio para ver qué tal iba, devoraba con sus ojos las infinitas variedades y formas del lujo de la moda. (172)

> Straight away she began looking into shop windows, attracted by anything pretty, rich or sumptuous. This was her greatest delight when out in the street, and the origin of the very lively appetites that so disturbed her, giving her intense delight and acute suffering at one and the same time. Without ceasing to gaze at her appearance in the window to see how she was looking, her eyes devoured the infinite varieties and shapes of luxury and fashion. (Clark 111)

This thick narrative moment captures Isidora, the stunning window shopper, as she exhibits an undoubtedly modern sense of self: she examines her reflection overlaying sumptuous luxury goods encased in glass. This layered image brilliantly illustrates the problematic nature of modern feminine subjectivity. The bourgeois woman emerges, necessarily, through the market, dependent on the hypervisual, self-commodifying regime of beauty. Isidora as the shopper illustrates Deborah Parson's observation that in the nineteenth century "commodities and the principle of spectacle become constitutive of identity" (53). Her social worth threatens to be marketized just like the commodities with which she would adorn her body. But for the impoverished Isidora, the glass display is a dazzling trap: at once a mirror – the objectification of her own image and a seemingly indispensable accessory in her beauty regimen – and the crystalline container that stands between her and the commodities she so adores but cannot buy. The *escaparate* ("shop window") thus serves as a subtle reminder that sumptuous goods remain financially out of reach to the liminal protagonist who skirts the edge of bourgeois society. To afford these sumptuous goods, Isidora herself must become a beautiful commodity – a dazzling social trap.

Women's consumption sparked a great deal of unease in *fin-de-siglo* Spain, for as Bridget Aldaraca and Alison Sinclair have both noted, luxury (*lujo*) was thought to be a gateway to lust (*lujuria*) – i.e., adultery and prostitution.[5] Bourgeois order – reliant to a great extent on a free-market logic – threatens to dissolve into disorder. Elizabeth Wilson has observed that prostitution in the nineteenth century was readily associated with tenets of the French Revolution, as it "was not only a real and ever-present threat to morals; it was also a metaphor for disorder and the overturning of the natural hierarchies and institutions of society" (n.p.). Fittingly, in Galdós's first adultery novel, *La de Bringas* (set against the backdrop of the 1868 Revolution), Rosalía engages in sex work to pay off a debt incurred from shopping. Leigh Mercer has written extensively on this problem of female consumerism in Spain, noting that bourgeois women found themselves in a "double bind" as consumers (63). Mercer explains: "While there existed a strong societal desire to keep women separate from the dirty and dangerous urban marketplace, the promotion of women as consumers was essential to the success of the new means of production this segment of society was cultivating. In an ironic twist of fate, female consumerism in this era become one of the most productive and industrious elements of the burgeoning capitalist economics of Europe" (63). Indeed, as *La de Bringas* perfectly demonstrates, Rosalía (unlike her miserly husband) is a proper capitalist, precisely because both shopping and sex work promote the circulation of capital.

Commenting on *La desheredada*, Luis Fernández Cifuentes has poignantly argued that "Isidora's initial steps in the city are also the beginning of a slow process that will make of her noble beauty a sign for sale, a luxury-good, the most expensive commodity in the city of Galdós" (308). Isidora, however, is not only a commodity – she consumes and is consumed. And she brokers the sale of her body by choice, revelling in the financial worth of her commoditized beauty. As a sex worker, she selects her clients while simultaneously refusing courtship from marriageable suitors. As Rita Felski puts it, "both seller and commodity … [the prostitute's] body yielded to a number of conflicting interpretations; seen by some contemporary writers to exemplify the tyranny of commerce and the universal domination of the cash nexus, it was read by others as representing the dark abyss of a dangerous female sexuality linked to contamination, disease, and the breakdown of social hierarchies in the modern city" (19). Galdós airs out these fears, especially the assumption that in a market economy, women's financial (and sexual) autonomy, while important for the circulation of capital, inherently carries with it the potential for women's wilful "thingification."

In this way, the glitz, refinement, and frivolity of modern life all constitute the crude reality of poverty and sex for sale laid bare in what the naturalist writer Eduardo López Bago (Galdós's more radical contemporary) would have termed a "novela fea" ("ugly novel").[6] The window shopper stubbornly believes she is of noble lineage and longs for the social and legal confirmation of her blue blood. These circumstances ironically lead her to capitalize on the only asset she has: her beauty. Therein lies the novel's "ugliness." Isidora's stunning beauty belies her poverty, and her poverty belies her sense of grandeur.

La desheredada and Crowd Science

From Galdós to Zola, Pedro Felipe Monlau to Gustave le Bon, the massing of people – the multitude – was an object of politically charged intellectual inquiry and debate throughout the nineteenth century.[7] As early as 1847, Monlau wrote of the ills that originated from crowds specifically in relation to political events. In *Elementos de higiene pública*, he writes: "Sobreviene una conmoción política, un trastorno social, y millares de hombres se vuelven locos, y quizás criminales, antes de que hayan tenido tiempo de reflexionar lo que hacen, ni de examinar en virtud de qué impulso obran" ("Out of nowhere a political commotion, a social disturbance erupts, and thousands of men go mad, even becoming criminals, before they have time to reflect on what they do, or examine by virtue of what impulse they act"; 684). Ordinary men *en masse*, as it were, not only eclipse the individual but also devolve into criminal insanity in the face of sudden "political commotion." Views such as this one registered elite fears of popular uprisings in the nineteenth century. Susanna Barrows convincingly shows that "crowd science" emerged in response to fears of revolt and revolution in nineteenth-century France. For his part, Robert Nye notes that "the vast majority of recorded observations of crowd behavior have been made from *above* by members of the upper classes, who have had the most to lose from the depredations of mobs" (5; emphasis in original). The very notion of a crowd, in fact, appears to discursively delegitimize the political will of the people by casting them as an irrational horde. Historian Pablo Sánchez León argues that while in other European countries it was possible "to imagine an autonomous multitude capable of decisive intervention political processes that brought about modernity," (17) the political conditions in Spain proved challenging in this regard. Sánchez

León goes on to argue that in Bourbon Spain: "a politically mobilized people deprived of representation within a resiliently corporate society was successfully dismissed as the manifestation of a contemptible and threatening crowd, a conception that endured with some fluctuations through the rest of the eighteenth and well into the nineteenth century, until the first establishment of democracy" (17). For Sánchez Leon, the political distinction between plebe (which he likens to the crowd) and the people lies at heart of this problem in Spain, arguing that: "the plebe is a counter-concept coined to deny and exclude a political subject in partaking with the people" (17).

Gender is perhaps a surprising but important consideration here, for the fear of crowds emerged in a context in which the twinned anxiety around women's autonomy and popular uprisings coursed through *fin-de-siècle* Europe. Daniel Pick in his study on degeneration theory argues that "Women were seen by Le Bon and Tarde ... as not only the passive victims, but also the active agents of revolutionary disorder ... the quintessential embodiment of political anarchy" (93). Pick goes on to argue that, for some, this gendered fear of political anarchy stemmed from the belief that the "'periodicity' of the female body had a particular relation to social atavism, the relapse into 'bloodletting' and anarchy; women were seen as peculiarly cruel and irrational during menstruation" (94). Gustave Le Bon, who described crowds as "primitive beings," gendered them feminine. Le Bon went so far as to say that "[c]rowds are everywhere distinguished by feminine characteristics, but Latin crowds are the most feminine of all" (59). Thus, in addition to Spanish crowds having a special proclivity towards "feminine" (i.e., irrational, deindividuated) behaviour, according to Le Bon, the conventional depiction of crowds aligned with fears of populations that posed a threat to social order. Indeed, crowd theorists portrayed their object of study: "violent, bestial, insane, capricious beings whose comportment resembled that of the mentally ill, women, alcoholics, or savages" (Barrows 5). The feminization of crowds seems to further delegitimize their collective political will, since women were not full citizens, further bolstering Sánchez León's claim that the irrational, menacing crowd counterposes the political entity that is "the people."

José Ortega y Gasset would later, in 1930, attribute Spain's political problems to crowds, or more precisely what he terms the "lleno" ("fullness") of modern urbanity (130):

> Las ciudades están llenas de gente. Las casas, llenas de inquilinos. Los hoteles, llenos de huéspedes. Los trenes, llenos de viajeros. Los cafés, llenos de consumidores. Los paseos, llenos de transeúntes. Las salas de los

médicos famosos, llenas de enfermos. Los espectáculos, como no sean muy extemporáneos, llenos de espectadores. Las playas, llenas de bañistas. Lo que antes no solía ser problemas, empieza a serlo casi de continuo: encontrar sitio. (130)

Cities are full of people. Houses, full of tenants. Hotels, full of guests. Trains, full of passengers. Cafes, full of consumers. Promenades, full of pedestrians. Offices of famous doctors, full of sick patients. Performances, as long as they are not too extemporaneous, full of spectators. Beaches, full of bathers. What tended not to be a problem before, has nearly become a constant one: finding space.

At first glance, Ortega y Gasset's "lleno" presents a problem of space, privacy, and individuation. "Ya no hay protagonistas" ("There are no longer protagonists"), Ortega y Gasset laments, "solo hay coro" ("only choruses"; 131). But crowds can imply a redistribution of power to the people, the dissolution of age-old hierarches. Thus, Ortega y Gasset's writings on the matter exhume a longing for a time when people occupied their correct social station. The problem, I suggest, has less to do with "encontrar sitio" ("finding space") as it does hierarchy – *cada uno en su sitio* ("everyone in their proper place"). Crucially, the diffusive quality of the modern "lleno," what Ortega y Gasset eventually calls "la masa" ("the mass"), does not necessarily imply the multiplication of bodies:

En rigor, la masa puede definirse, como hecho psicológico, sin necesidad de esperar a que aparezcan los individuos en aglomeración. Delante de una sola persona podemos saber si es masa o no. Masa es todo aquel que no se valora a sí mismo – en bien o en mal – por razones especiales, sino que se siente "como todo el mundo." (133)

In effect, the mass can be defined, as a psychological act, without the need to wait for an agglomeration of individuals to appear. Standing before just one person and we can determine if he is mass or not. Mass is all that does not place a value on itself – good or bad – for special reasons, and instead feels "like everyone else."

Ultimately, Ortega y Gasset's desire to understand the masses enfolds a fear of the proliferation of the common and the ordinary – in other words, the loss of social distinction.[8]

La desheredada anticipates this fear of becoming "como todo el mundo" ("like everyone else"). Such a fear underwrites the untranslatable notion of *cursi* – to be tacky, aspirational, kitsch – a dreaded label that clings to the aspirational women of Galdós's *novelas contemporáneas*, of which *La desheredada* is the first.[9] When Isidora rejects Joaquin Saldeoro's offer to provide her with a more comfortable life in exchange for (the narrative implies) sexual favours, the marquis hurls the dreaded insult at her, screaming "Cursilona!" ("Pretentious upstart!"; *La desheredada* 237; Clark 180) as she frantically flees his home. Anxieties around the democratization of society, *lo cursi*, and the crowd as an agent of social upheaval course through the intellectual channels of Restoration Spain and fin-de-siècle Europe more broadly.[10]

With his finger on the pulse of the nation, Galdós showcases these anxieties about feminine *cursilería*, the crowd, and democratization in *La desheredada*. Published in 1881 and set in the early 1870s, the novel presents a complex and noteworthy meditation of gendered subjectivity and individuation at odds with an ideology of blood purity. The tension between the individual and the crowd, or the protagonist and the chorus as it were, weaves itself into the novel's plot and reveals the limits of narrative omniscience – a point to which I will return at the chapter's close. Questions of social rank – class *and* caste – come into sharp relief as they intersect with gender. Women's sexual and financial autonomy, marriage, and female beauty all play crucial roles in the novel's ensanguined plot. Isidora Rufete believes she is not a Rufete, but rather the granddaughter of the Marchioness de Aransis. As such, throughout Isidora's obsessive quest for social distinction, she incessantly expresses a marked distaste for *lo ordinario* ("the common").

The Aristocrat

Like the other protagonists studied in this book, Isidora fixates on her matrilineal inheritance: "mi madre ... fue hija de una marquesa" ("my mother ... was the daughter of a marquesa"; *La desheredada* 110; Clark 48). In contrast to *Doña Luz* and *La Regenta*, however, *La desheredada* distorts the chastity bind, as Isidora has no real aristocratic bloodlines to speak of. If in the antiquated Vetusta, Ana Ozores was bound by early modern codes of blood purity and honour, Isidora, in a markedly modern Madrid, clings to a fantasy borne by novel reading (110). In *La Regenta*, Ana Ozores's reading is thought to prompt her early menstruation, while in *La desheredada* fiction reading further fuels Isidora's delusional attachment to blood. When Isidora's attempts to convince her aunt, La Sanguijuela, of her secret aristocratic origins, she retorts: "Me parece que tú te has hartado de leer esos librotes que llaman novelas" ("It seems to me you've been reading too many of those fat books they call novels"; 110; 48). With both *La Regenta* and *La desheredada*, we see strong connections between the woman reader and the creation of blood fictions. In the case of the latter, aristocratic birthright appears outmoded in a modernizing world in which bloodlines have lost their lustre and social rank seems increasingly determined by taste and sartorial style.

For the purpose of my argument, I am interested in the fact that Isidora manoeuvres two distinct but coterminous modes of social identification: aristocratic birthright and bourgeois self-fashioning. Jo Labanyi rightfully notes that the narrator fuses Isidora's sense of birthright with the idea of merit: "With Isidora's inheritance, Galdós is, of course, specifically dealing with the question of the aristocracy – i.e., the right to wealth and position by birth into a certain class. But it is worth noting that Isidora does not hinge her claim to an inheritance solely on her supposed noble birth; she considers that she merits a position in society, even if she is not entitled to it by rank, because of her innate qualities of beauty and taste: a 'birthright of merit' rather than of class" ("The Political Significance of *La desheredada*"). Colin McKinney, for his part, has examined Isidora's identity quest through the Bourdieusian concept of distinction, which relies heavily on cultivation of taste. McKinney argues that Isidora navigates a "thin road between distinction and *cursilería*" (55). The latter leads Isidora into a cycle of poverty and prostitution, while the former, a seemingly anachronistic Cervantine fantasy, takes on the characteristics of a modern neurosis.

In "Family Romance," first published in 1908, Sigmund Freud writes that the "freeing of the individual, as he grows up, from the authority of his parents is one of the most necessary though one of the most painful results brought about by the course of his development" (156). Throughout this process, the child becomes increasingly aware of his once idealized parents' flaws, and in response he creates a "fantasy in which both parents are replaced by others of better birth" (157). This description uncannily captures the plight of Isidora, who never abandons this fantasy. *La desheredada*, predating Freud's essay by nearly thirty years, provides a somewhat sympathetic description of Isidora's neurotic condition:

Salvo algunas ligeras neuralgias de cabeza, Isidora gozaba de excelente salud. Tan sólo era molestada de frecuentes y penosos insomnios, que a veces la hacían pasar de claro en claro las noches. La causa de esto parecía ser como una sed de su espíritu, que se fomentaba, sin aplacarse, de audaces previsiones de lo futuro, de un perpetuo imaginar hechos que pasarían, que tendrían que pasar, que no podían menos de tomar su puesto en las infalibles series de la realidad. Era una segunda vida encajada en la

vida fisiológica y que se desarrollaba potente, construida por la imagi-
nación, sin que faltase una pieza, ni un cabo, ni un accesorio. (114)

Apart from slight neuralgia headaches, Isidora enjoyed excellent health.
The only things that troubled her were frequent disturbing bouts of
insomnia that sometimes kept her awake the whole night long. The cause
seemed to be akin to a thirst of the mind which was brought on relent-
lessly by daring visions of the future, the perpetual imagining of things
that would happen, which had to happen, and could do no less than take
their places in the infallible chain of events called reality. It was a second
life enclosed within physical life and it unfolded with great potency, constructed by her imagination and lacking not a single fragment, piece or
accessory. (Clark 52)

This "second life" leads Isidora to claim that the couple that raised her
are not her biological parents, believing instead that she is the foundling
of an aristocratic mother:

No somos hijos de don Tomás Rufete ni de doña Francisca Guillén. Esos dos
señores, a quienes yo quiero mucho, muchísimo, no fueron nuestros padres
verdaderos. Nos criaron fingiendo ser nuestros papas y llamándonos hijos,
porque el mundo ..., ¡qué mundo éste! (109)

We are not the children of Don Tomás Rufete nor of Doña Francisca
Guillén. Those two people, whom I love very dearly, were not our true
parents. They brought us up pretending to be our parents and calling us
their children, because the world ... what a world! (47)

Isidora's neurosis is apparently passed on by her father, who resides, at
the start of the novel, in Leganés, an historical insane asylum. Doomed
by quixotic delusions of grandeur, which find their expression in blood,
hers is both a disease of inheritance and an inherited disease. Isidora's
"mad" blood makes her a modern, feminine rewriting of Don Quix-
ote and at once a proto-Freudian neurotic. It is notable that "Family
Romance" is read as a theory of the novel – i.e., romance as a *roman*.
Marthe Robert, commenting on Freud's essay, remarks that "[t]he novel
wants to be believed just like the story the child used to invent to compensate for life's disappointments" (168). In the context of *La desheredada*, Isidora's quest for the social and legal recognition of her imagined
bloodlines may be a meta commentary, on the part of Galdós, on the
fictionality of naturalist novels and their desired approximation to lived
and scientifically scrutinized realities.

The novel calls upon the reader to distinguish reality from fiction. Possessing "el don de imaginar fuerte" ("her gift of a highly developed imagination"; 95; 34), Isidora's fantasies engulf her sense of self, entirely eclipsing her social reality.[11] But in typical Galdosian fashion, there is no immediacy to the truth. Instead, reality must be laboriously sussed out by the reader.[12] Indeed, Galdós makes the dizzying effect of this novelistic "lleno" or the aesthetics of the crowd – the blurred lines of distinction in a sensuous thicket of bodies – a readerly experience. The aesthetic excess of this blood novel has a maddening effect – the truth is mediated by competing frames and varying scales that are key to keep abreast of the truth. In this way, *La desheredada* initiates a play with frames and scale that we see further developed a few years later in the famous opening paragraphs of *La de Bringas* in which the reader gets lost in the narrator's meticulous description of what we eventually discover is artwork made entirely of human hair. Like Bringas himself, who temporarily goes blind as a result of this work, Galdós masterfully shows that myopic vision and the proliferation of detail do not necessarily amount to greater comprehension. One must see the frame to gain a fuller picture of reality.[13]

Similarly, *La desheredada* begins not from a place of epistemological mastery, rather it begins from disorder. The first chapter commences abruptly with the conclusion of another novel, so the title indicates: "Final de otra novela" ("The End of Another Story"). By beginning *La desheredada* with the story of Tomás Rufete, Galdós (following the tenets of naturalism) isolates the point of transmission of Isidora's hereditary disease while inventing a fictional, novelistic genealogy. Tomás Rufete's unfiltered bureaucratic rant forms the opening lines of the novel:

> – ¿Se han reunido todos los ministros …? ¿Puede empezar el Consejo … ¡El coche, el coche, o no llegaré a tiempo al Senado! … Esta vida es intolerable … ¡Y el país, este bendito monstruo con cabeza de barbarie y cola de ingratitud, no sabe apreciar nuestra abnegación, para nuestros sacrificios con injurias, y se regocija de vernos humillados! Pero ya te arreglaré yo, país de las monas. ¿Cómo te llamas? Te llamas envidiópolis. (67)

> Are all the ministers gathered together? Can the Cabinet meeting begin? The carriage, the carriage, or I'll not be at the Senate House in time! This life is insufferable … And the country, that blessed monster with barbarism for a head and ingratitude for a tail, the country doesn't know how to appreciate our self denial, pays us for our sacrifices with insults, and rejoices to see us humiliated! But I'll set you to rights, you land of apes. What's your name? You're called *Envyopolis*. (7)

That Tomás's speech initially appears decontextualized – without a narrative frame – is significant because it temporarily authorizes his discourse, privileging his words over those of the narrator. In turn, the reader may sympathize or even laugh with the embittered speaker, but soon enough things begin to feel amiss. It takes times to comprehend that Tomás has a mental illness, but the narrator provides incremental hints along the way. Language is a first indicator: "El que de tal modo habla (si merece nombre de lenguaje esta expresión atropellada y difusa en la cual los retazos de oraciones corresponden al espantoso fracciona-miento de ideas)" ("The man speaking [if that halting, diffuse expression in which odd lines from speeches reflect the terrible fragmentation of thought may be called language]"; 68; 8). And physiognomy follows: "es uno de esos hombres que han llegado a perder la normalidad de la fisonomía y con ella la inscripción aproximada de la edad" ("the man in question is one of those who have come to lose normal facial expression, and with it, some approximate indication of age"; 68; 8). Even as the visual comes into play, signs (linguistic or phenotypic) cannot easily be deciphered:

> ¿Hállase en el punto central de la vida, o en miserable decrepitud? La movilidad de sus facciones y el llamear de sus ojos, ¿anuncian exaltado ingenio, o desconsoladora imbecilidad? No es fácil decirlo, ni el especta-dor, oyéndole y viéndole, sabe decidirse entre la compasión y la risa. (68)

> Is he in the middle of his life, or in miserable decay? The mobility of his features and those blazing eyes, are they signs of exalted talent or heart-breaking imbecility? It is not easy to say which, nor does the onlooker, hearing and seeing him, know how to choose between compassion and laughter. (8)

The appearance of a doctor suddenly brings this dystopian reality into focus – medicine works as a discursive frame through which we come to understand, at least *from the doctor's perspective*, that Tomás has a mental illness.[14] The doctor administers a sedative, and Tomás begins to direct his speech to a tree trunk. But are we, as Tomás's spectator, to laugh with or feel compassion for him? Galdós arms his narrator with ambiguous words, leaving ample room for doubt. This ambiguity, along with the narrative's initial authorization of Tomás's speech, and the distortion of the novel's temporality leads us to question the origins of Tomás's madness. Medicine only provides one frame to interpret Tomás's story. Is he truly a madman or simply a politically disgruntled civil servant too long sedated by doctors and subjected to the "domador de locos" ("asylum keeper"; 73; 12) to know? We do not have access to this unwritten novel.[15]

We are in Leganés, the narrator belatedly informs us, Madrid's historic psychiatric ward.[16] A heterotopic space the narrator deems a "triste colonia" ("miserable colony"; 72; 11) and likens to "locales primitivos" ("primitive places"; 71; 10), Leganés is at once modern and antiquated, a colony within the metropolis, a space that confines the nation's internal others.[17] Liana Ewald shows that Leganés was a mansion-turned-insane-asylum once inhabited by dukes, an architectural palimpsest layered with historical significance. According to the memoirs of Leganés's former administrator, Eduardo Viota y Soliva, the official name of the psychiatric ward – Hospital de Dementes de Santa Isabel de Leganés:[18] "pays homage to the aristocracy, with 'Isabel' referring to Isabel II, the Bourbon monarch deposed in 1868, and 'Leganés,' to Don Diego Messía de Guzmán, Marquis of Leganés and proprietor of the mansion in the seventeenth century" (Viota y Soliva 29). "The denomination *santa* canonizes them both" (Ewald 371).

Significantly, in 1868, General Prim led a military rebellion against the crown, effectively pushing Isabel II into exile, and set off the liberal revolution known as *La Gloriosa*. The aftermath of *La Gloriosa* hazily backlights the novel's plot, beginning with the unsteady years of Amadeo de Savoy's brief reign preceding the establishment of the First Republic. It is notable, too, that Savoy coincides with the Paris Commune of 1871, which appears indirectly in the narrative when the anarchist Juan Bou names Adolphe Thiers as an example of a "sanguijuela del pueblo" ("[leech] feeding on the people"; 127; 279).[19] The Paris Commune, of course, spurred a deep anxiety about crowds across Europe, including Spain. Barrows convincingly shows that crowd scientists such as Le Bon in large part were responding to the political tumult that stemmed from the Paris Commune. That the commune came on the heels of the Spanish liberal revolution is no insignificant detail. Historian José Álvarez Junco describes at the length the political reverberations of this event in Spain as citizens across the political spectrum responded to this event. He writes:

> La inestabilidad, la confusión y el dinamismo caracterizaban la coyuntura política española de 1871. Recién iniciado el último ciclo de la Revolución liberal, contralaba el timón una monarquía constitucional – la de don Amadeo –, que trataba de sostenerse ante el creciente empuje republicano y la renovada combatividad carlista … Una tentativa revolucionaria tan abiertamente amenazadora y tan cercana como la Comuna de París habría de ser la piedra de toque ante la que no era posibles medias tintas ni

veleidades demagógicas, revistiendo así un carácter decisivo en el proceso de clarificación de las actitudes políticas en [España] nuestro país. (1)

Instability, confusion, and dynamism characterized the political conjuncture of 1871. Having recently initiated the final cycle of the liberal Revolution, the ship's helm was taken by a constitutional monarchy – that of Don Amadeo – which tried to sustain itself amid a growing republican push and renewed Carlist combativeness ... A revolutionary attempt so openly threatening and close by as the Paris Commune was likely the touchstone for which there were no possible half-measures or demagogic whims, covering up a decisive character in the process of clarifying the political attitudes in [Spain] our nation.

The political uprising in Paris sparked a great deal of debate in this moment of great instability.

Álvarez Junco's study of the Paris Commune includes a compendium of ideologically diverse opinion pieces contemporary to the period. A brief survey of the articles shows that across the political spectrum, the language used to depict the crowds of the Paris Commune mirrors the pejorative sentiments of crowd scientists that dominate at the end of the century. The authors refer to crowds as "turbas de facciosos" ("factious mobs"; 23), "una masa de hombres cegados" ("a mass of blinded men"; 23), "una masa de bandidos" ("a mass of bandits"; 54), "los bárbaros de la civilización moderna" ("barbarians of modern civilization"; 79), "salvajes" ("savages"; 79), "criminales, no hombres políticos" ("criminals, not political men"; 87), and "los jugadores, los borrachos, los asesinos, los esclavos de todos los vicios más repugnantes" ("gamblers, drunks, murderes, slaves of the most reviling vices"; 119). We can assume that contemporary readers of *La desheredada* would recall these images in relation to both the Paris Commune and the political upheavals in Spain.

Galdós, being the master of realist irony, thus brilliantly chooses Leganés, whose patron "saints" are its former aristocratic proprietor and the recently deposed queen, as the disorderly starting point for a novel rife with anxieties pertaining to blood, sovereignty, madness, and the unruly potential of crowds. It is fitting that Galdós presents us with the first depiction of a crowd inside the Hospital de Dementes de Santa Isabel de Leganés: "El patio es estrecho. Se codean demasiado los enfermos, simulando a veces la existencia de un bendito sentimiento que rarísima vez habita en los manicomios: la amistad. Aquello parece a veces una bolsa de contratación de manías. Hay demanda y oferta de desatinos" ("The yard is narrow. The inmates rub shoulders [elbows] with one another too much, sometimes simulating a blessed feeling rare in lunatic asylums: friendship. The place sometimes seems like a Stock Exchange for transacting business in manias. There are bids and offers for deranged nonsense"; 72–3; 12). Notably, the passage begins with a description of space. The patio is narrow, and thus we understand that to a large extent the crowd forms not organically through some common interest or "political commotion," but rather that this is a *lleno* that forms in response to the lack of space. Contact between individuals occurs through elbowing, which, contrary to what the image of *codear* (elbowing) suggests – aggressivity, frenzy, competition, individualism – it simulates a sign of friendship. The irony is that it is only simulation because, again, this group does not congeal through a common emotion or desire that functions as the bonding agent of crowds.[20] Instead, what we have is the agglomeration of individuals who fail to interact but instead simply coexist side by side with one another: "Se miran sin verse. Cada cual está bastante ocupados consigo mismo para cuidarse de los demás. El egoísmo ha llegado aquí a su grado máximo" ("They look at each other without seeing. Each one is too occupied with himself to take any notice of the rest. Here egoism has reached its ultimate peak"; 73; 12). There is oddly nothing about these interactions that would necessarily indicate that these men are unwell. In fact, this passage, when decontextualized, captures the banal reality of life in an urban centre – anonymity, atomization, indifference, egotism, the lack of mutual regard, etc. *Cada uno en su sitio.*

Galdós presents the reader with an image of the crowd that goes against the dominant narratives of the time. In Leganés, the crowd is not antithetical to the ideal of the individual. It is not the reckless horde ("psychological crowd") that Gustave Le Bon so feared. In this masterful description, the crowd in the *manicomio* seems counterintuitively conducive to individuality (*el egoísmo*). In so doing, it renders the individual – a cornerstone of modernity – disturbingly strange and alienating. One longs for the simulation of friendship to become real, for sociality to heal the egotism of this crowd. But if for a moment the narrative frame disappears from view, leading the reader to forget that this is in fact a description of an insane asylum, the narrator goes on to say "los locos refinan su locura con el mutuo ejemplo, cómo perfeccionan sus manías" ("lunatics refine their madness through mutual example, how they perfect their manias"; 71; 11).[21] What initially mirrored the experience of anonymity and human density in a modern city now devolves into deranged animalistic behaviour: "Los imbéciles yacen por el suelo. Parecen que está pastando. Algunos exaltados cantan en un rincón. Hay grupos que se forma y se deshacen, si no amistad, hay allí misteriosas simpatías o antipatías que en un momento nacen y mueren"

("The lunatics lie on the ground. It looks as if they are grazing. Some over-excited ones sing in a corner. Groups form and disband, for if there is no friendship, there are mysterious likes and dislikes that are born or die in an instant"; 72–3; 12). Until now, the focus on crowds and mental illness has been gendered masculine. However, Galdós ends his depiction of Leganés with a female crowd. "¡Las locas!" ("The mad-women!") the narrator exclaims (76). Leganés is a liminal space: "Estamos en el lugar espeluznante de aquel Limbo enmascarado de mundo" ("Now we are in the most horrifying part of that Limbo disguised as the world"). And mental illness is, apparently, a gendered affair: "Los hombres inspiran lástima y terror; las hijas de Eva inspiran sentimientos de difícil determinación. Su locura es, por lo general, más pacífica que en nosotros, excepto en ciertos casos patológicos exclusivamente propios de su sexo" ("The men inspire pity and fear; the daughters of Eve inspire feelings hard to define. Their madness is, for the most part, more peaceful than ours, except in certain pathological cases peculiar to their sex"; *La desheredada* 76; Clark 16). If the men in Leganés mimic the quiet grazing of cows ("Parece que están pastando" ["It looks as if they are grazing"]), women cluck about like hens: "Su patio, defendido en la parte del sol por esteras, es un gallinero donde cacarean hasta veinte o treinta hembras con murmullo de coquetería, de celos, de cháchara frívola y desacorde que no tiene fin, ni principio, ni términos claros, ni pausa, ni variedad" ("Their courtyard, protected from the sun by reed mats, is a chicken run where up to twenty or thirty females cackle in their murmured flirtations and jealousies, a frivolous discordant prattle which has neither beginning nor end, nor distinct expression, nor pause nor variety"; 76; 16). There are crowds here in this palace turned asylum, but no social collectives of which to speak. Leganés – where the "sanguijuelas del pueblo" ("leeches feeding on the people"), i.e., the aristocracy, once resided – functions as a house of social death, a sepulchre of the nation's vitality.

The Crowd

"También la hermosa mitad tiene sus jaulas de dobles rejas. No serían mujeres si no necesitaran alguna vez estar bajo llave" ("The fair sex also has its cages with double bars. They would not be women if they did not sometimes need to be under lock and key"; *La desheredada* 76–7; Clark 16). If confinement, a trope that persists throughout Spanish literary history from Zayas to Galdós, is a persistent condition of women's gendered identity, then Isidora's ambulatory movement – one that leads her to the crowded streets of Madrid – takes on particular political valences, deviating from a long history of woman's confinement.[22] Leigh Mercer, in her monograph *Urbanism and Urbanity: The Spanish Bourgeois Novel and Contemporary Customs (1845–1925)*, contests the conventional notion that bourgeois women were confined to the home and, in turn, the public sphere was antithetical to their honour. Instead, Mercer forcefully demonstrates that market demands rendered bourgeois women vital consumers, compelling them to appear in public spaces (museums, parks, promenades, shops, etc.) through a kind of scripted, social performance that entailed publicly visible acts.[23] Isidora, in Mercer's view, fails to be cognizant of these collectivized visual practices (74), adhering to a seemingly démodé model of distinction. In fact, her persistent attachment to bloodlines will lead her to appeal to courts. Tellingly, Isidora will later be jailed in the novel, not for her unruly activity as a woman but for her attempts to climb the social ranks by falsely claiming her connections to an aristocratic family. I am less invested in whether Isidora consciously performs these visual practices as I am compelled by the contrast between the well-scripted movement of the promenade with a male companion, as opposed to the frenzied, corporeally dense movement of the anonymous multitude, where no bourgeois woman ought to be seen.

Throughout the novel, Isidora repeatedly asserts her aristocratic origins: "a mí no me correspondía compartir las penas y la miseria de Tomás Rufete, porque aunque le llamo mi padre, y a su mujer mi madre, es porque me criaron y no porque yo sea verdaderamente su hija" ("I was not meant to share the sorrows and misery of Tomás Rufete, because although I call him my father, and I call his wife my mother, that is because they brought me up, and not because I am really their daughter"; *La desheredada* 24; Clark 24). She derives her sense of distinction from her imagined blue blood. As she explains to her aunt, pointedly known as la Sanguijuela ("the Leech"): "Usted no es mi tía. Usted no tiene mi sangre" ("You are not my aunt. You are not of my blood") 112; 50). Like Doña Luz, Isidora believes "el pueblo" ("common people") to be synonymous with filth and that any form of contact will lead to social contagion. Isidora's unremitting belief in her aristocratic origins manifests as an aversion towards the *pueblo*: "¡Qué odioso, qué soez, qué repugnante es el pueblo!" ("How odious, coarse and repulsive common people are!"; 113; 51). Her hatred for commoners mirrors the disavowals of social climbers captured by federal republicans in *La igualdad* (1871): "En esos regios salones, donde todo convida a la ambición y al despotismo, se albergan hombres nacidos de la nada, hombres nacidos de la nada, elevados de esas mismas turbas que hoy contemplan con repugnancias porque les recuerdan su pasado" ("In these regal salons, where everything invites ambition and despotism, men born of nothing gather, men born of nothing, elevated from these very hordes which today contemplate with repugnance because they remind them of their past"; Álvarez Junco, "Los Rojos" 128).

While Isidora has an unrelenting desire to be in public, in her meanderings in Madrid she recoils upon contact, direct or otherwise, with *el pueblo*. On one occasion she lies to her family to explore the city with one of her many suitors, the medical student Miquis. After an outing at the Casa de Fieras – something she regards as designed for consumption by the lower classes – the two dine at a local tavern, where the depiction of filth and food are refracted through Isidora's gaze:

> Compareció sobre el mantel una tortilla fláccida que, por el color, más parte tenía de cebolla que de huevo, y Miquis la dividió al punto. El vino que llegó como escudero de la tortilla era picón y negro, cual nefanda mixtura de pimienta y tinta de escribir. El plato, mal llamado fuerte, que siguió la tortilla, y que, sin duda debía la anterior calificación a la dureza de la carne que lo componía, no gustó a Isidora más que el local, el vino y la dueña del puesto. Con deprecio mezclado de repugnancia observó la pared del ventorrillo, que parecía un mal establo, el interior de la tienda o taberna, las groseras pinturas que publicaban el juego de la rayuela, el piso de tierra, las mesas, el ajuar todo, los cajones verdes con matas de evónimos, cuyas hojas tenían un costra de endurecido polvo, el aspecto del público de capa y mantón que iba poco a poco ocupando los puestos cercanos, el rumor soez, la desagradable vista de los barriles de escabeche, chorreando salmuera. (*La desheredada* 126)

There appeared on the tablecloth a limp omelette [*sic*] which, judging by its smell, had more onion than egg in it, and Miquis immediately cut it in two. The wine that arrived as squire to the omelette was sharp and black, like an unholy mixture of pepper and ink. The ill-named "main" course that followed the omelet, and which, no doubt, owned its description to the hardness of its meat, did not please Isidora any more than the place, the wine or the lady of the house. With a mixture of disdain and repugnance she observed the inn wall, which looked like a dilapidated stable, the interior of the tavern, the crude pictures showing pitch-and-toss, the earth floor, the tables, all the furniture, the green stands with evonymus [*sic*] bushes, whose leaves had a crust of hardened dust, the common people in cloaks and shawls who were gradually occupying the seats near by [*sic*], the crude talk, the unpleasant sight of barrels of pickled fish, leaking brine. (Clark 64)

When Isidora exclaims, "¡Qué ordinario es esto!" ("How vulgar all this is!") Miquis, the medical student, doesn't fear contagion: "A mí me encanta el contacto del pueblo" ("I love being in contact with the people"; 127; 64). It is in this very moment that Miquis then playfully calls Isidora an aristocrat and leech: "aristócrata, sanguijuela del pueblo … Si digo que te he de cortar la cabeza … Pero será para comérmela" ("my aristocratic friend, blood-sucker [leech] of the poor … I tell you I ought to have your head cut off … But it will only be to eat it"; 127; 65). Miquis's joking, coquettish comments position Isidora as a bloodthirsty social parasite – who ought to be beheaded and consumed – draining the nation of its crimson vitality.

Isidora's consistent hatred and visceral disdain for the poor makes it all the more shocking that she would later venture into the crowded city streets at night. What has precipitated this singular event is her visit to the Palace of Aransis. This well-known chapter is entitled "Anagnórisis"[24] – the crucial moment of self-discovery in Greek drama. Significantly, the date is 11 February 1873, the very day Amadeo de Savoy abdicated the crown. Joaquín de Pez spoke to Isidora about "los graves sucesos políticos del día" ("the grave political events of the day"; 259; 204), which she summarily ignored, not having a penchant for politics. Isidora approaches the palace and is led inside by the concierge. She eagerly awaits the Marchioness, and everything hangs on this encounter. The narrator paints the waiting period as an intense expanse of suspension, a threshold moment:

> Instante único, tremendo; ángel con el pie levantado y las alas extendidas, que va a volar y no se sabe si dirigirá su vuelo al suelo o al infinito; instante soberano; dogal que oprime la garganta; espada de un cabello suspendida; es hermano del instante en que se nace o en que se muere, del instante en que se hunden los imperios, y de aquel, no conocido todavía, en que se acabará el mundo. (263)

> It was a unique, a tremendous moment; like an angel with foot poised and wings spread, about to fly not knowing if the flight will be to the earth or the infinite; a supreme moment; a tightening noose about the throat; a sword suspended by a hair; akin to the moment of birth and death, the moment when empires crumble, the moment as yet unknown when the world shall come to an end. (208)

The Marchioness appears in all her grandiosity. She is, to Isidora, the "imagen de la dignidad y la nobleza, como reina y madre de reyes" ("the very picture of dignity and nobility, like a queen and mother of kings"; 263; 209).

Isidora anticipates that this long-awaited moment of recognition will be her grand homecoming. But the Marchioness is distant and unaffectionate. Stunned, Isidora feels as though she is dying: "Se sentía morir" ("She felt she was going to die"; 264; 209). Indeed, the Marchioness denies any relation to Isidora, to which Isidora responds "Señora ... la voz de la sangre me ha llamado hace tiempo, la voz de la sangre me pone ahora a los pies de la madre de mi madre" ("*Señora* ... the voice of my true blood has called me for many years; the voice of my true blood places me now at the feet of my mother's mother"; 265; 210). The Marchioness, recognizing Isidora's extraordinary beauty, kindly acknowledges her good intentions, but rejects her nonetheless, calling her birthright claims "farsas estudiosas o capítulos de novelas" (267) ("carefully prepared farces or novelettes"; 267; 212), and suggests that she is either an imposter or demented. In a final plea, Isidora offers to show documentation of their relations, but to no avail, as the Marchioness refuses to see them. After this devasting moment of rejection, Isidora finds that her godfather Relimpio is waiting for her, and together they go out into the night.

If "Anagnórisis," intended to be the climactic moment of truth and recognition, initiates a kind of dying, then the following chapter, befittingly entitled "Igualdad. Suicidio de Isidora" ("Equality. Isidora's Suicide"), represents the protagonist's social death. Readers often feel misled by this chapter title, since Isidora does not, in fact, end her life – though the narrative certainly flirts with the possibility. As she and Relimpio plunge into the night, they pass by a bridge under construction that seems to invite suicide "– Cuando este puente se acabe – dijo Relimpio en tono de mucha autoridad – no servirá sino para que se arrojen de él los desesperados" ("'When this bridge is finished,' said Relimpio in a very authoritative tone, 'it will be of no use at all, except for despairing souls to throw themselves from the top'"; 272; 216). Unphased by his macabre remarks, Isidora boldy retorts, "¡Quia! Eso es muy bajo" ("Surely not! It's too low"; 272; 217). They pass by a tavern in which an inebriated man exclaims, "Ya todos somos iguales" ("Now we're all equal"; 272; 217) – a reference to the Republic that will be established after the dethroning of Amadeo, the constitutional monarch.[25] Relimpio then murmurs to Isidora, "El rey se va, renuncia la corona" ("The King's leaving, giving up the crown"; 272; 217). Isidora contemplates suicide, thinking to herself, "no debía vivir más tiempo" ("she should not go on living"; 273; 217). This is a fleeting thought, as even suicide seems *cursi*, and thus wholly unappealing to her:

Todos los medios de apartarse voluntariamente de la vida le parecían dolorosos, antipáticos y aun cursis. Heridos su orgullo y su dignidad, muertes sus ilusiones, algo ataba aún a la vida, aunque no fuera más que la curiosidad de goces y satisfacciones que no había probado todavía … No, morir, no. Tiempo había para eso. (273)

Every method of departing voluntarily from this life seemed to her to be painful, unpleasant and even affected [*cursi*]. With her pride and dignity wounded and her illusions shattered, something still bound her to life, even though it might be no more than a curiosity to experience the delights and satisfactions she had not yet tasted … She did not want to die. No. There was plenty of time for that. (217–18)

In place of actual suicide, what we have is a symbolic death followed by a social rebirth – one that comes into sharp focus as Isidora ventures into the dense bustle of nocturnal Madrid.

With little regard for her own safety and much to Relimpio's chagrin, Isidora insists on further wandering the streets at night unaccompanied. The avuncular Relimpio, who views Isidora's extraordinary beauty as a liability, makes veiled references to the threat of sexual violence: "¡Ir tú sola, de noche, por esas calles! ¡En Madrid hay mucho atrevido! Te lo digo con franqueza, porque yo no soy ningún anacoreta. A los pícaros españoles nos gustan tanto las hembras bonitas …. No, hija, no. No puedes andar sola de noche" ("Let you go alone at night through these streets! There's many a bold rogue in Madrid. I tell you frankly because I'm no hermit myself. We Spanish rascals like pretty girls so much … No, my girl, no. You can't go around alone at night"; 274; 218).

Ignoring these admonitions, Isidora charges into the city centre with Relimpio stubbornly by her side. Nocturnal Sol, as the narrator describes it, is a beating heart. "Adelante" ("Onward"; my translation) the narrator commands, as if simultaneously beckoning to the reader and Isidora, "La Puerta del Sol, latiendo como un corazón siempre alborozado, le comunicó su vivir rápido y anheloso. Allí se cruzan las ansiedades; *la sangre social* entra y sale, llevando las sensaciones o sacando el impulso" ("The Puerta del Sol, beating like a heart permanently stimulated, revealed its fast moving breathless life. There human anxieties meet and mingle; the *blood of society* [social blood] flows in and out bringing excitement and emotions or removing the motive force of life"; 274, my emphasis; 219, my emphasis).

Believing her mother was an aristocrat, Isidora's sense of distinction relies on a notion of blood-based exclusively. In this sense, blood remains a closed circuit: the aristocratic caste. It is therefore notable that the narrator describes la Puerta del Sol as the channels of social blood, where the crimson fluid ceases to be the precious possession of the nobility. This blood flow is boundless and collectivized by the presence of an anonymous multitude. Sol is abuzz with energy, populated by an anonymous, dizzying crowd: "un río de gente" ("a river of people"), "una marea humana" ("a tide of humanity"; 274; 220). In contrast to the fixity and purity that aristocratic blood emblematizes, the illusions to water (*río, marea*) further the imagery of fluidity, mixing, and unboundedness that social blood invokes at the start of the passage. Masked carnival participants and republican demonstrators populate this indiscriminate sea of people.

The scene is as much revolutionary as it is carnivalesque. Isidora fearlessly immerses herself in the anonymous crowd, demonstrating that her disgust for *el pueblo* is momentarily suspended. In *Crowds and Power*, Elias Canetti describes the crowd's capacity to erode an individual's fear of touch:

> It is only in a crowd that man can become free of this fear of being touched. That is the only situation in which the fear changes into its opposite. The crowd he needs is the dense crowd, in which the body is pressed to body; a crowd, too, whose physical constitution is also dense or compact, so that he no longer notices who it is that presses against him. As soon as a man has surrendered himself to the crowd, he ceases to fear its touch. Ideally, all are equal there; no distinctions count, not even that of sex. (16)

This is the effect the crowd has on Isidora. Her fear of contagion vis-à-vis the pueblo recedes as she plunges into a rising tide of anonymity that erases all sense of distinction. The crowd, writes Anne McClintock, is a "threshold place ... the place where social boundaries were permanently on the edge of breakdown" (81). And this breakdown, this mixing of social strata, manifests through physical proximity and touch: "In its insolent promiscuity, merchants and clerks, prostitutes and streetsellers, bankers and beggars mingle, touch and pass each other" (81). Crucially, as Isidora's beliefs are suspended, she takes pleasure in the anonymous physical touch of the crowd: "A Isidora *le gustaba* aquella noche, sin saber por qué, el choque de las multitudes y aquel frotamiento de codos" ("That evening, without knowing why, Isidora liked the crush of people and the rubbing of shoulders [elbows]"; *La desheredada* 275, my emphasis; Clark 220).

Sara Muñoz has described this scene as a moment of collective seduction: "Como el *flâneur*, Isidora busca su asilo y se deja seducir por la muchedumbre" ("Like the *flâneur*, Isidora searches for her asylum and she allows herself to be seduced by the crowd"; 95). Framing this as a form of seduction, as Isidora's moral misstep, may obscure the radical potential of the crowd. What interests me here is that in this instance the individual body ceases to be an end point of identity, and pleasure exists apart from conventional sexual relations. Gender, too, recedes from view as the aggregation of bodies appears as a collective of unsexed elbows and arms. The touch of the multitude is disarming, threatening to render meaningless individual subjectivity and agency. It allows for collectivized forms of pleasure that sharply deviate from the well-scripted reproductive couple form. One effect of this is that distinction, and thus the individual, threatens to dissolve in the "marea humana" ("tide of humanity"), and thus gender, class, and caste may momentarily cease to be meaningful forms of social organization and hierarchy.

For a moment, however, it is worth reflecting on the fact that this transformative form of touch impresses upon Isidora's body. The repeated *codazos* ("elbowing"), *roces* ("brushing"), and *empujones* ("pushing") of the crowd "wound" Isidora's nervous system: "Sus nervios saltaban, heridos por las mil impresiones repetidas del codazo, del roce, del empujón, de las cosas vistas y deseadas" ("Her nerves were tingling, excited [wounded] by the endless repeated impressions of the jostling [elbowing], brushing, pushing crowd, of things seen and desired"; *La desheredada* 275; Clark 220). Any mention of female nerves in the realist novel conjures up associations with hysteria. Indeed, in the nineteenth century, nerves – imperceptible to the human eye – are arguably as important in defining sexual difference as genitalia. In *Higiene del matrimonio* (1876) Monlau writes: "Solamente la mujer goza de aquella impresionabilidad del sistema nervioso, de aquella disposición afectiva, de la cual el histerismo no es mas que un modo particular, una especie de exageración" ("Only women have an impressionable nervous system, an affective disposition, of which hysteria is only one particular mode, a kind of exaggeration"; 550). No sooner does Monlau identify this unique female attribute than he links it to the gravest gendered pathology – perfectly illustrating what Foucault termed the "hysterization of women's bodies" (104). As such, even as doctors and moralists idealized woman's biological pre-disposition to maternal affection, the tenderness that stemmed from their hypersensitive nerves remained tethered to the unnerving specter of hysteria. As Foucault put it, "the Mother, with her negative image of 'nervous woman,' constituted the most visible form of this hysterization" (104). But while Monlau warned of the excess of female excitation, in the above-cited quote his use of the term "gozar" – to have, literally to enjoy – ("solamente la mujer goza de aquella impresionabilidad del sistema nervioso") unwittingly connotes an affirmative sense of pleasure in relation to the female nervous system. In a feminist rereading of this statement, we might translate Monlau's words as "Only woman enjoys/takes pleasure in an impressionable system" rather than the conventional translation "Only woman possesses an impressionable nervous system." In this light, it is significant Isidora's "injuries" do not preclude the possibility of pleasure.[26]

Indeed, sensuous, pleasurable touch transforms Isidora's sense of self: "¡Cuántos hombres, y también cuántas mujeres! El contacto de la muchedumbre, aquel fluido magnético conductor de misteriosos apetitos, que se comunicaba de cuerpo a cuerpo por el roce de hombros y brazos, entró en ella y la sacudió" ("How many men there were and women too! Contact with the masses, that fluid magnetic conductor of mysterious desires which flows from one body to another as shoulders and arms rub against each other, entered into her and shook her profoundly"; *La desheredada* 276; Clark 221). In the crowd, visibility dramatically recedes in favour of "nervous" impressions and sensorial transformations – all narrated from the vantage point of Isidora. This sensuous experience is analogous to Ana Ozores's pleasures of the flesh. A significant difference here, of course, is that Isidora's realization of pleasure takes place in an anonymous, gender-diverse multitude rather than with a male suitor or by herself. This is also remarkably different than what we saw with the crowd in Leganés. There, visibility reigned as a disciplinary force. We could see the crowds – visualize and hear them – and they were explicitly segregated on the basis of gender.

The political crowd certainly presents a potential source of violence, including sexual violence, in the novel – hence Relimpio's horror at Isidora's desire to venture into the streets. Nonetheless, this is now the second instance in which Galdós presents his reader with a surprisingly tame crowd. In this way he diverges from contemporary crowd theorists and fiction writers like Zola, whose crowds confirmed elite fears of unruly masses. What is more, the "sangre social" that courses through the veins of the carnivalesque, Republican multitude contains a curative potential. The antidote for Isidora's neurosis is precisely that which she avoids: physical contact with ordinary people. Indeed, throughout the narrative the protagonist has persistently asserted her birthright to aristocratic privilege, all is momentarily suspended in this sensuous encounter with the crowd:

> Al penetrar en las calles bulliciosas, cuya vida y animación convidan a los placeres y a intentar gratas aventuras, sintió la joven que se amenguaba su profundísimo pesar, como el dolor agudo que cede a la energía narcótica calmante. Se sintió halagada por el contacto de la sociedad percibió en su cerebro como un saludo de bienvenida, y voces simpáticas llamándola a otro mundo y esfera para ella desconocida. (274)

> As they made their way deep into the maze of noisy streets, where the
> life and the excitement invite people to taste pleasures and embark on
> delightful adventures, the young woman felt her profound sorrow ease,
> like a sharp pain surrendering to a soothing drug. She felt herself cajoled
> by contact with society; she noted in her mind something like a welcom-
> ing greeting, and kind voices calling her to a world unknown to her. (219)

The crowd, while erotically stimulating, has a calming, analgesic effect
on Isidora. Just as the voices of blood summoned her to the estate of the
Aransis, it is now the sensations enabled by social blood which beckon
her to this pleasurable state of collectivity.

Isidora, whose illness is both of and about blood, now revels in the
possibility of anonymity and the sensual chaos the Republican multitude offers. This is the chance to explore "la curiosidad de goces y satisfacciones que no había probado todavía" ("a curiosity to experience
the delights and satisfactions she had not yet tasted"; 273; 217–18),
which give her the will to live. Upon her contact with the crowd,
Isidora momentarily abandons her quest for distinction ("ilusiones
despedazadas y muertas" ["dead, shattered illusions"]): "Y como la
humana soberbia afecta desdeñar lo que no puede obtener, en su interior hizo un gesto de desprecio a todo el pasado de ilusiones despedazadas y muertas. Ella también despreciaba una corona. También ella
era una reina que se iba" ("And as human pride pretends to despise
what it cannot obtain, in her heart she dismissed with scorn all the
past with its dead, shattered illusions. She scorned a crown too. She
also was a queen who was leaving"; 274; 219). The lyrical lines that
close out this passage are deceptively simple. The chiastic structure
("Ella también … También ella") performs – in the spirit of *Carnaval* –
a syntactic inversion that enfolds politically subversive semantics.
Isidora aligns herself with the republican protestors who show their
disdain for royalty. In an instant, she herself becomes the dethroned
queen who must depart from Spain. The first "también" – signifying
"she too" – points to Isidora's affinity with the anti-dynastic republicans, while the second "también" takes on the additional meaning
of "furthermore" or even "besides," an acknowledgment of the fact
that she has recently entered the midst of political and social sea
change. The repetition of "también" and the inverted structure reinforce the relationship of antithesis of republicans towards birthright
and monarchs (Isabel II and Amadeo de Savoy). Isidora's opposing
movement from one side to the other effectively renders her formal
aristocratic self socially dead. This transformation is symbolic anarchic bloodletting.

Moreover, the infusion of social blood from the multitude momentarily awakens Isidora to a political reality that frames her aristocratic dreams as an expired hold over of the *antiguo régimen*, effectively curing her delusions of grandeur. It is a revolution of sorts, but one that occurs without struggle or violence. Indeed, Galdós offers a rather ambivalent depiction of crowds that radically diverges from his contemporaries', going out of his way (it seems) to acknowledge their non-violent presence:

> Menudeaban los grupos, todos pacíficos. No eran hordas de descamisados, sino bandadas de curiosos. Se oía decir aquí y allí: "La República, la República," pero sin gritos ni amenazas. Se hablaba con frialdad de aquella cosa grande y temida. No había entusiasmo ni embriaguez revolucionaria, ni amenazas. La República entraba para cubrir la vacante del Trono, como por disposición testamentaria. No la acompañaron las brutalidades, pero tampoco las victorias. Diríase que había venido de la botica tras la receta del médico. Se le aceptaba como un brebaje de ignorado sabor, del cual no se espera ni salud ni muerte. (275)

> Groups were gathering, but they were all peaceful. They were not ragged hordes but bands of curious onlookers. Here and there you could hear: "The Republic, the Republic," but with no shouts or threats. That great and dreaded issue was spoken of dispassionately. There was no wild enthusiasm or revolutionary intoxication, no threats. The Republic was coming in to take over a vacant throne, as if by legal authority on the execution of a will or testament. Its arrival was not accompanied by violent outbreaks, but there were no victories either. You might say it had come along from the pharmacy on a doctor's prescription. It was accepted like a medicine with an unknown taste, from which you expect neither health nor death. (22)

Elizabeth Amann has compared Galdós's tame image of a political crowd to Flaubert's *L'Education sentimentale* (1869) in its depiction of the Revolution of 1848, arguing that "both novels represent the political event as more spectacle and social gathering than real uprising" (455).

In offering this pacific description, Galdós may have been responding to the fears of political assembly and popular uprisings that circulated in Spain following the bloodbath that surrounded the Paris Commune. As Álvarez Junco notes:

> Los republicanos se encuentran en situación más difícil que las anteriores [las tradicionalistas católicas y la prensa liberal monárquica], pues

> parte del programa comunero coincide con el suyo, mas de ningún modo
> quieren ser confundidos con "las hordas" y dejar en manos de sus enemi-
> gos el arma propagandística terrible que supondría identificar para siem-
> pre el credo republicando y la Comuna. Por eso necesitan "distanciarse"
> de los comuneros con condenas aún más iracunda e inequívocas que las
> anteriores. (2–3)

> The republicans find themselves in a more difficult situation than the pre-
> vious groups [the Catholic traditionalists and the liberal monarchic press],
> since part of the Commune's program coincided with theirs, thus in no
> way did they want to be confused with "the hordes" and leave this terrible
> propagandistic weapon in the hands of their enemies who might forever
> identify the republican's creed with that of the Commune.

Indeed, Álvarez Junco's description seems to neatly capture Galdós's disavowal of the "shirtless horde," an image that conforms more to the Zolaesque depiction of the crowd. At the same time, there is a marked ambivalence to the narrator's tenor. He notes that the peaceful crowd neither commits atrocities nor wins victories – perhaps commenting on the ineffectiveness of a lukewarm liberal revolution and the need for a kind of anarchic bloodshed (i.e., the beheading of the king) to expunge the *antiguo régimen* once and for all. With this in mind, we can see the blood of the crowd inoculates Isidora against aristocratic pretense. But only momentarily.

As Isidora "hangs" from Relimpio's protective, patriarchal arm, she remains precariously on the edge of dissolution. Let us recall that Relimpio stubbornly clings to the protagonist as she walks on unsteady terrain, made slippery by mysterious black soap: "El piso húmedo, untado de una especie de jabón negro, era resbaladizo; pero ella se sostenía bien, y en caso de apuro *se colgaba del protector brazo de su padrino*" ("The wet pavement, smeared with a sort of black grease, was very slippery; but she kept her balance well, and in case of dif-ficulties would *hang on to the protecting arm of her godfather*"; *La deshere-dada* 275, my emphasis; Clark 220, my emphasis). Like *La Regenta*'s Ana Ozores, who sloshes around in the symbolically charged mud of Vetusta, Isidora risks a literal and symbolic slippage, yet crucially she "hangs" from Relimpio's protective, patriarchal arm, which holds her steady. His supervision prevents Isidora from fully realizing a process of deindividuation. Isidora does not, I argue, "melt into the crowd" (Tsuchiya 39); rather, she remains on its edge. Relimpio restrains Isi-dora, though he is not strong enough to control her rebellious nature, as we shall soon see.

At the same time, his paternal hold also ironically authorizes, permits in a way, Isidora to experience the magnetic current of the crowd while safely remaining on its edge. In other words, she grazes the threshold of de-individuation and delights in this *possibility* of dissolving into the crowd. Crucially, while on the edge of the crowd, Isidora becomes distracted by the glimmering storefronts that line the city's streets: "Isidora observó que en ella renacía, dominando su ser por entero, aquel su afán de ver tiendas, aquel apetito de comprar todo ... Se miraba en los cristales" ("Isidora noticed that once again she was being dominated completely by the rebirth of that desire of hers to look into shop windows, that yearning to buy everything ... She looked at herself in the shop windows"; 274; 219). In her encounter with the crowd, then, Isidora remains in a liminal position, caught between the world of the aristocracy (which she has momentarily abandoned), the revolutionary promise of the crowd, and the seductive allure of the "abierto bazar" ("open market"; 274; 219). McKinney notes that Isidora and other members of the petite bourgeoisie "find themselves precariously perched near the end of a social boundary, liable to slip into the nearby depths of the lower class unless they can gain a surer footing within the middle class" (57). Isidora, thus, is a kind of threshold subject, operating at the boundary and the intersections of diverse social worlds. Here, I am thinking of Anne McClintock's analysis of the nineteenth-century flaneur (building on Walter Benjamin's prior formulation) as a liminal figure: "the flaneur is still on the threshold, of the city as of the bourgeois class. Neither has yet engulfed him; in neither is he at home. He seeks refuge in the crowd" (81). Relatedly, Akiko Tsuchiya notes the critical potential in Isidora's contact with the crowd, calling her the "female flaneur par excellence" (37–8).

As the blood of aristocracy and the crown ceases to be precious, another kind of symbolic bloodletting occurs. Isidora and Relimpio make their way to Calle de la Montera. There, carts of freshly butchered meat, still dripping with blood, pass before Isidora's eyes: "El ruido era infernal. Subían los carros de la carne con las movibles cortinas de cuero chorreando sangre, y su enorme pesadez estremecía el suelo" ("The noise was infernal. Meat carts were coming up the street, with their swaying leather coverings dripping with blood, and their enormous weight making the ground tremble"; *La desheredada* 275; Clark 220). Of course, carnival (from Latin *carn-* ["flesh"] and *levare* ["to put away"]) is the festival in which one consumes meat for the final time before Lent. The colossal weight of the carts is enough to quake the already unsteady ground coated in unctuous black soap, making the threat of slippage all the more imminent. Here, I am reminded of Deleuze and

Guattari's description of a dream in which crowds, particularly at the point of a threshold, take centre stage:

> I am on the edge of the crowd, at the periphery; but I belong to it, I am attached to it by one of my extremities, a hand or a foot. I know that the periphery is the only place I can be, that I would die if I let myself be drawn into the center of the fray, but just as certainly if I let go of the crowd. That is not an easy position to stay in, it is even very difficult to hold, for these beings are in constant motion and their movements are unpredictable and follow no rhythm. They swirl, go north, then suddenly east; none of the individuals in the crowd remains in the same place in relation to the others. So I am in perpetual motion; all this demands a high level of tension, but it gives me a feeling of violent, almost vertiginous happiness. (29)

What is striking about this passage is that the edge of the crowd represents a delicate boundary that gives way to death on either side of the divide. So too, I argue, Isidora finds herself in a similarly unstable position facing symbolic deaths on all sides. The blood of freshly butchered meat may serve as a reminder of symbolic, anarchic bloodletting that Isidora's abandonment of the aristocracy entails. It also, however, emblematizes the goriness involved in flesh for sale – a clear metaphor and foreshadowing of sex work.

Indeed, no sooner does Isidora encounter the raw meat than she suddenly desires to head back towards Sol. "¿Otra vez?" ("What, again?"; *La desheredada* 275; Clark 220) Relimpio asks. And she remarks that she wants to get to Congress. In front of Congress and coming upon Calle del Turco, Relimpio stops in the exact spot where General Prim, the leader of the revolution, was recently assassinated. "Aquí mataron a D. Juan Prim. Todavía están en la pared las señales de las balas" ("Here's where they killed Don Juan Prim. The bullet marks are still in the wall"; 278; 223). In this instance, Isidora, oblivious to the significance of this site of political bloodletting, attempts to free herself of Relimpio's hold: "Déjeme usted sola – dijo a su padrino –. Yo tengo que hacer" ("'Leave me on my own,' she said to her godfather. 'I have things I must do'"; 276; 221). Apologetic, she slips away, fleeing the scene with the marquis Joaquin Saldeoro to whom she sells herself: "Isidora echó a correr, llegose a él, *se le colgó del brazo*. Hubo exclamaciones de sorpresa y alegría ... Después siguieron juntos, y se perdieron en la niebla" ("Isidora began to run, reached him and took his arm [*hung onto his arm*]. There were exclamations of surprise and joy ... Then they went on together and were lost in the fog"; 278, my emphasis; 223, my emphasis). Isidora's full submersion into the crowd is impeded as she remains anchored down by the physical arms of patriarchy: a father figure on one end and lover-purchaser on the other. Both prevent her from being subsumed by the pleasurable, democratic multitude. Here, I diverge from Sara Muñoz's claim that "la unión de Isidora con la masa contribuye a canalizar sus deseos sexuales al unirse del brazo de Pez, su futuro amante" ("The union of Isidora with the masses contributes to the channeling of her sexual desires as she joins Pez, her future lover, by the arm"; 95). Joaquin, in my view, undercuts Isidora's union with the multitude rather than embody the culmination of desires stoked by the collective. If the crowd – and its social blood – presented the possibility of a pleasurable cure for Isidora – the deindividuation and the antidote to her delusions – Joaquin enables her re-entry as a beautiful commodity – "a sign for sale" (Cifuentes) – into the circulation of the market-driven city, the open bazaar.

The Prostitute

Isidora exits the crowd at Puerta de Sol. The bustling city centre also occupies the novel's temporal centre. Leaving the threshold of collectivized anonymity, she disappears into the fog with Joaquin. An ethereal opacity that challenges narrative omniscience, the fog is an occlusive matter that momentarily obfuscates the narrator's vision. After tracking Isidora's movement through the city, Relimpio too rather abruptly loses sight of his cherished goddaughter. To some degree, the fog is liberatory for Isidora, allowing her to finally escape Relimpio's authority. But the fog also consumes her, and so too does Joaquin.

By contrast, the nebulous relations between Isidora and Joaquin – of which the salacious transaction (we imagine) occurs behind closed doors – Isidora's sensual epiphany in the crowd comes across in rich detail. This experience of collective excitation exceeds, no doubt, the social codes of chastity, but nonetheless Galdós makes the authorial decision to bring it into the representation with great poetic force. Indeed, Isidora's encounter with the crowd comes through with vivid, tactile description. Like Ana Ozores's epiphanic moment of pleasure, intellectual lucidity and sensorial knowledge accompany this fleeting moment of blurred boundaries, allowing the reader to imagine an affective and tactile experience.

The narrative details that allow us to sense the crowd begins to illustrate political theorist Jason Frank's notion of the "living image of the people": "the novel idea that collective assemblies, crowds, and mass protests, [in the Age of Democratic Revolutions] were no longer understood merely as factious riots or seditious rebellions, but instead as living incarnations of the people's authority, sublime expressions of the vitality and the significance of popular will" (n.p.). Indeed, in Galdós, it is not so much that we visualize or surveil the crowd in a disciplinary sense – we do not get a sense of its forms, its lines, it colours – rather we *feel* the crowd – its impressions (*codazos*), its electric current (magnetism) – as sight gives way to multitudinous touch. This sensorium, moreover, holds a radical potential.

Isidora's sensual experience attests to the emotion's breaking down of boundaries. That is: "the emotions refuse the organization of experience in tidy categories, undoing the binary oppositions inside/outside, individual/collective, mind/body, thought/feeling, and reason/emotion that have been erected to contain them ... emotions [are] a form of thought and knowledge, and a major component of social life – including in the nineteenth century, which attempted to relegate them to a feminine intimate sphere" (Delgado et al. 2). This, we might say, is the seed of a crowd aesthetic that derails "realist vision" – to borrow Peter Brooks's words – and challenges the notion of a violent, irrational mob.

Crucially, Akiko Tsuchiya has argued that the crowd allows Isidora to "escap[e] the gaze and the authority of the masculine narrator" (39). The opacity of the fog, which descends on the city just as we encounter Joaquin, forces the narrator to recede – he no longer attends to Isidora's affective state. There is something extraordinary worth dwelling on here. Not only does fog signify a kind of narrative impotence – the unnarratable – it also suggests that more important things merit narrative space and sensorial attention. Isidora's encounter with the crowd affirms the generative force of anonymized touch, rendering meaningless the couple form and the boundaries that demarcate the individual, gendered subject. Visual markers of identity become useless signs that lose their social currency. The masked carnival goers – by hiding their faces – defy the kind of disciplinary or "infallible super-vision" (D.A. Miller 23) that stalks the tantalizingly beautiful Isidora throughout the narrative.[27] Thus, the fact that visibility recedes in the face of the crowd sharply contrasts with the visual regime of bourgeois female subjectivity. No one appears to notice the window shopper's beauty – it is of no value to the crowd. Instead, what we have is a moment of visual and disciplinary suspension that gives way to a sensual, revolutionary epiphany – one that betrays the "voz de la sangre" ("voice of my true blood"; *La desheredada* 265; Clark 210) – indeed, blood-based distinction has no place here. Life in the crowd is bodied forth through transient collective tactile pleasure that erases distinction – in stark opposition to the "segunda vida" ("second life"; 114; 52) of Isidora's heady neuralgias.

The crowd is antilinear and appears to have neither origin nor end-point in *La desheredada*. Instead, it swirls in the novel's centre. (If we recall that novel opens with the truncated end of another novel [one that does not exist], Galdós seems, from the outset, to challenge the idea of linearity, discreteness, and totality.) Here, the crowd may elicit fears such as the ones Ortega y Gasset would later identify. The modern *lleno* would entail the fatal bloodletting of the protagonist, threatening to make the crowd the new subject of the novel. This does not quite illustrate Frederic Jameson's provocative claim that Galdós's fiction lacks any real protagonist – what he terms "waning protagonicity" – but that the crowd as a subject may challenge the notion of the individual and, in turn, the protagonist as we know it. *Ya no hay protagonistas solo hay coro.*

Galdós, I contend, is not quite ready to dispense with female protagonists, nor the idea of the modern subject – there is still much to be explored here as he debuts his *novelas contemporáneas*. Instead, what I have attempted to show in this chapter is how an attention to blood shows the struggle of the modern female subject emerging in a dialectical tension between self-fashioning (the window shopper) and birthright (bloodlines). Galdós, however, entertains the idea of a third possibility, that social blood – the blood of the multitude – yields the potential to resolve this conflict. This struggle mirrors that of the political battle between Republicans and monarchists, but it also exceeds it – critiquing more broadly the problem of gendered subjectivity under modernity.

In a recent study on populations and the Victorian novel, Emily Steinlight trenchantly challenges the widely accepted notion that the subject of the novel is the "modern individual in society" in relation to a social totality (13) and instead "finds fiction's point of departure in a surplus of humanity" (10). Fiction's timely intervention occurs just as the social sciences, Steinlight notes, attempt to account for and regulate surplus populations (e.g., Malthus). The novel, rather than attempt to control populations, yields the "potential to give aesthetic expression to the scope of what its represented world has yet to accommodate" (17). Galdós's narrative fiction, from *La desheredada* buds a new crowd aesthetic – predicated on collective, non-gendered tactility – that perhaps never fully blossoms – much in the way that Republicanism is undercut by the Restoration of the Bourbon monarchy.

The novel's close, "Muerte de Isidora. Conclusión de los Rufetes," which takes place under the Restoration, gestures towards yet another symbolic death. Crucially, Galdós loops back to Isidora's reflection in a mirror:

Isidora, pues ella misma era y no una vana imagen, se miró largo rato en el espejo. Aunque este era pequeño y malo, ella quería verse, no sólo el rostro, sino el cuerpo, y tomaba las actitudes más extrañas y violentas, ladeándose y haciendo contorsiones. La ligereza de su ropa era tal, que fácilmente salían al exterior las formas intachables de su talle y todo el conjunto gracioso y esbelto de su cuerpo. (495)

Isidora, for it was she and no vain image, looked at herself in the mirror for a long time. Although the glass was small and badly pitted, she wanted to see not only her face but her body, and she was taking up the most strange and outrageous poses, turning this way and that, contorting herself. The lightness of her clothing was such that you could easily see the flawless shape of her figure and the slender grace of her body. (452–3)

Ill and deranged, Isidora contemplates her lascivious image not in the lustrous glass display we saw at the novel's start and again on the edge of the crowd, but in a small, imperfect mirror. Relimpio, once taken by her beauty, now finds Isidora's investment in her own appearance disturbing:

Don José se quedó lelo, frío, inerte, cuando oyó estas palabras, pronunciadas claramente por Isidora: "Todavía soy guapa …, y cuando me reponga seré guapísima. Valgo mucho, y valdré muchísimo más." (495)

Don José remained stupefied, cold and motionless, when he heard these words, clearly pronounced by Isidora: "I'm still pretty … and when I'm better again, I'll be very pretty indeed. I'm worth a lot, and I shall be worth a great deal more." (453)

This symbolic death, then, is not one that gives way to the generative, vitalizing power of the collective, but the dehumanizing force of the market that consigns Isidora to the realm of objects. Isidora's reflection is no longer super imposed over luxury goods on display. She blatantly and unapologetically quantifies her own beauty in market terms.

Surrounded, once again, by two paternal figures – Miquis and Relimpio – she plots her escape.

Salió, efectivamente, veloz, resuelta, con paso de suicida; y como este cae furioso, aturdido, demente en el abismo que le ha solicitado con atracción invencible, así cayó ella despeñada en el voraginoso laberinto de las calles. La presa fue devorada, y poco después en la superficie social todo estaba tranquilo. (500)

So she went out, swiftly, resolutely, with the firm step of a person about to commit suicide; and just as such a person falls raging, confused and demented into the abyss that has lured him on irresistibly, so she fell headlong into the vortex, the labyrinth of the streets. The prey was devoured, and shortly afterwards, on the surface of society, everything was peaceful. (458)

Scholars have interpreted this scene as one in which Isidora is fully and finally subsumed by a crowd based on the assumption that the streets of the capital are filled with people. But upon careful inspection of the novel's end, it is clear that, oddly, there are no crowds to speak of now. Galdós depicts the streets of the capital as eerily depopulated, a vacant, impersonal labyrinth, an abyss. At the novel's close, Isidora fails to be the leech (*la sanguijuela del pueblo*) – the aspirational bloodsucking aristocrat – and the social blood of the republic does not flow through her veins. Instead, with a "suicidal pace," she hastily submits to the vice of the market-driven streets. Order is restored: the prostitute fully subsumes the window shopper, and she is, in turn, gobbled up by the modern labyrinthine city.

Chapter Four

Transfusions: Queering Kinship in *Fortunata y Jacinta: Dos historias de casadas*

> *To enter into a gift exchange as a partner,*
> *one must have something to give.*
> *If women are for men to dispose of,*
> *they are in no position to give themselves away.*
>
> Gayle Rubin, "The Traffic in Women"

Blood – at once a sacred signifier and vital fluid – colours the pages of *Fortunata y Jacinta*; it is named over seventy times in the novel. In its material form, blood sticks to boot soles, drips from animal flesh, and flows from Fortunata's expiring post-partum body. At the lower rungs of society, the materiality of blood appears hyper perceptible, assaulting the senses, while among the ruling classes of Madrid blood operates as a phantom signifier: an invisible symbol of their caste identity. Indeed, *Fortunata y Jacinta* exhibits a world in which the "symbolics of blood" (Foucault, *History of Sexuality I*) exists alongside blood's crude materiality. This duality – blood as a symbol of distinction and blood as visceral, fluid matter – structures, to borrow Gil Anidjar's words, the "hemophiliac economy" that binds the novel's social web. In such an economy, the value of purportedly pure blood – that of the elite caste – is regulated through marriage, or more precisely, via the "traffic of women," to use Gayle Rubin's formulation. Thus, the central protagonist Juanito Santa Cruz dutifully marries his first cousin Jacinta. There, in the ruling classes, blood remains unseen, flowing in a closed circuit. By contrast, the highly aestheticized shedding of physical blood, like that of the hemorrhaging Fortunata – Juanito's plebeian lover and mother to his only son – marks those bodies that inhabit spaces of social precarity. Through an examination of blood's myriad forms, this chapter advances a nuanced understanding of caste, kinship, and intimacy in Galdós's seminal adultery novel. To this end, I approach blood as a wholly intimate fluid: the crimson plasma that sustains human life, a conduit of sexual relations, and an agglutinative agent that binds kin.

Throughout this book blood congeals around origins, but in this final chapter I want to begin with a hematic end. At the novel's close, Fortunata narrates her own death as she hemorrhages: "Parece que me voy en sangre ... Hijo mío, Dios me quiere separar de ti; y ello será por tu bien ... Me muero; la vida se me corre fuera, como el río que va a la mar" ("It feels like I'm losing blood. Oh, my son, I'm dying; life's flowing out of me like a river running into the sea"; *FJ* II 765; Moncy Gullón 801).[1]

As Fortunata's body drains of blood, she dictates her will, which effectively bequeaths her son to Jacinta. This is a watershed moment in the narrative, one that has generated significant scholarly attention. Megan L. Kelly has argued that "[t]he death of Fortunata is clearly pivotal in that the resolution of the plot hinges precisely upon the fact that she dies: the adoption of Juan Evaristo ensures that there is a secure heir to the Santa Cruz family, and Jacinta has the child she has longed for" (12). For her part, Camille Cruz Martes proposes that we view Fortunata's death through the trope of substitution deployed throughout the novel, arguing that this ambiguous and contradictory sacrifice is "[l]a gran sustitución en la novela" ("the greatest substitution of the novel"; 144). Frederic Jameson makes a similar claim, viewing Fortunata's death as a return to "equilibrium achieved by swap: Jacinta will receive Fortunata's child as her own, and Fortunata will become a saint and go to heaven" (100). Curiously, three of these accounts focus on Fortunata's death as a utilitarian elision from the plot, while negating (perhaps unintentionally) her active role in this transaction. Nuria S. Pastor is the only scholar, to my knowledge, who has examined this act from the vantage point of a gift economy, thus recuperating Fortunata's active role in this exchange. Pastor argues that "[c]uando Fortunata sacrifica a su hijo, éste adquiere un enorme valor simbólico pues representa la deuda que la burguesía contrae con la madre" ("when Fortunata sacrificies her son he acquires an enormous symbolic value – he represents the debt that the bourgeoisie incurs with the mother"; 268). This debt, Pastor notes, can never be repaid, moreover, "el orden social se restituye cuando Fortunata muere en la casa donde nació y los burgueses consiguen el hijo que necesitan para perpetuarse" ("the social order is restored when Fortunata dies in the house in which she was born, and the bourgeoise obtain the son they need to perpetuate themselves"; 268).

Even in this case, however, the word "sacrifice" frames Fortunata as a martyr or selfless mother and detracts from the agentic power that undergirds the act of giving – emblematized by Fortunata's wilful intentionality. Pastor does, however, rescue an affirming aspect of her death. When the flesh and blood of the protagonist die, Pastor claims, "[l]a esencia de Fortunata quedará eternamente personificada en su hijo" ("Fortunata's essence will remain eternally personified in her son"; 268). We might think of this "essence" as materialized from Fortunata's blood. In this way, bequeathing Pituso operates as a kind of blood transfusion, one which forever morphs the Santa Cruz y Arnaiz genealogy. From this point of departure, I want to offer a more agentic, subversive account of Fortunata's death and will. In what follows, I will argue that the act of giving her son to her lover's wife can be read as a feminist gesture, one that queers traditional gender roles by upending patriarchal kinship as we know it.

By framing this relation as queer, I do not mean to suggest that Fortunata and Jacinta's fleeting union exemplifies a kind of lesbian erotics – though one could conceivably make a case for it. Instead, I am drawing on Juana María Rodríguez's lucid explanation of queer as mode of critique and resistance: "'Queer' is not simply an umbrella term that encompasses lesbians, bisexuals, gay men, two-spirited people, and transsexuals; it is a challenge to constructions of heteronormativity. It need not subsume the particularities of these other definitions of identity; instead it creates an opportunity to call into question the systems of categorization that have served to define sexuality" (Rodríguez 24). Following this assertion, I want us to consider how Fortunata and Jacinta's shared parentage instantiates a non-normative social arrangement – one that simultaneously undoes the patriarchal structure of kinship around which the force of gender identification coheres while also highlighting the impossibility of the fantasy of blood purity upon which this hemophiliac economy depends.

To grasp the subversive force of Fortunata's gift to Jacinta, we must first understand the diverse forms that blood takes in the novel. Galdós represents blood in its most crude material state (e.g., a bloody steak), blood as pigment (e.g., the blood-coloured slums), and blood in hallucinatory visions (e.g., a room filled to the ceiling with Maxi's blood). All the while, blood, as in bloodlines, also functions as a subcutaneous symbol of distinction and exclusivity. Thus, for the members of the caste, blood becomes a "site of difference" (Anidjar 19). Far from incidental, this duality structures the social hierarchy of *Fortunata y Jacinta*. In fact, the social world of Galdós's Madrid is ordered according to those who bleed and those whose blood remains contained and invisible. Fortunata, Mauricia, and Maxi occupy the social periphery of Madrid, and all are associated with abundant blood flow. Mauricia, like

Fortunata, bleeds profusely in her final moments of life upon suffering a blow to the head:

> – Si tiene rajada la cabeza en salva la parte … afirmó Papitos dando a conocer gráficamente las dimensiones de la herida –. Y echaba la mar de sangre … que corría por la calle abajo, como corre el agua cuando llueve. (*FJ* II 372)

> "She's split her head wide open," stated Papitos, thus giving a graphic description of the size of the wound. "And she was spouting blood all over, it was running down the street like the water when it rains." (Moncy Gullón 540)

Maxi, Fortunata's feeble husband, in his illness, has a hallucinatory vision of blood: "Soñaba que te habías marchado … y yo te había cogido de un pie, y tú tirabas, y yo tiraba más, y tirando se me rompía la bolsa del aneurisma, y todo el cuarto se llenaba de sangre, todo el cuarto hasta el techo" ("I dreamed that you'd left … and then I was holding onto you by your foot and you were tugging away, and I pulled you harder and then the aneurysm sac in my head broke open and the whole room was full of blood … the whole room, even the ceiling"; *FJ* II 435; 582). And in his failed confrontation with Juan, Maxi bleeds from his forehead, while Juan remains unscathed. Viewed together, these images – a hemorrhaging mother, a sea of blood, a blood-filled room – are viscerally horrific. What this propensity for bleeding demonstrates is that the "marginal subjects" (to borrow Tsuchiya's words)[2] are associated with flow and the crude materiality of blood. By contrast, Juan's precious blood, the blood of the elite caste, is rarely (if ever) exposed. Instead, it remains invisible and must be protected and carefully managed.[3]

Bloodlines, Origins, Essence

Purity and mixing prove key to understanding Galdós's grand, four-part adultery novel. Here, I turn to Tony Tanner's compelling definition of adultery as the mixture of "what should be kept separate by bringing the wrong things together in the wrong places (or the wrong people in the wrong beds)" (13). Paraphrasing Tanner, adultery or adulteration threatens form, collapsing boundaries between interior and exterior (18). Social mixing is certainly the bread and butter of modern urbanity. Set during the transition from Revolution to Restoration (1869–76), Galdós's first-person narrator traces, at the start of the novel, the shifting economic conditions and ideologies that engendered a more capitalist, modern Madrid. The introduction of market economies, a national currency, and new modes of consumption form the backdrop of this post-revolutionary period during which a rising middle class upsets the centuries-old hierarchy of the feudal nobility.[4] This era of modernization – the Restoration marking the beginning of economic reform – witnessed the failures of the 1868 revolution and constitutional democracy and the increasing sentiments of national impotence prompted by Spain's precipitous imperial decline on the global stage. Unsurprisingly, anxieties around the shifting internal (class, caste, gender, nation) and external (empire, colonialism, European modernity) markers of identity abound.

Amid this cultural ferment, the narrator details the web of incestuous relations that controls the nation's capital. Stephen Gilman has characterized the first quarter of this 1,000-page novel as "a book of genesis" or an "arboreal allegory" (294, 295). While scholars have commented extensively on the formation of class identity in *Fortunata y Jacinta*, which, according to Harriet Turner, is determined by, above all, money (Turner, *Galdós: Fortunata y Jacinta* 37), far less attention has been given to bloodlines and none (to my knowledge) to the iconography of blood, both of which breathe life into *Fortunata y Jacinta*'s arboreal plot and ensanguined aesthetic, respectively.

Powerful kinship relations and elite caste identity congeal through blood's agglutinative force. When Barbarita, the mother of the novel's protagonist Juanito Santa Cruz, worries that her son may be sexually corrupted during his trip to Paris, her husband Baldomero reassures her that "[Juanito es] de casta honrada, tiene la formalidad en la masa de la sangre" ("[Juanito is] well-bred, it's in his blood"; *FJ* I 214; 9). Indeed, elite families treat blood not only as a marker of social status but also as a guarantor of moral probity: blood underwrites both *la casta* (caste) and *la castidad* (chastity). In the interest of maintaining the exclusivity of the caste, incest serves as a biopolitical strategy for securing bloodlines: Barbarita arranges for Juanito to marry his first cousin and childhood playmate, aptly named Jacinta – the Spanish equivalent of Hyacinth, meaning "born to the purple" (Turner, *Galdós* 55). The future of the caste, however, reaches a point of crisis when Juanito and Jacinta fail to produce an heir.

While this is not the Spain of the *antiguo regimen* ("old regime"), the elite families of Madrid value birth as a form of symbolic capital and one that challenges the mobile social constructions of bourgeois identity. This complicates the assertion that Juanito Santa Cruz is the "prototipo de la clase media española decimonónica" ("prototype of the Spanish nineteenth-century middle class"), since conventional conceptions of the bourgeoisie do not account for his sense of distinction (Cruz Martes 114). It would be fruitful to underscore the fact that the bourgeoisie typically define themselves in opposition to blood-based hierarchies, which have long been associated with the aristocracy. As Eric Hobsbawm explains, the bourgeoisie is: "a body of persons of power and influence, independent of the power and influence of traditional birth and status. To belong to it a man had to be 'someone'; a person who counted as an individual, because of his wealth, his capacity to command other men or otherwise influence them" (244). Early on, in a passage that is laden with hypocrisy, the novel's unreliable narrator comments on the lack of importance of birth:

> Es curioso observar cómo nuestra edad, por otros conceptos infeliz, nos presenta una dichosa confusión de todas las clases, mejor dicho, la concordia y reconciliación de todas ellas. En esto aventaja nuestro país a otros, donde están pendientes de sentencia los graves pleitos históricos de la igualdad. Aquí se ha resuelto el problema sencilla y pacíficamente, gracias al temple democrático de los españoles y a la escasa vehemencia de las preocupaciones nobiliarias ... esta confusión es un bien ... *El nacimiento no significa nada entre nosotros.* (*FJ* I 347; my emphasis)

> It's strange to see how our times, which are unfortunate in other ways, present us with a happy confusion of social classes or, rather, their harmony and reconciliation. In this respect our country is ahead of others, where serious historical suits for equality are awaiting a verdict. The problem has been solved here and peacefully, thanks to the democratic spirit of Spaniards and our less vehement concern about aristocratic status ... This confusion is good ... *Birth means nothing to us.* (81; my emphasis)

In this national scenario, the narrator draws an oxymoronic image of "paz y armonía" ("peace and harmony") that boasts of a happy confusion of classes and "un socialismo atenuado e inofensivo" ("inoffense form of socialism"; *FJ* I 347; 80–1) supposedly unknown to other nations. He smooths over the class tensions of this period, but perhaps more significantly, he strategically disavows the ways in which the middle class was interconnected with the nobility. In nearly the same breath, the narrator frames the union of the nobility with a rising merchant class as an entanglement of the old and the new: "Ya tenemos aquí, perfectamente enganchadas, a la aristocracia antigua y el comercio moderno" ("With this we have a perfect link between the old aristocracy and the modern business world"; *FJ* I 349; 82). What follows this declaration of class harmony is a detailed genealogy of all the intermarried commercial families of the novel identified by their surnames, their regional origins, and current economic standings. For the narrator, who is closely tied to the central family of the novel, these relationships are allegedly not determined through birth but are simply following the liberal logic of capitalism. What determines class position, according to the narrator, is, first, education and comportment and, second, money. He explains: "La otra determinación positiva de clases, el dinero, está fundada en principios económicos tan inmutables como las leyes físicas, y querer impedirla viene a ser lo mismo que intentar beberse la mar" ("The other positive class distinction, money, is based on economic principles as immutable as the laws of physics, and trying to alter them would be like trying to swallow the sea"; *FJ* I 348; 82). The detailed mapping of the commercial family origins makes clear, however, that despite the narrator's prior claim that birth has no importance to "us," blood and lineage serve as powerful markers of distinction and exclusion independent of capital.

The Santa Cruz y Arnaiz family clings to the narrative of their origins while suspiciously scrutinizing those of others. Yet perhaps the greatest irony of all is that the surname Santa Cruz, as Harriet Turner has noted, is a *converso* surname: "[t]he family's cult of respectability and decency – cleanliness of the individual and social body – carries a residue of inquisitorial obsession with purity of blood, the name Santa Cruz suggesting that of converted Jews" (*Galdós* 37). This, combined with her concerns for maintaining the insularity of the caste through "succession," makes clear that their own investment in the reproduction of their bloodlines is more than just a residue of early modern blood purity statutes: it works as a form of compensation for and a disavowal of their own muddied history. Nonetheless, their fixation on bloodlines and the silence around the possibility of *converso* origins, papers over this past, and their lineage remains largely unquestioned in the novel. The tedious genealogical mapping suggests that in the cultural milieu of the modern capital, notable bloodlines ensure a kind of symbolic power that cannot be acquired through the accumulation of economic capital alone. The narrative illustrates, as we shall soon see, that changing economic conditions in Spain produced an unstable dependence among the elite caste defined by bloodlines, an emergent bourgeoisie defined by economic status, and the urban poor, which both of these groups exploited.

Juan Santa Cruz y Arnaiz is the sole heir to the family fortune acquired through the textile and garment trade with China via the Philippines; his father was a partner in the *Real Compañía de las Filipinas*, a short-lived enterprise that was quickly overcome by the British domination of transpacific commerce. Far from being oblivious to "las preocupaciones nobiliarias" ("concern about aristocratic status"), the family seeks to forge its social identity not solely through economic prosperity but also through maintaining the allusion of pure bloodlines. They accomplish this through intermarriage within the extended family. In fact, Bárbara Arnaiz and her husband Baldomero Santa Cruz are themselves distant cousins. When Bárbara discovers through a family friend that her son, Juan, has been romantically involved with a plebeian woman (whom we later learn is Fortunata), she quickly arranges for him to marry his first cousin Jacinta. Juan, without hesitation, agrees. Jacinta's family ties make her an ideal candidate for marriage, even though her parents have experienced financial strain in recent years, further indicating the primacy of bloodlines over economic success in establishing social status.

With this blood union between cousins, all is well in the Santa Cruz-Arnaiz home until, two years into the marriage, Jacinta still has not produced an heir. Her presumed sterility juxtaposed with Fortunata's fertility sets the narrative into motion, revealing the failures that underlie the social practices and biopolitical techniques, such as incest, that secure ostensible blood purity. Male sexual behaviour remains outside of this formulation of purity even though paternity marks one's membership in a family. Managing the impossible balancing act between (the appearance of) chastity on the one hand and (the essence of) fertility on the other, women like Jacinta were tasked with securing the future of the caste. Barbarita consoles the forlorn Jacinta, but as a patriarchal mother she also secretly "deseaba tanto como Jacinta la aparición de un muchacho que perpetuase la casta y les alegrase a todos" ("she shared Jacinta's wish for a child to appear to perpetuate the Santa Cruz line [caste] and make them all happy"; *FJ* I 346; 80). Barbarita, after all, needs a grandson to secure her own status in the social world of elites. Without an heir to continue the caste, the future of the Santa Cruz y Arnaiz name and fortune is at risk of dissolution, and Bárbara begins to lose any "esperanzas de sucesión" ("hope for a sucessor"; *FJ* I 346; 81). The shame of Jacinta's barrenness is further amplified by her mother's and sister's hyperbolic fertility: the mother, blessed with "una fecundidad prodigiosa" ("prodigious fertility"; *FJ* I 257; 30), gave birth to seventeen children; her two older sisters are pregnant year after year, and her younger sister, who even "married down," gave birth to twins. Jacinta's chaste disposition makes her an iconic *ángel del hogar* ("angel of the hearth"), but her failure to become a mother makes her an incomplete woman. Her presumed sterility can be read as the excess or logical end point of the ideal of blood purity;[5] the slippage between sterile (as pure and clean) and sterility (as barren) becomes painfully clear when read against Fortunata's fertile working-class body, which Jacinta deems filthy.[6]

Edibility, Flow, and Abjection

Fortunata first appears in the novel during Juan's visit to "Madrid primitivo" ("old Madrid"; *FJ* I 283; Moncy Gullón 43), where he intends to visit his ill and bed-ridden friend Estupiñá. This scene is set in a building, the entrance to which "[e]fectivamente, parecía la subida a un castillo o prisión de Estado" ("[a]s a matter of fact, it did seem like the ascent to a castle or a state prison"; *FJ* I 283–4; 43), which was occupied by a poultry shop, or "tienda de aves." Upon entering, Juan pauses to survey the abundant stacks of eggs and deplumed poultry carcasses. The narrator recounts Juan's empathic reaction to this bloody scene only moments before he meets his soon-to-be lover:

> Daba dolor ver las anatomías de aquellos pobres animales, que apenas desplumados eran suspendidos por la cabeza, conservando la cola como un sarcasmo de su mísero destino. A la izquierda de la entrada vio el Delfín [Juan] cajones llenos de huevos, acopio de aquel comercio. La voracidad del hombre no tiene límites, y sacrifica a su apetito no sólo las presentes sino las futuras generaciones gallináceas. A la derecha, en la prolongación de aquella cuadra lóbrega, un sicario manchado de sangre daba garrote a las aves. Retorcía los pescuezos con esa presteza y donaire que da el hábito, y apenas soltaba una víctima y la entrega agonizante a las desplumadores, cogía otra para hacerle la misma caricia. (*FJ* I 283)

> It was painful to see the anatomy of those poor birds; they'd hardly been plucked when they were strung from their heads, their tail feathers still jaunty, like a sarcastic remark on their miserable fate. To the left of the entrance the Dauphin [Juan] saw boxes packed with eggs, the business' supply. Man's voracity is limitless, and sacrifices not only the present but also future gallinaceous generations. To the right of that lugubrious square space, in another area, a paid assassin besmirched with blood was executing the hens. He wrung their necks with the speed and cleverness that come from experience, and when he had scarcely let go one victim and turned the agonizing creature over to the pluckers, he would grab another to caress her in the same way. (Moncy Gullón 43)

It is against this bloody backdrop that Fortunata comes into view. The significance of this textual still life – the interrupted promise of reproduction (eggs) and the cold-blooded reality of flesh for sale (dead hens) – exhibits the mundane cruelty of everyday practices that sustain human life.[7] Moreover, painting Fortunata as the bird-woman invites the reader to identify the poultry business with Estupiñá and Juan's sexual exploits with different working-class women ("diferentes aves" ["different birds"]) – further emblematized by the tropes of slaughter and the impersonal, excessive consumption of birds. Sarah King describes this scene as a "replica in microcosm of the destructive role which [Juan's] own amorous appetite will play in the lives of the women with whom he comes in contact; especially Fortunata, who becomes through antonomasia 'la víctima'" (81).

In linking the consumption of animal blood and flesh to Juan's love affairs with working-class women – which he euphemistically dubs "la manía de lo popular" ("craze for the popular"; my translation) – Galdós enfolds a complex mediation on intimacy, caste, and ultimately, humanness. This affectively charged description of slaughter shows this literal and figurative meat market as jamming reproductive life cycles (las futuras generaciones gallináceas ["future generations of galliformes"]). It is worth noting that later in the novel, Juan will (momentarily) express remorse about these sexual adventures when he confesses: "Los hombres, digo, los señoritos, somos unos miserables; creemos que el honor de las hijas del pueblo es cosa de juego" ("Men, us *señoritos* I mean, are a rotten lot; we think that the honor of a village girl is just a toy for us"; *FJ* I 334; 73). The narrator closes his description with a macabre, erotic twist when he describes the blood-drenched feather plucker as a serial assassin ("un sicario") "caressing" one "victim" after another – a clear transference of responsibility that displaces and obscures Juan's complicity and feelings of guilt in this future affair.

This passage is notable for its sensational depiction of blood and the ways in which it overwhelms and assaults the senses. Blood flow becomes gender and class specific. It conjures up the blood of menstruation, which at the time was heavily commented on by medical hygienists. In fact, Pedro Felipe Monlau in his *Elementos de obstetricia* (1833), rather gratuitously remarks that "Hipócrates dice que [la sangre de las reglas] es parecida á [*sic*] un animal recien [*sic*] degollado" ("Hippocrates says that [menstrual blood] looks similar to that of a recently beheaded animal"; 95). Juan's blood remains contained as an invisible signifier of distinction, protected by boundaries and hermetically sealed in the caste. In contrast, the blood of plebeian women is depicted as fluid, messy, and made available for consumption. Unlike the contained, imperceptible blood of the caste, blood in the *tienda de aves* ("poultry shop") knows not the trappings of social exclusivity and remoteness. Far from being a sacred phantom signifier, blood lies exposed in its crudest material form, viscerally conjoining the erotics of alimentation and reproduction with systematic slaughter. And through the intricate workings of metonymy as risen from its contextualization in the novel's rhetoric elsewhere, it aestheticizes the sexual "slaughter" of working-class women. What is more, the fact that Juan appears via his nickname "Delfín" – derived from *Dauphin de France*, the name given to the blood heir to the French throne – positions his "blue" blood in sharp contrast to the blood-stained poultry shop.

What this scene reveals, then, is that the hierarchy between Juanito and Fortunata is marked by blood. The social world of modern Madrid was divided between those who bleed and those who do not.[8] The blood of the latter remains an invisible, phantom signifier of distinction, encased in protective skin. Debased material blood, uncontained and grotesquely portrayed, assaults the senses; it spatters and stains. It is precisely this messiness – the viscous, sticky quality of the hens'/ Fortunata's blood – that leads me to conceptualize its stubborn, unruly potential. For stickiness, as Mary Douglas succinctly writes, "is a trap, it clings like a leech; it attacks the boundary between myself and it" (38). The leech, which can be seen as either parasitic or curative, is a particularly suggestive image here. Juan, the parasitic leech, feeds off Fortunata's abundant fluidity.

And yet, consuming Fortunata is not a simple affair. Her blood "clings like a leech." It cannot simply be washed away. The lure of Fortunata's flesh – emblematized by the bloody poultry – once again recalls Tanner's notion of adulteration. Her unruly blood crosses boundaries – to build on Douglas's formulation – mixing with Juan's and becoming an obdurate stain on his protected lineage. Jo Labanyi identifies a kind of "miscegenation narrative" that structures Juan's relationship with Fortunata (*Gender and Modernization* 192). According to this colonial logic, Fortunata is forced into the role of a "native female" as a "superior breeder" that can be absorbed into the nation through her coupling with a white man (192). I propose a different reading – that Fortunata's reproductive coupling with Juan perverts his precious bloodlines. Thus, rather than being absorbed into the national family (via colonial conquest), she alters its course. Read in this way, by wielding an unexpected power over Juan, Fortunata threatens Juan's autonomy, his cleanliness, and the delicate boundaries that enclose his precious blood. As a "superior breeder," she penetrates the closed blood economy of the caste. The lure of her irresistible flesh brings him closer to the threat of adulteration that messiness of her blood unleashes.

This is not to say that Juan exercises no power over the women he "consumes." Fortunata's edible, erotic animality initially adheres to what Kyla Wazana Tompkins identifies as the status of "thingness" that certain social bodies inhabit as they become "reduced – debased – into animal fleshiness" (30).[9] Tompkins elaborates: "Those that are eaten are not persons but things, and their thingness is the result of a system of social degradation. For a human to take the place of an animal means they become the object of a similar social degradation. To be socially degraded, then, to be completely other with relation to the human, is one of the conditions of being edible" (30–1). Significantly, throughout the novel, Fortunata is described in terms of alimentation. Villalonga spots her in the street lavishly dressed in Parisian clothes and recounts "Está de rechupete" ("She looks good enough to eat!"; *FJ* I 556; my translation). By contrast, the jealous Jacinta describes Fortunata in terms of filth and revulsion by noting that poor women smell of onions (*FJ* I 314). But Fortunata's "edibility" as a quality of social debasement is not as straightforward as it initially appears. There are notable instances in which characters are afflicted by what Kevin Larsen has termed "alimentary madness." The first time Feijoo encounters Fortunata, he thinks to himself "Esta mujer me vuelve loco" ("I'm wild [crazy] about this woman"; *FJ* II 295; 488) and shortly thereafter, "Me la comería" ("I could devour her"; *FJ* II 297; 489). Thus, those who long to "eat" Fortunata find themselves "consumed" by her. Such alimentary madness, of course, takes on undeniably erotic undertones. This affliction even appears to affect Jacinta and Juan during their honeymoon, where both obsess over Juan's affair with Fortunata and devour a "*montón de cadáveres* [de pájaros] fritos" ("a pile of fried [bird] corpses"; *FJ* I 323; 66).

And, while the poultry shop scene is initially framed in terms of male sexual appetite ("la voracidad del hombre" ["the voracity of men"]) and the sexual exploitation of plebeian women, the narrator inverts the analogy by foregrounding female sexual agency and consumption. In fact, his desire for Fortunata often undermines his very autonomy. Shortly after the narrator describes the bloody poultry shop, Juan spots Fortunata for the very first time, and in this oft-cited passage she appears bird-like to him in her sexualized grandiosity:[10]

La moza tenía pañuelo azul claro por la cabeza y un mantón sobre los hombros, y en el momento de ver al Delfín, se infló con él, quiero decir, que hizo ese característico arqueo de brazos y alzamiento de hombros con que las madrileñas del pueblo se agasajan dentro del mantón, movimiento que les da cierta semejanza con una gallina que esponja su plumaje y se ahueca para volver luego a su volumen natural. (*FJ* I 284)

> The girl wore a light blue scarf on her head and a large, heavy shawl over
> her shoulders, and the minute she saw the Dauphin she swelled up at
> him, I mean she put her hands on her hips and raised her shoulders with
> that characteristic gesture that low-class women of Madrid have, filling
> out their shawls with a movement that reminds you of a hen ruffling
> her feathers and swelling out before coming down to normal size again.
> (Moncy Gullón 44)

Like King, Stephen Gilman positions Fortunata as the victim in this
scene, "flushed from cover by two skilled and avid hunters, Juanito
and Galdós" (78). But Fortunata, the *rara avis*, is no ordinary bird.
Her body swells ("se infló") with erotic power – recalling male avian
mating rituals – as she appears before Juan sucking a raw egg from its
shell: "Por entre los dedos de la chica se escurrían aquellas babas gela-
tinosas y transparentes. Tuvo tentaciones Juanito de aceptar la oferta;
pero no: le repugnaban los huevos crudos" ("The jellyish, transpar-
ent drool slipped through the girl's fingers. Juanito was tempted to
accept the offer, but no; raw eggs were repulsive"; *FJ* I 286; Moncy
Gullón 44). This highly ambivalent moment lends itself to multiple
interpretations. For starters, the egg, particularly in Spanish, symbolizes both male (testes) and female (ovum) fertility. Is this a harbinger
of Fortunata's fatally marked reproductive future with Juan – their
first-born dies – or is Fortunata the castrating mother vis-à-vis Juan?
Either way, eggs are a source of physical nourishment, and the sight
of their consumption functions as an almost fetishistic erotic pleasure.
Here, the act of eating serves as a "metalanguage for genital pleasure
and sexual desire" but also becomes "a site of erotic pleasure itself"
(Tompkins 5). Erotic pleasure, as we shall see, is haunted by the spectre of death – not Fortunata's (as was the case at the start of this scene)
but Juan's.

Forbidden temptations are couched in cannibalistic terms – Fortunata the "gallina" ("hen") consumes an egg. The devouring mother
elicits fears of the abject, rendering Juan the frightful child that
must constitute himself as a subject through and against the maternal body. As Julia Kristeva has argued, "food is the oral object (the
abject) that sets up archaic relationships between the human being
and the other, its mother, who wields a power that is as vital as it is
fierce" (Kristeva 75–6). Fortunata, both the fowl destined for consumption and consuming animal, bespeaks what Anne McClintock
describes in male imperial discourse as "the simultaneous dread
of catastrophic boundary *loss* (implosion), associated with fears of
impotence and infantilization and attended by an *excess* of boundary

order and fantasies of unlimited power" (26). McClintock goes on to note that the "fear of engulfment expresses itself most acutely in the cannibal trope" (27). Juan's gaze, directed at Fortunata, appears both desirous and anxious: the consumer fears being consumed, gobbled up.

There are strong undercurrents of infancy, maternity, and abjection in the scenes of eroticism in *Fortunata y Jacinta*. Juan's masculinity frequently recedes in his relationships with women, which often mimic the mother–child dynamic. That the narrator uses the term "baba" ("drool") to describe the runny egg is no insignificant detail, "baba" being a bodily fluid associated with infants. Drool drips from the mouths of young children who have not been disciplined to contain this internal fluid. The 1884 entry of "baba" in *Diccionario de Real Academia Española* includes the expression "caérse á uno la baba" ("to drool"): "con que se da á entender, ó que uno es bobo, porque de cualquiera cosa se queda como persuade, ó el gran gusto que le ocasiona el primor con que dice ó hace alguna cosa la persona que es de su cariño" ("understood to mean that either one is dumb, because they can be fooled by anything; or the great pleasure that is occasioned by the delicacy with which an endearing person speaks or acts"). "Baba" thus emblematizes Juan's affective state, "stupefied" by the pull of undisciplined pleasure ("el gran gusto" ["the great pleasure"]), causing a momentary lapse in judgment (i.e., making him "dumb"). Fittingly, "baba" resembles infant speech as they begin sounding out words. We might imagine that for Juan this is a transient moment of inarticulate infancy prompted by Fortunata, the engorged mother hen. Juan "el bebé" pleasurably gazes at the "baba," which renders him "bobo."

Crucially, it is the instantiation of disgust (*repugnancia*) that restores Juan's moral superiority in the face of Fortunata's erotic maternal force. Tempted by the "baba," Juan threatens to break out of his bourgeois mode of decorum and accept the half-eaten runny egg. He then quickly thinks to himself: "no: le repugnaban los huevos crudos" ("no; raw eggs were repulsive"). Here, disgust interrupts unruly desire and keeps Juan away (for now) from Fortunata's sticky trap. The complexity of this act is further illuminated when considering Sara Ahmed's claim that disgust "functions to maintain power relations between above and below, *through which 'aboveness' and 'belowness' become properties of particular bodies, objects and spaces*" (*The Cultural Politics of Emotion* 89). And yet, the threat of Juan's sinking to Fortunata's level does not entirely vanish. Ahmed further elaborates that the person who feels disgust remains open "to being affected by those who are felt to be below" (89).

With significant differences, Galdós duplicates the erotic mother–infant dynamic in Juan's relationship with Jacinta. The married cousins enact fetishistic scenes of desire through the role play of mother and infant:

> ¡Qué gusto ser *bebé!* – murmuró el Delfín–. ¡Sentirse en los brazos de la mamá, recibir el calor de su aliento y ...!
>
> Pasó otro rato, y Juan, despabilándose y fingiendo el lloriqueo de un tierno infante en edad de lactancia chilló así:
>
> – Mamá ... mamá ...
>
> –¿Qué?
>
> –Teta.
>
> Jacinta sofocó una carcajada.
>
> – *Ahola* no ... teta caca ... cosa fea ...
>
> Ambos se divertían con tales simplezas. Era un medio de entretener el tiempo y de expresarse su cariño.
>
> – Toma teta – díjole Jacinta metiéndole un dedo en la boca; y él se lo chupaba diciendo que estaba muy rica, con otras muchas tontadas, justificada sólo por la ocasión, la noche y la dulce intimidad. (*FJ* I 508)

"It's so nice to be a *bebé*," murmured the Dauphin; "be in your mother's arms, and feel the warmth of her breathing and ...!"

> Another stretch of time, and then Juan, waking up and imitating the whimper of a tender infant being nursed, bleated:
>
> "Mamá ... Mamá ... "
>
> "What?"
>
> "Nipple."
>
> Jacinta stifled a laugh.
>
> "Not now ... it's bad [caca] ... dirty ..."
>
> They both found such silly phrases amusing. It was a way of killing time and showing their affection.
>
> "Here, my nipple," said Jacinta, putting a finger in his mouth; and he sucked it, saying it was delicious and other foolish things, justified only by the occasion, the night, and their sweet intimacy. (184)

According to the narrator, Juan and Jacinta derive mutual pleasure from the mother–son role play. In so doing, they fetishize the idealized domestic scene of chaste mother and innocent male infant. In the same way, the infantilist fetishism between Juan and Jacinta, which derives its symbolic force from the cult of domesticity, allows the couple to side-step, or symbolically compensate for, Jacinta's infertility – a marker of her insufficiently gendered role in the family.[11]

Of course, the eroticization of motherhood diverges from the bourgeois moral order of the family, in which sex is only a means to reproduction rather than a pleasurable end in itself. For Juan and Jacinta, sex does not yield reproduction, and what is more, the multiplicity of real and imagined familial relations that these two embody – husband–wife, cousin–cousin, mother–son – renders the nuclear family a site of incest. Familial relations meant to uphold the structure of patriarchal kinship instead serve as fodder for subversive gendered imaginings.

For Juan, this erotic play opens up a space of fantasy that permits the performance of a submissive role through which he becomes dependent on the nourishing, sexualized body of an all-powerful mother (like Barbarita, the barbaric noblewoman). Jacinta, on the other hand, anxiously oscillates between positions of agency, objectification, and abjection. Juan demands "teta," but Jacinta denies him. We might, initially, read this as a powerful act of refusing consent. At the same time, what is striking here is that Jacinta verbally defiles her own body by calling her breast "caca" and "cosa fea" ("ugly thing"; my translation).[12] By substituting "caca" for breast milk, Jacinta summons forth the abject, "the horrors of the maternal bowels" (Kristeva 53). Disarmed by Juan's erotic infantile play, Jacinta deliberately mispronounces the word "ahora" ("now") as she says "ahola no." She too becomes infantile as she diminishes the potential of her imagined maternal power.

At the end of this scene, Jacinta offers Juan her finger as a substitute: "Toma teta" ("Here, my nipple"). The finger as substitution for the breast, though undeniably phallic, ultimately desexualizes their role play. Historically, as Jennifer Smith reminds us, medical doctors compared maternal breasts and men's penises, noting similarities in regard to erection, secretion, and sexual pleasure ("The Wet Nurse" 45). Of course, there are limits to the representability of the naked female body in Spanish realism – it is impossible to imagine Galdós depicting Juan playing at suckling Jacinta's actual breast – but the substitution also points to Jacinta's sexual frustration within their "sterile life" (Turner "Family Ties"). The refusal of her breast diffuses the erotic energy that had been built up by Juan. Finally, Juan renders Jacinta's body edible – he sucks her finger-breast, calling it "rica" ("delicious"). Once again, fluidity comes into play here, represented by the imagined breast milk Juan pretends to suckle from Jacinta's breast.[13] Yet, what becomes painfully clear is that Jacinta is emphatically not a lactating mother.

Jo Labanyi has pointed to the ways in which medical hygiene gendered concepts like flow and blockage, particularly in relation to female sterility: "The childless wife is a special problem. Pulido (1876:14) warns that female sterility can cause serious physical and mental disturbances requiring medication or internment. For this bodily economy is strictly gendered: men's problem is over-expenditure of resources but women's problem is blockage, impeding natural flow. Blocked bodily fluids and energies, particularly those linked with women's reproductive function, were liable to fester and go rotten; women have to take care to 'sluice out' their 'dark drains' regularly" (*Gender and Modernization* 216). While the narrative does not reference menstruation – as in the case of *La Regenta* – Jacinta's body is nonetheless marked by the absence of flow, in this case the flow of breast milk. If fluidity has historically been gendered feminine, Jacinta, as a member of the elite caste, is insufficient in this regard. She remains inadequately gendered when compared to women like Fortunata whose bodily effluvia take up ample narrative space. Like the caste itself, the "childless wife" is excessively hermetic.

Fortunata certainly presents as robust and fertile, yet her fluidity also possesses a subversive, unrestrained quality. Robin Ragan, in her study on menstruation in nineteenth-century Spain, uncovers a pharmaceutical ad in *El hogar y la moda* (1898), which reads: "Una mujer bien reglada, es garantía de buena salud, hermosura, y riqueza de sangre. Cuando este flujo falta o presenta irregularidad en sus periodos, es señal clara que en la mujer se desarrolla la Clorosis o Anemia" ("A woman with a regular cycle ['well-regulated' woman], is a guarantor of good health, beauty, and a wealth of blood. When this fluid is absent or presents irregularities during her periods, it is a sign that the woman is developing chlorosis or anemia"; 49). This ad serves as a testament to the fact that the abundance and regularity of menstrual flow signalled health and fertility. But Fortunata also fails to be "una mujer bien reglada" ("a well-regulated woman") in the sense that her flow is excessive. Her blood and "baba" are at once visceral signs and edible matter, vital fluids, and erotic oozings. Sticky and unruly, they also threaten to entrap the male subject. They function as what Sara Ahmed would term "sticky signs" that entail "a transference of affect" (91). Indeed, Fortunata's sexual deviance becomes Juan's sexual shame. The precious blood of the caste may course through his veins, but he cannot escape the taint of his sexual exploits. The blood of the caste, as his parents believe, does not guarantee him immunity. Instead, Fortunata's blood stubbornly sticks to seducers and accomplices alike. The narrator remarks that Estupiñá frequently had "pegadas a las botas, plumas diferentes aves" ("the feathers from different birds stuck to his boots") and Juan "[l]as cogía a salir, como las había cogido él, por más cuidado que tuvo de evitar al paso los sitios en que había plumas y algo de sangre" ("picked them up on his way out, just as Juanito was picking them up now, no matter how carefully he tried to avoid them"; *FJ* I 283; 43). Juan's attempts at keeping his boots clean prove futile. In effect, we might say that both men leave the building "emplumados" ("covered in feathers") – an image evocative of the Spanish equivalent of tarring and feathering, a form of corporal punishment and public shaming reserved for *alcahuetas* ("procuress") in medieval and early modern Spain (Beusterien 412). Galdós's revisioning of this historically feminine imagery (the tarred and feathered *alcahueta*) radically subverts the gendered nature of sexual shame and castigation, challenging Baldomero's belief that the blood of the caste grants immunity. Elizabeth Grosz writes that "[b]ody fluids attest to the permeability of the body, its necessary depending on an outside, its liability to collapse into this outside (this is what death implies), to the perilous divisions between the body's inside and its outside" (193). The collapse of these boundaries – those that ensure the distinction between Juan and Fortunata – threatens the social order upon which the exclusive caste depends. And yet the caste faces a crisis of fluidity. Jacinta does not give body to the notion that "[w]omen's corporeality is inscribed as a mode of seepage" (203). Ultimately, as she hemorrhages, Fortunata's abundant blood will provide the necessary flow that will allow Jacinta to forge her own kin.

Signs, Surface, Skin

"¡Oh!, el rojo abundaba tanto, que aquello parecía un pueblo que tiene la religión de la sangre" ("There was *so* much red everywhere that blood seemed to be the religion of these people"; *FJ* I 431; 133). So goes the narrator's description of "el cuarto estado" ("the slums") where the city's poor reside. In contrast to the urbane quarters of the social elite,[14] in the slums blood-coloured hues abound: "Telas rojas, arneses rojos, collarines y frontiles rojos con madroñaje arabesco. Las puertas de las tabernas también de color de sangre" ("Red material, red harnesses, red collars and yokes with berry-shaped tassels, Arabic style. The doors to the taverns were blood-colored, too"; *FJ* I 431; 133). Leaving the world of refinement momentarily behind, Jacinta, with the self-important philanthropist Guillermina as her guide, ventures into the capital's crimson underbelly with the intention of illegally purchasing the child whom they believe to be Juan's illegitimate son. In light of her reproductive crisis, it serves Jacinta to believe that the tainted blood of Juanito's bastard son can metamorphose into the immutable, incorruptible proof of membership to the caste. Of course, after bringing Pituso home we learn that the child is "counterfeit." Indeed, en *el cuarto estado* where life is at once excessively colourful and drab, resplendent and dreary, signs prove highly deceptive.

That this working-class neighbourhood is painted in the colour of blood adds complexity to the idea that perceptible blood functions as a marker of social debasement. Once again, it is the *pueblo* that "bleeds" red. But in the slums, blood becomes metaphorized and highly aesthetic, taking on the signifying form of vivid colour. Before we examine the colour of blood, it is crucial to turn back to an earlier chapter of the novel in which Galdós's narrator deploys a chromatic-affective schema to illustrate the geopolitical hierarchy of European imperial powers. As colours correspond to social class and represent emotive states, the narrative erects a structure of feeling that maps on to north–south relations, couched in a story about fashion:

> La sociedad española empezaba a presumir de *seria*; es decir, a vestirse lúgubremente, y el alegre imperio de los colorines se derrumbaba de un modo indudable. Como se habían ido las capas rojas, se fueron los pañuelos de Manila. La aristocracia los cedía con desdén a la clase media, y ésta, que también quería ser aristócrata, entregábalos al pueblo, último y fiel adepto de los matices vivos. (*FJ* I 250)

> Spanish society began to flatter itself by fancying that it was "serious," that is to say, it began to dress mournfully: our happy empire of bright colors was plainly fading away. Manila shawls went the way of red cloaks. The aristocracy haughtily relinquished them to the middle class, who, wishing to be aristocratic, cast them off to the proletariat, whose loyalty to bright colors was eternal. (Moncy Gullón 26)

The narrator recounts the changing enterprise of the Santa Cruz y Arnaiz family, whose wealth is derived in large part from the textile industry. In the mid-nineteenth century, so the story goes, England, France, and Belgium began to dominate the world of fashion: "se apuntaba la invasión lenta y tiránica de los medios colores, que pretenden ser signo de cultura" ("you could see the beginnings of the slow, tyrannical invasion of mixed or secondary colors, which presume to be a sign of refinement"; *FJ* I 250; 26). Spain, Europe's exotic southern neighbour, upper-class Spanish society at least, needed to adopt the sober colours of northern sensibility.

Philippe Perrot, in his study on fashion, argues that this sort of abandonment of colour was integral to the consolidation of bourgeois identity: "The new dress embodied the ideological justification for and social legitimacy of the bourgeoisie. Clothing reaffirmed the concepts of modesty, effort, propriety, reserve, and 'self-control,' which were the basis of bourgeois 'respectability.' They combined a moral rejection with their political rejection of color" (32). Thus, "bajo la influencia del Norte de Europa" ("under the influence of northern Europe"), the well-to-do Spaniard would have to don English colour, specifically "los grises que toma de su ahumado cielo" ("the grays that it gets from its smoky gray sky"; *FJ* I 251; 26) and leave its bloody hues to the poor – the "primitives" of the metropolis. This political rejection of colour, or what anthropologist Michael Taussig calls the "banishment of the vivid" (11), not only points to the imperial hierarchy internal to Western Europe but also evokes Spain's history of colonization in the Americas. Here, I uphold Taussig's claim that "the combustible mix of attraction and repulsion towards color" can be attributed "to the Western experience of colonization as colored Otherness" (9). Like the poultry shop, *el cuarto estado* (where blood-coloured signs abound), functions as a "color danger zone" "where exquisite care has to be exercised as regards to what otherwise comes across as the pollution and transgressive quality of bright color" (12). The dangerous potential of colour lies in its vivid, unrefined qualities. Bright primary colour paints the slums: "azules, rojos, y verdes" ("blues, reds, and greens"). Confirming Taussig's earlier claim, these bright hues represent "los colores vivos y elementales que agradan a los salvajes" ("basic colors [vivid colours] that appeal to primitive peoples"; *FJ* I 430; 133). As Madrid's colourful poor become equated with the colonized people of the Americas, Jacinta and Guillermina's philanthropic quest at best aligns itself with the civilizing mission of Spanish colonialism and at worst evokes the transatlantic slave trade as they seek to buy Pituso with a handsome sum of cash.

Further extending this colonial discourse, *el cuarto estado* in the eyes of Jacinta is framed as a heterotopic space populated by unsightly bodies: ragged women, mangy cats, prematurely aged Moorish women, and blind men (*FJ* I 437). Though in Madrid, Jacinta has gone far from the social trappings of well-to-do society. The slums appear otherworldly, producing a disorienting affect for Jacinta and the narrator alike. Nothing is at it seems. The outward signs of age, race, and gender become dizzyingly mottled. The illegibility of signs intensifies as Jacinta and Guillermina are confronted by a horde of children, drenched in what is thought to be shoe polish or varnish used to print "papel de luto" ("mourning paper"; *FJ* II 440; 139). The narrator explains:

Era una manada de salvajes, compuesta de dos tagarotes como de diez y doce años, una niña más chica, y otros dos *chavales*, cuya edad y sexo no se podía saber. Tenían todos ellos la cara y las manos llenas de chafarrinones [manchas] negros, hechos con algo que debía de ser betún o barniz japonés del más fuerte. Uno se había pintado rayas en el rostro, otro anteojos, aquél bigotes, cejas y patillas con tan mala maña, que toda la cara parecía revuelta en heces de tintero. Los pequeñuelos no parecían pertenecer a la raza humana, y con aquel maldito tizne extendido y rebosado por la cara y las manos semejaban micos, diablillos o engendros infernales. (*FJ* I 438)

It was a bunch of savages, made of two awkward-looking beanpoles who were about ten and twelve, a younger girl, and two other small fry whose age and sex were unascertainable. They all had their faces and hands full of black stains from what must have been tar or the strongest kind of Japanese varnish. One had painted stripes on his face; another, glasses; still another, a mustache, eyebrows, and sideburns, so clumsily that his face looked as if it had been dipped in the dregs of an inkwell. The little things didn't look as if they belonged to the human race. With that grimy soot spread and rubbed into their faces and hands, they looked more like monkeys, miniature devils, or some such infernal offspring. (138)

This denigrating description points to the inscrutability of the poor children as well as the narrator's limited gaze. As Lisa Surwillo has observed, the narrator "describe pero no llega a descifrar el fenómeno de los niños ennegreciedos" ("describes but is unable to decipher the phenonomen of the blackened children"; "Pituso en Blackface" 192). Otherwise omniscient, here the narrator fails to discern the children's gender and age – in fact, they appear entirely inhuman to him (and Jacinta). Thus, in this otherworldly corner of Madrid, the members of the caste (the narrator included) find themselves at an epistemic impasse unable to understand what they see. And it is also here in *el cuarto estado*, that pigment – specifically ink, which is a "vehículo de la lectura" ("vehicle for reading"; "Pituso en Blackface" 192) – fails to manifest as printed language and instead enters the ambivalent, unstable realm of signs.[15]

Pituso, the imposter, is among this group of blackened children. With his hair and skin completely drenched in ink, he is the only one who appears black from head to toe. At first glance, Jacinta believes Pituso's blackness to be a visual inheritance of his father's sexual transgressions, his so-called manía por lo salvaje ("mania for savage things"). Thus, "la mancha del pecado era tal, que aun a la misma inocencia extendía su sombra" ("the stain left by the sin had spread its shadow over innocence itself"; 142). Jacinta construes Pituso's blackness as an outward sign of Juan's sullied bloodlines. The children, the narrator remarks, are stained with "chafarrinones negros" ("black stains"). The 1884 definition of *chafarrinón* includes the entry "chafarrinada" and "Echar uno un chafarrinan," which is defined as follows: "Hacer una cosa indigna, *que desluzca su linaje"* ("to do something disgraceful *that darkens one's lineage"*; *DRAE*; my emphasis). In this case, blood manifests as visible blackness.

Blackness, moreover, exceeds the metaphorical dirt and tainted bloodlines of the Santa Cruz caste. It is more than mere sin when we consider the colonial overtones that colour this scene. The blackened children, as Lisa Surwillo has shown in her groundbreaking article "Pituso en Blackface," evoke the nineteenth-century theatrical practices of blackface, or *teatro de bufo*. As slavery was abolished during the writing of the novel (1886), this rather timely provocation is one that, according to Surwillo, allows Galdós to articulate a critique of racial identity:

> Galdós representa la diferencia de "casta" de una manera innovadora que complementa su función cultural. La cara negra postiza del supuesto heredero de Juanito Santa Cruz, conseguido por tramites irregulares pone en tela de juicio la idea de que la identidad (individual o racial) se percibe en la apariencia y cuestiona las relaciones de poder entre la burguesía española y la clase obrera, por una parte, y los esclavos coloniales, por otra. (189)

> Galdós represents "caste" difference in an innovative way that complements its cultural function. The artificially blackened face – achieved by unusual means – of Juanito Santa Cruz's supposed heir throws into question the idea that (individual or racial) identity is perceived by appearance and questions the power relations between the Spanish bourgeoise and the working class on the one hand and colonial slaves on the other.

The visual schema of racial and class identity, which we so readily associate with the nineteenth century, falters. In the end, "[l]a cuestión de la raza y el linaje se desarrolla como algo relacionado con el color de la piel, pero distinto de él" ("the question of race and lineage develops as something related to but different from skin color"; Surwillo, "Pituso and Blackface" 194).

Not at all unique to the case of Spain, blackness was a trope associated with working-class people in nineteenth-century Europe. In *Imperial Leather*, Ann McClintock details the ways in which marginal groups within white European society, particularly female domestic servants, were typed as slaves, primitive, and black, figuring as what she terms "anachronistic humans" (42). For her part, Stoler argues that "racial etymologies of the language of class ... place the making of racial discourse, and a discourse on [African] slavery in particular, as formative in the making of a middle-class identity rather than as a late nineteenth-century addition to it" (123–4). Fortunata is typed as black on multiple occasions in the narrative that (to my knowledge) have never been examined in the criticism. In fact, Agnes Moncy Gullón's English translation of the novel elides these mentions altogether. Juan, calls Fortunata black – at once a fetishization of her class and a racist term of endearment – repeatedly calling her "nena negra" ("black girl"). Moncy Gullón translates these instances as "my little squirrel" (478–9), "baby" (615, 616), or simply omits them (614). And on at least one occasion, Fortunata internalizes this identity, thinking to herself that "trabajaría *como una negra*" ("I would work like a black woman") – a clear reference to enslaved African women (*FJ* I 841; emphasis in original) or in Moncy Gullón's words "work like a dog" (407), a euphemistic translation that unconsciously reflects the ways in which Black women have historically been associated with animality. Using blackness or the figure of the enslaved African woman as a designation for a working-class Spanish woman illustrates the ways in which a modern racial grammar (an epidermal schema) has begun to shape the politics of exclusion and the maintenance of the social hierarchy in the metropolis long structured around blood. The elision of blackness from the modern English translation bespeaks our reluctance to confront it.

Moreover, the pollution of blood is haunted by a discourse of hygiene that conjures up a long history of race and colonization. Surwillo explains: "En la novela la burguesía española cultiva una limpieza y blancura corporal que la marcarán como europea, a diferencia tanto de las poblaciones 'salvajes' que conforman su imperio americano como de las que habitan en la capital" ("In the novel the Spanish bourgeoisie cultivate a corporeal cleanliness and whiteness that would mark them as European, in contrast to both the 'savage' populations that comprise their American empire and the ones that live in the capital"; 197–8). Ideas around cleanliness and dirtiness, thus, cannot be divorced from the discourse of race, yet the formulation of identity-as-surface, as we have seen throughout the novel, is far from stable.

From the point of view of the reader, it is clear the children have artificially darkened their skin. Pituso appears with black ink dripping from his hands, his clothing stained by the hands of the other children. The mother of one of these unruly children appears furious that the children have stolen her ink (used for printing "papeles de luto" ["mourning papers"]) and slaps one of the children across the face "sin miedo a mancharse ella también" ("with no fear of dirtying herself too"; *FJ* I 439; Clark 138). The children's "misuse" of this black substance, intended for printing, acts almost as an excessive representation of European notions of savagery and excess. Blackness – both as pigment and as race –

comes to stand in for Pituso's social status, i.e., his blood relation to Fortunata the *nena negra*, throwing into question the likeness between Pituso and Juan.

Jacinta is offended by Pituso's unruly behaviour and lack of supervision. Her disapproval stems from her utter inability to understand why a child could be allowed to look this way, covered in toxic varnish. "¿Será veneno eso?" ("Do you suppose it's poison?"; 444; 142) she asks herself. This scene emphasizes how Pituso initially relishes his performance, his "papel de mico" ("role as a monkey") in stark contrast to the bourgeois fetish of all things white and clean. The monkey-like Pituso has not learned the self-discipline of the bourgeoisie, and having been raised by "savages," he has been educated contrary to the class and caste of his father. Put another way, he has not been sufficiently racialized as a member of the caste. In his own childlike way through play among the other children, Pituso irreverently mocks bourgeois anxieties about identity by acting or dressing like a monkey or a native of the colonies, an act of play in which he and the other children "[gozan] íntimamente en la sorpresa y terror que sus espantables cataduras producían en aquellas señoriticas tan requetefinas" ("secretly enjoying the surprise and terror their frightful looks produced in such refined, delicate ladies"; 438; 138).

Pituso's state of pollution horrifies Jacinta, who initially mistakes him for a black "savage," but it lasts only long enough for her to recognize that his blackness is mere paint. Jacinta then begins to imagine that Pituso's blackness is her husband's "mancha del pecado" ("stain of sin"). She *reads* his blackness literally, that is, as a sign. Pituso's filth in the end, rather than fully repelling Jacinta, in fact motivates her all the more to "purchase" and raise him, fulfilling at once a maternal and missionary calling. She is appalled by the fact that in *el cuarto estado* the adults refuse to wash him: "Que lo laven. ¿Por qué no lo lavan?" ("He should be washed. Why won't they wash him?"; 444; 142). Anne McClintock historicizes the Victorian obsession for all things clean and white (e.g., clothing and bodies), establishing that it was not merely a consequence of economic surplus. In her analysis of racist soap advertisements, for example, McClintock argues that the commodity "emerged commercially during an era of impending crisis and social calamity, serving to preserve, through fetish ritual, the uncertain boundaries of class, gender and race identity in a social order felt to be threatened by the fetid effluvia of the slums, the belching smoke of industry, social agitation, economic upheaval, imperial competition and anti-colonial resistance" (McClintock 211). In *Fortunata y Jacinta*, the narrator notes that white linens come of fashion once public water becomes readily available in

Madrid. But whiteness takes on a clear moral valence when Fortunata enters the Micaelas convent so that she may "adecentarse y pulirse" ("to become decent and polished"; *FJ* I 609; Clark 251). This sudden shift in Fortunata's belief system comes as a result of the "examen de conciencia" ("self-examination"; my translation), which she undertakes as part of her admittance to the convent. Through this experience, Fortunata contemplates the Host, which speaks to her in her own colloquial language on the topic of marriage. Fortunata calls her newly minted sense of discipline and commitment to chastity *la idea blanca* ("the white idea"), evidencing an internalization of a notion of bourgeois purity. It is no coincidence that Fortunata models her fantasy of female domesticity after Jacinta herself, who is emblematic of bourgeois chastity. As Rosa Elena Ríos Lloret observes:

> La exaltación de la pureza y su calificación de cualidad natural femenina se extendía a la representación física ideal de una mujer, pero también a todo lo que la rodeaba. Así, el blanco se convierte en el color de la joven. Blanco es el traje de su comunión, el de su presentación en sociedad, el de su boda. Como blanco tiene que ser su comportamiento, su forma de moverse, de hablar, de mirar. (193)

> The exaltation of purity and its signification of natural feminine quality not only extended the physical representation of a woman but also everything that surrounded her. Thus, whiteness became the colour of the young woman. Whiteness is the colour of a communion dress, of her dress when debuted to society, of her wedding dress. White must be the colour of her behaviour, her form of moving, of speaking, of looking.

"White behaviour" or *la idea blanca* is the essence of chastity (*castidad*). Like many idealized female characters of this period, she is purity incarnate: "Jacinta era la pureza misma" ("Jacinta was purity itself"; *FJ* I 305; Clark 55) and looks as though she were a doll with "su figura y cara porcelanescas" ("delicate proportions and figure and porcelain face"; 298; 52).

When Jacinta, however, brings Pituso home, her sister is not convinced: "Sonreía Benigna, y si no hubiera sido por consideración a su querida hermana, habría dicho del *Pituso* lo que de las monedas que no sonaban bien: *Es falso*, o por lo menos, *tiene hoja*" ("Benigna smiled; if it hadn't been for the consideration she had toward her beloved sister, she would have said the same thing about Pituso that her husband had said about the coins that didn't ring true: 'He's a fake.' Or at least, 'Something's fishy'"; 517; 190). Benigna tells Jacinta: "Hija, no he visto un salvaje igual. El pobrecito ... bien se ve entre qué gentes se ha criado"

("Dear, I've never seen such a savage! Poor little thing. You can tell what sort of people he's grown up among"). To which Jacinta replies: "Mejor … Así le domesticaremos" ("All the better. We'll simply tame [domesticate] him"; 527; 196). Believing him to be Juan's son, his blood deems him salvageable, unlike the other "savage," monstrous children.

Jacinta entertains something of a colonial Pygmalion fantasy here, believing she can recreate Pituso in her own image by bathing/whitening him – just as it is done in Victorian soap ads – an act that is at best emblematic of baptismal rebirth or at worst forced conversion. "Domestication," however, proves to be more difficult than Jacinta had imagined. The act of bathing is received as a foreign and violent imposition to Pituso. And when Jacinta presents Pituso to Barbarita, not yet convinced that he is Juan's son, the latter thinks to herself "¿Qué casta de nieto era aquel?" ("What sort [caste] of grandchild was he?"; 521; 192). When Jacinta reveals the news to Juan, he confesses that his son with Fortunata is dead and scolds her for having participated in this risky transaction he calls a "mal negocio" ("bad business"; 534; 201). Just as Benigna had suspected, this Pituso is a fraud.

The narrative attention to the paint dripping from Pituso's hands juxtaposed with Jacinta's initial reaction of racially motivated fear points to the novel's self-reflexive play with colour and signs, disguise and visibility – the stuff of representation. That Pituso's blackness is falsified – not even skin deep – destabilizes the notion of visible signs as trustworthy signifiers. In fact, this chapter confirms Stoler's claim that sexuality, race, gender, and class "hinge on visual markers of distinction that profess to – but poorly index – the internal traits, psychological dispositions, and moral essence on which these theories of difference and social membership are based" (133–4). At the same time, this blood-as-ink schema exposes bloodlines as a vacant signifier, having no tangible form to confirm its authenticity. Not incidentally, this reanimates early modern and modern conceptions of race, which hinge on the opposition of lineage (blood) and the visible (skin). *Fortunata y Jacinta* exposes the unremitting tenets of early modern and colonial identity paradigms rooted in blood, precisely at a historical moment in which, throughout the Western world, racialized identity becomes increasingly sutured to the idea of visibility and surface, i.e., skin colour and phenotype. Rather than collapse race and caste, here Galdós adeptly plays with the tensions between surface (colour) and depth (bloodlines), metaphor and matter – getting to the heart of realist aesthetics.

Throughout the novel, as I have already argued, visible signs become faulty indicators of identity. This time, the revelation is presented from the point of view of the imposter child. The narrator deploys free indirect style to depict an epiphany as Pituso marvels at Jacinta's gloves: "No tenía él ni idea remota de que existieran aquellas manos de mentira, dentro de las cuales estaban las manos verdaderas" ("He didn't have the slightest notion that there were such things as those 'fake hands,' inside which were real ones"; *FJ* I 473; Clark 160). In the context of the Bourbon Restoration, where identity becomes increasingly tethered to appearance and self-presentation and meaning becomes inextricably bound to representation, the social elites in *Fortunata y Jacinta* espouse a form of distinction that precedes this modern, visible schema. Thus, as I have already noted in chapter three, two primary modes of identification come into tension: the preservation of elite exclusivity through blood and lineage contrasted with new, malleable modes of bourgeois self-fashioning: namely, sartorial style, education, and hygiene.[16]

Given the impossibility of confirming the truth of one's blood, the novel's characters seek to ascertain signs of authentic and fraudulent identity, respectively, even as these signs themselves become increasingly suspect and easily falsifiable. For them, identity remains firmly rooted in Spain's history of exclusivity based on a system of blood-based, i.e., caste, identity. The former, established through birth, takes on blood as an invisible symbol of distinction, while the latter hinges on education and the mutability of appearances achieved through disciplinary and performative modes of power. Juan illustrates this duality when he tells his wife: "Hija de mi alma, hay que ponerse en la realidad. Hay dos mundos, el que se ve y el que no se ve" ("Look, dear, you've got to face reality. There are two worlds, the one you *can* see and the one you *can't see*"; 342; 78, emphasis in original).

Madrid's social elites uphold the fiction of bloodlines and its presumed linkage to authenticity. This is particularly paradoxical for Juanito Santa Cruz, who claims to prefer material reality to fiction. As a university student, he reportedly fried an egg during class instead of listening to the lessons of metaphysics. For Juanito, "Vivir es relacionarse, gozar y padecer, desear, aborrecer y amar. La lectura es vida artificial y prestada" ("Living was relating to others, enjoying and suffering, desiring, hating and loving. Reading was artificial borrowed life"; 209; 7). Befittingly, he sums up his theory of representation in an alimentary example:

No paraban aquí las filosofías de Juanito, y hacía una comparación que no carece de exactitud. Decía que entre estas dos maneras de vivir, observaba él la diferencia que hay entre comerse una chuleta y que le vengan a contar a uno cómo y cuándo se la ha comido otro, haciendo el cuento muy a lo vivo, se entiende, y describiendo la cara que ponía, el gusto que le daba la masticación, la gana con que tragaba y el reposo con que digería. (209)

Juan's philosophical theories didn't end here; he made another comparison that was not wholly inaccurate. He claimed that the difference between these two ways of living was like the difference between eating a chop yourself and having someone tell you how and when someone else ate it, making the story a really good one of course – describing the expression on the person's face, his pleasure from chewing the meat, his satisfaction upon swallowing it, and then his placid digestion. (7)

Juan may be the "the richest repository of metaphor," to borrow Turner's words, engaging in endless substitution and replacement (e.g., replacing his wife with a lover), but he himself disdains the world of signs, desiring the world of raw materiality – one that he finds in Fortunata, but Fortunata's enticing edibility – "her real animal nature ('res'), her native rawness and fidelity" – expires and gives way to the realm of letters and the law "lex" ("Metonomy and Metaphor" 889).

The Gift of Blood

In this concluding section, let us return to the starting point of this chapter: Fortunata's bloody death. Megan L. Kelly has pointed to the ways in which death is an unnarratable moment in *Fortunata y Jacinta*, arguing that in the case of Fortunata, this draws attention to the "primacy of materiality" and "the inherent vulnerability of the body" (22). What I find extraordinary about this scene is not the narrative silence that follows death, but rather the focus on Fortunata's self-narration as she anticipates her dying. The attention to the primacy of Fortunata's materiality is met with lexical force. This is particularly significant given Fortunata's marked inarticulateness throughout the novel.[17] As Fortunata's blood gushes forth, so too does language. The hemorrhaging mother refuses medicine and instead demands "pluma y papel" ("pen and paper"), ordering Don Plácido to write as she dictates a will. The narrator relays Fortunata's thought process as she anxiously edits aloud:

> En fin, siga usted poniendo lo que le digo … "No quiero morirme sin hacerle a usted una fineza, y le mando a usted, por mano del amigo D. Plácido, ese *mono del Cielo* que su esposo de usted me dio a mí, equivocadamente …" No, no, borre el *equivocadamente*; ponga: "que me lo dio a mí robándoselo a usted …" No, D. Plácido, así no, eso está muy mal … porque yo lo tuve … yo, y a ella no se le ha quitado nada. Lo que hay es que yo se lo quiero dar, porque sé que ha de quererle, y porque es mi amiga. (*FJ* II 766–7)

Well, anyway, keep writing what I say. "I don't want to die without doing you a kind deed, and I'm sending you, in care of our friend Don Plácido, the little 'angel face' that your husband gave me by mistake." No, cross out "by mistake" and put "that he gave me, stealing him from you." But no, Don Plácido, not like that; it sounds awful … because it was me who had him, me, and nobody took anything away from her. What I mean is that I want to give him to her because I know she'll love him and because she's my friend. (Moncy Gullón 802)

In this crucial moment of the narrative, we bear witness to Fortunata's thought process as she lays claim to her son. At the start, she speaks of Pituso as a misdirected gift from Juan – one that, in turn, robbed Jacinta of a child. But she immediately revises this statement, realizing that Pituso is a product of her own labour: "yo lo tuve … yo" ("It was me who had him, me"). Whereas the norms and laws of Spanish society attributed the custody of children to their fathers, Fortunata defies *la patria potestad* and asserts that Pituso is both hers and hers to give away.

Providing a legal analysis of this scene, Jo Labanyi explains that "[w]ills were the only contract, apart from the marriage contract, that all nineteenth-century Spanish women were legally entitled to make" (182). By creating a will, Fortunata makes known that she is a "free individual" (183). That she gives him to the childless Jacinta, the wife of her child's father, is no insignificant act. Labanyi argues that "[i]t is this final contract between women that empowers Jacinta to dictate the terms of a de facto legal separation to Juanito (what at the time was called 'divorcio' 'divorce'). Jacinta hereby not only declares Juanito free, but establishes her own claim to freedom" (183). In exercising liberal contractual power, Fortunata sets into motion a process that begins with her realization as a modern subject and ends with Jacinta's liberation from her philandering husband.

To fully appreciate the political promise of Fortunata's "gift" to Jacinta, I turn to Gayle Rubin's well-known theorization of kinship and gender in "The Traffic in Women." Rubin advances a feminist reading of Claude Lévi-Strauss's *Elementary Structures of Kinship*. For Lévi-Strauss, patriarchal kinship systems rely on the exchange of women between men. Through this so-called traffic in women, men secure "sexual access, genealogical statuses, lineage names and ancestors, rights and *people*" (Rubin 177). The distinction, therefore, between giver and gift or man and woman takes shape through kinship alliances, making gender an effect of that system: "To enter into a gift exchange as a partner, one must have something to give. If women are for men to dispose of, they are in no position to give themselves away" (Rubin 179). Fortunata's will radically alters the patriarchal kinship and the caste genealogy around which the entire edifice of Galdós's narrative is erected. The very title of the novel *Fortunata y Jacinta: Historia de dos casadas* (*Fortunata and Jacinta: Stories of Two Wives*) underscores the centrality of heterosexuality and patriarchal kinship to women's gendered identity. But Fortunata and Jacinta unite as mothers of the same child, and, by participating as givers in this exchange, they radically transform what it means to be a mother and ultimately a woman in patriarchal society. Occupying the position as giver, Fortunata's defiance adheres to what she (prior to drafting the will) theorizes as "the law of blood," overriding the laws of the state:

> Yo soy madre del único *hijo de la casa*; madre soy, bien claro está, y no hay más nieto de don Baldomero que este rey del mundo que yo tengo aquí ... ¿Había quien me lo niegue? Yo no tengo la culpa de que la ley ponga esta o ponga otro. Si las leyes son unos disparates muy gordos, yo no tengo nada que ver con ellas. ¿Para qué han hecho así? La verdadera ley es la de la sangre. (*FJ* II 691)

> I'm the mother of the only "son in the family," I'm the mother, it's very plain; the only grandson Don Baldomero has is the king of the world that I've got with me here. Would anybody dare try denying it? It's not my fault if the law says such and such. Laws are a lot of stupid nonsense and I don't have anything to do with them. Why did they make them like that? The real law is blood ties. (Clark 752)

Even the narrator himself echoes this view, noting that "el tal nene era un Rubín, pero por fuerza de la sangre ... era preciso darle el título del monstruo [Juan]" ("the child was a Rubín, but the strength of blood ties would overpower ... he would deserve the title of monster [Juan]"; 676; 742).

Defying the norms of the caste, which uphold legitimacy as a strictly paternal issue, Fortunata constructs her own kinship system, which legitimates and valorizes matrilineal inheritance and intimacy between women. This gift of blood – this transfusion – alters the linearity of the caste, forever tainting, even as it reanimates, its genealogy. It is fitting, then, that her son takes the name Pituso, derived from Fortunata's own nickname Pitusa. By occupying the role of the "giver" and testatrix in her will, Fortunata embodies what Sara Ahmed has called a *wilful* feminist by "not willing to be owned" (*Living a Feminist Life* 74). If, as Rubin has suggested, gender is an effect of patriarchal kinship, then ultimately, Fortunata's will transforms the terms of gender identity. By "bequeathing" her son to Jacinta rather than Juanito, Fortunata gestures towards the possibility of "get[ting] beyond gender" by "overthrow[ing] kinship" – or at least kinship as it was conceived of in nineteenth-century Spain (Rubin "Sexual Traffic" 66, qtd. in Ramberg).[18] Jacinta, for her part, appears to follow suit. Upon receiving Fortunata's "gift" and leaving Juan, the narrator remarks: "También ella tenía su idea respecto a los vínculos establecidos por la ley y los rompía con el pensamiento" ("She too, had her notions on lawful ties, and broke them"; *FJ* II 780; Clark 812).

Thus, Fortunata, on her death bed, deploys liberal contractual power not only as an act of self-actualization, but as a radical queer gesture that forges new kin based not on heterosexual marriage but on same gender parentage and matrilineal inheritance. As Harriet Turner put it: "As the 'first mother' of the new child and heir, Fortunata imagines momentarily a new, 'feminist' family: herself as 'la mamá primera,' Jacinta, and Guillermina as second and third in a radically new, 'holy' and 'Trinitarian' family of women" ("The Realist Novel" n.p.). Her unconventional legal bond with Jacinta, moreover, enables a queer sociality – a bond that allows for the "nonnormative logics and organizations of community" (Halberstam 6) and a mode of critique that challenges the patriarchal structure of kinship that renders women property.

Pituso, the product of Fortunata's labour, embodies this queer bond through the mixing of blood (Jacinta's and Fortunata's) – all of this just moments before the wilful protagonist's body drains of blood. Laura Connor links Fortunata's hemorrhaging body to the initial scene of carnage in the poultry shop: "It is significant that Fortunata bleeds to death after confronting and attacking Juanito's new paramour, Aurora Fenelon: having exerted herself too soon after giving birth, she hemorrhages and dies, underlining the comparison between her and a mother hen hung up to drain it of blood" (167). But Fortunata's final flow is, to borrow the words of Elizabeth Grosz, "engulfing, difficult to get rid of" (193). It exceeds her thingification as mere flesh destined for consumption. Instead, Fortunata's animate fluids "seep, they infiltrate, their control is a matter of vigilance, never guaranteed" (Grosz 194). Rather than sidestepping an alliance system based on blood, Fortunata penetrates the closed caste system, proving its bloodlines to be both vulnerable and unprotected. Thus, while Juan remains *emplumado* ("tarred and feathered") – stained by his extra-caste coupling – Fortunata legally alters Jacinta's fate with *pluma y papel* ("quill and paper"). Throughout the narrative, Galdós invites his readers to consider the value construed by the hierarchical tension between the realm of the discursive (bloodlines) and the material (blood) – emblematized by those who bleed (in a rather spectacular and visceral way) and those whose blood remains invisible. In this final moment, Fortunata – consigned to the precarious realm of materiality – appropriates the discursive as her only recourse to an afterlife, but one that is born of ink and forever bonded in the fleshy futurity of her son.

The Bleeding Body

In 1875, Francisco Cortejarena, member of the *Real Academia de Medicina*, published an article entitled "Ligeros apuntes acerca del efecto de las evacuaciones sanguíneas de la mujer" ("Brief Notes on the Effect of Blood Evacuations in Women").[1] A doctor of gynecology and obstetrics, Cortejarena responds to the medical preoccupation with a woman's ability to sustain substantial blood loss, of which menstruation is only one example: "Hay un hecho de observacion [*sic*], y es que la mujer tolera mejor las evacuaciones sanguíneas que el hombre" ("There is one fact established by observation and that is that women tolerate evacuations of blood better than men"; 17).[2] This propensity for bleeding does not derive exclusively from women's sex. Rather, in a surprising turn in the article, Cortejarena explains that several forms of hemorrhaging in *male* bodies result from what we now call gender:

> Hay hombres-mujeres, y vice-versa; los hombres de vida sedentaria, que gastan poco en las funciones de relación, cuyo género de vida se parece más al de la mujer, vemos que tienen almorranas, y segun [*sic*] la edad, si es joven, tiene epistasis [*sic*], hemorragias por varios puntos; cuando adulto, hematemesis, melena, hematuria; y si bien esto no sucede siempre, veremos en equivalencia afecciones humorales artríticas, pérdidas de varias especies, y si no hay esto, engordan, se ponen obesos. (258)

> There are men-women, and vice versa; men of a sedentary life, that expend little on the functions of relation, whose lifestyle more closely resembles that of a woman, we see that they have hemorrhoids, and depending on the age, if he is young, he will have epistaxis [nasal hemorrhage], hemorrhages at various sites; as an adult he will have hematemesis [vomiting of blood], melena [bloody stools], hematuria [blood in the urine]; and if this does not always occur, we will see the equivalent humoral arthritic

affections, losses of all kinds, and if not these, they gain weight, they become obese.

Within this line of thinking, male blood loss becomes a physiological consequence of a social aberration (e.g., a sedentary man). Bleeding appears not to be an effect of sex – inevitably stemming from a woman's biology – but gender, illustrated by his claim that effeminate men will, in one form or another, bleed. Put bluntly, *men who act like women will bleed like women.*

This complex conceptualization of the body has a notable early modern feel to it – conjuring up images of menstruating Jewish men (Dopico Black 3) – Galdós's Maxi being a modern example of this – and more broadly, the body as a fluid and mutable entity. At the same time, it reads as strikingly postmodern. Cortejarena links physiological changes in the body (i.e., hemorrhaging) to a gendered lifestyle (i.e., sedentariness), unwittingly challenging the deterministic force of biology and the notion of fixity so readily associated with nineteenth-century scientific approaches to the body. This *doubly* fluid gendered body – that is to say, the mutable body from which blood readily flows – challenges Vanita Seth's claim that in this very period, the body becomes "an immutable passive object" with "deterministic significance," "packaged in discrete, inflexible categories" (175). Indeed, Cortejarena's notion of the body in flux unsettles such widely held assumptions about the fixity of "modern" corporeality and the supposed biologically determined identities – namely, sex and race – they are thought to enfold.[3] However, blood loss in women – whether involuntary (e.g., menstruation) or medically induced (e.g., bloodletting), a source of endless cultural curiosity and fear, problematically appears in this gynecology article as proof or even a source of women's physical resilience. That is, women appear immune or even strengthened after several rounds of bloodletting, something men – Cortejarana observes – are not equipped to endure (17). But blood is messy matter, and the novels studied here tell a somewhat different story about gender, bleeding, and life – one that scrutinizes the fragility of gendered bleeding bodies, rather than exalt their resilience.

In this closing reflection, I want to gesture towards an unexpected, critical potential of Galdós's realist aesthetic, which lays bare the material reality of gender, perhaps at the expense of delineating the genre's own discursive limitations and at odds with the masculinist anxiety around gendered bleeding that infuses these major novels. I do so, moreover, in the spirit of Tobin Siebers's call for a theoretical account of embodied social experience. Siebers writes: "without a theory that can verify how social identities are embodied in lived experience, how they become real, it is not clear that we can understand what oppression actually is and how it works" (297).

To begin, I would like to briefly probe the function of the *real* in Spanish realism. For Akiko Tsuchiya, realism – despite being predicated on the hegemonic notions of the real – affords space to the expression of fantasy: "The literary text has always been a space of desire and fantasy. Such is the case even of realist (or naturalist) fiction, which is presumably modelled on 'the real,' however this notion might be defined by existing social and cultural conventions" (213). Harriet Turner, for her part, reflects on the complex rendering of the real in Galdós's oeuvre. She writes:

> Galdós sketches out a kind of "equation" for realism, positioning what is known or factual – *exactitud* – in relation to beauty – *belleza*, that is, invention, aesthetic design. What is "real" happens. It is a process of exchange and transformation taking place in the mind of narrator, character, and reader, and thus this "real thing" eludes words. It is not always susceptible to naming. Rather the "real thing" precipitates, as it were, from the conjunction, the consequence, of one term and the other, establishing a dialectical structure that involves the roles of narrator, character, and reader. This concept of a dialectical realism reiterates, on another level, those triangular structures so prominently featured in the plots of the Spanish realist novel. ("The Realist Novel" n.p.)

The real can only emerge through the triangular relationship between the narrator, reader, and character ("The Realist Novel" n.p.). Turner's reading of Galdós's dialectical realism, beautifully illustrates his complex treatment of the real that lies somewhere in between the factual and the aesthetic. Thus, the real in Galdós diverges from this facile notion of mimesis – that the realist novel is a mirror reflection of reality depicting an uncomplicated attachment to the primacy of tangible objects and things. As Hazel Gold puts it: "[r]eality [for Galdós] is not something to be corresponded to but rather to be-recreated narratively and experientially. Pure idealism exhibiting no connection to the concerns of the accidental, material world may become unacceptable" (72). Taken together, these views suggest that the real in Galdosian realism is always undergirded by the realm of fantasy and aesthetic creation, but it remains, crucially, tethered to materiality.

This relationship between the discursive and the material speaks to recent debates within feminist new materialism, which take shape precisely around the tension between the fixed immutable body versus the body as the object of cultural inscription. This school of thought has emerged in response to the highly impactful discursive-linguistic turn in feminist theory from which the familiar concept of gender as a "social construction" has proliferated, alongside other identifications, most notably (and more complicatedly so) race. Indeed, the social construction model seems to have become the de facto blueprint for identificatory categories within postmodern theory, without a sufficient account – as feminist scholars of new materialism have claimed – of the body's irrefutable materiality. New materialists have widely critiqued Judith Butler's work in *Gender Trouble*, namely, the theory of gender performativity, for privileging discourse over the body, or to be more precise, for denying the existence of a material body prior to discourse. For example, Claire Colebrook has argued that "Butler does not want to see language or difference as a form imposed upon matter, but she nevertheless allows matter to remain that which can only be posited after the event – as that which must have been 'before' the recognized performance of the self" (68). Of course, Butler's subsequent book, *Bodies That Matter: On the Discursive Limits of Sex*, attempted to respond to such critiques. Here, Butler argues that the "regulatory norms of 'sex' work in a performative fashion to constitute the materiality of bodies, and more specifically, to materialize the body's sex, to materialize sexual difference in the service of the consolidation of the heterosexual imperative" (2). Here, Butler attempts to explain precisely how bodies come to *matter*, by arguing, poetically and rather paradoxically, that they materialize *discursively*. Over the course of these two paradigm-shifting works, the body's physiological attributes – its fluids and functions – nevertheless remain largely unaccounted for. In the words of Stacy Alaimo and Susan Hekman:

> While no one would deny the ongoing importance of discursive critique and the rearticulation for feminist scholarship and feminist politics, the discursive realm is nearly always constituted so as to foreclose attention to lived, material bodies, and evolving corporeal practices. An emerging group of feminist theorists of the body are arguing, however, that we need to find a way to talk about the materiality of the body as itself an active, sometimes recalcitrant, force. Women *have* bodies; these bodies have pain as well as pleasure. They also have diseases that are subject to medical interventions that may or may not cure those bodies. We need a way to talk about these bodies and the materiality they inhabit. ("Introduction" 3–4)

By recovering the materiality of the body and natural world abandoned in the era of the discursive turn, new feminist materialists seek not to reify the real nor completely discard the accomplishments of the prior feminist theories of gender. Instead, they seek to undo the "material/discursive dichotomy" by examining the intersection of the discursive and the material (6).

Such theories of the body, however, have not been without their pitfalls. We have already seen that a potential problem with new material feminism is the risk of treating the sexed body as fixed and universal. Elizabeth Grosz, whose groundbreaking book *Volatile Bodies: Toward a Corporeal Feminism* informs much of my thinking, falls into this essentialist trap. In this work, Grosz argues that the "specificity of bodies must be understood in its historical rather than simply its biological concreteness," further noting that "bodies are irreducibly sexually specific, necessarily interlocked with racial, cultural, and class particularities" (19). Yet in a subsequent discussion in the book on "women's corporeal flows," race and class (along with their historical locations) are altogether lost as the term "women" seems to repeat the universalizing move of so-called white feminism. Here, Grosz seems to contradict her earlier claims by asserting that menstrual blood and breast milk are signs of the "irreducible specificity of women's bodies, the bodies of *all* women, independent of class, race, and history" (207; emphasis in original). How can one adequately theorize blood and breast milk, for example, without properly accounting for the historical and cultural specificity of these symbolically loaded fluids? Can we speak of blood without, say, a meaningful account of its formation as a racial or religious concept? Grosz goes on to make the troubling, transphobic claim that "at best the transsexual can live out his fantasy of femininity … but can never feel like or be a woman" (207). This viewpoint – which oddly seems to foreclose any sense of the body's "volatility" – laid out in prior parts of the book – is surprisingly more rigid and essentializing than that of the nineteenth-century gynecologist Cortejarena.

Here is where I find the surprising, critical potential of Spanish realism, perhaps in spite of these male authors' own belief systems. It must be said, of course, that Galdós, Valera, and Alas were at best ambivalent towards women's emancipation and at worst explicitly misogynist and antifeminist (Jagoe, *Ambiguous Angels* 45–52, 120–6). In this respect, I reject Jameson's vacuous claim that "Galdós's sympathy with women is omnipresent and dispenses him from the suspicion of patriarchal bias" (101). Realist and naturalist novels on the one hand, as D.A. Miller has argued, enact a policing function – containing and tracking their deviant women and thus providing a corollary to the police *fiche* (21). At the same time, as I have noted previously, Tsuchiya has convincingly argued that in the Spanish context, "fiction betrays an equally powerful impulse to resist normativity, opening up new spaces of subjectivity (if not always of agency) and redefining the limits of what the dominant culture takes for granted as 'reality'" (5). In the social world of these blood novels, what counts as "reality" for the dominant culture – i.e., the elite caste – consistently operates at the level of discourse: symbolic blood, in other words bloodlines. If Cervantes's fiction exposed the "metamateriality" of *limpieza de sangre*, the attempt to make material that which was merely symbolic (Burk 27), blood novels reveal bloodlines to be, like the currency of the era, purely abstract, detached from any notion of visceral, material blood.

I recognize the irony of such an awareness coming from a *realist* tradition – a genre some equate with the reification of the real, against which modernism would subsequently rebel – yet Spanish realism, as Tsuchiya and others have documented, proves to be much more complex, contradictory, and self-reflexive than we tend to assume. As Gold explains: "Galdós avails himself to all the technique in mimesis' arsenal," and at the same time, "he necessarily lays bare those same devices to expose the novel's fictionality" (73). In the preceding chapters, I have delineated the distinct ways blood has functioned as one such complex and rich literary device – one whose simultaneous material and symbolic functions allow for realist authors to probe the very tenets and limits of the realist aesthetic. In Valera's *Doña Luz*, the novel's fictionality coheres around the falsified story of Luz's tainted blood. This fiction holds a powerful sway over the narrator himself, whose depiction of Luz's allure becomes tainted with racialized and colonial overtones made possible only by the false knowledge of her "mixed" blood. Valera's realism is steeped in a discourse of empire and domination, but as the story of Luz's bloodlines unravels (in an ironic Cervantine fashion) the fine-spun discourse of empire too suddenly becomes threadbare. Imperial nostalgia lingers in Clarín's *La Regenta*, where the early modern/modern dichotomy comes into question. Here, blood's material and symbolic duality comes to the fore as fiction and reality compete: in a very literal way, Ana's precocious reading impinges upon her bodily reality by provoking premature menstruation. With the celibate Don Víctor, reality falls short of fiction. An expert marksman and avid reader of Calderón's wife-murder plays, Víctor is unable to enact lessons of sanguinary justice when he is pathetically slain in a duel. In contrast to these profound but aesthetically bare moments, the rich sensorial details with which Alas conveys Ana's sexual pleasure threaten to exceed the diegetic bounds of the text, allowing for a feminist identification with the protagonist that betrays Alas's own misogynist beliefs. Galdós's *La desheredada* is a rare example in which the discursive power of blood is momentarily afforded to the people rather than a privileged member of the elite caste. If social blood, that of the crowd, had taken hold through the success of the First Republic, the novel form (in the first of the *novelas contemporáneas*) would have taken a radically different trajectory, annihilating the individual and thus the genre as we know it. *Fortunata y Jacinta*, published six years later, gestures towards this possibility. Fredric Jameson has provocatively described this as the end of protagonists – Ortega y Gasset's dread.[4] But Fortunata's rebirth is not in a crowd. Social blood is a moot point in Restoration Spain. At the close of this 1,000-page novel, Fortunata's enfeebled post-partum body hemorrhages as she wields the written word to compose a will. This legal fiction will render her ephemeral, physiological blood discursive – in a way, immune to her material expiration. These blood novels together exploit the discursive power of realist fiction yet remain undeniably invested in a tangible reality that seems ever ephemeral.

Above all, Spanish realism vividly depicts how blood's materiality is gendered through and through. These male novelists make plain their narrative investment in women protagonists all troubled by matters of blood. Blood, in many ways, breathes life into the fiction of gender. Tellingly, in these realist fictions we see the persistent return to gendered bleeding, rather than a biologically sexed, static body. More broadly, these novels tend to privilege the experiential: the body's tactility, fragility, and sensuous corporeality. Jo Labanyi has noted that in the nineteenth century "[m]en had bodies but women were bodies" (*Gender and Modernization* 217). Galdós's realism in particular, I contend, goes beyond the simple conflation of woman-as-materiality. It does not merely reinforce what Judith Butler describes as "the classical association of femininity with materiality," which "can be traced to a set of etymologies [linking] matter with *mater* and *matrix* (or the womb), and hence, with a problematic of reproduction" (*Bodies That Matter* 31). Instead, its aesthetic attention to the gendered, bleeding body speaks to the socially induced precarity of certain lives, particularly those marginalized subjects gendered feminine and excluded from and exploited by elite castes. In this way, it reveals the "ability to shed blood" (Foucault 147) therefore is far from universal. Realism, in these case studies, directs a critical aesthetic eye to the hierarchal system of blood-based exclusivity and the institution of patriarchy that relegate such women and effeminate men to the sphere of precarious materiality, one that often converges with a kind of racialized alterity – as we have seen in the case of Doña Luz, Maxi, Ana Ozores, and Fortunata. Attending to the embodied realities of its marginalized characters – Doña Luz's and Ana Ozores's physical desires, Fortunata's fatal hemorrhage, Maxi and

Mauricia's social-corporeal fragility, Jacinta's barrenness, Isidora's sensuous contact with the crowd – these blood novels unwittingly provide the possibility for culturally situated, feminist materialist critique.

The novels of Valera and Alas expose the fissures in the crumbling façade of blood purity – with all of its early modern and colonial historical baggage – while Galdós's sustained engagement with the materiality of blood points to a critical notion of the real by affording aesthetic space to those bodies burdened with the social sentence of materiality. This attests to the unruly and immanent nature of bodily fluids that Grosz advanced: "Body fluids flow, they seep, they infiltrate; their control is a matter of vigilance, never guaranteed. In this sense, they betray a certain irreducible materiality; they assert the priority of the body over subjectivity; they demonstrate the limits of subjectivity in the body, the irreducible specificity of particular bodies" (194). Paul Julian Smith makes a parallel claim in *The Body Hispanic* as he describes the body's enigmatic nature: "the body goes beyond experience (because it admits determinants unknown to the empirical subject); but it falls short of transcendence (because it admits no essence beyond or within itself)" (10). It is thus through the bleeding body that blood novels ultimately show us the limits of discourse, critiquing the vacancy of a reality construed as pure representation – reality as mimesis – to return to Labanyi's incisive definition of modernity (*Gender and Modernization*). This critique inevitably exposes the emptiness of an ideology of blood purity, whose power coheres precisely at the level of discourse. While the early modern period exhibited an impulse to materialize that which was rhetorically produced (through documents, the law, testimonies, etc.), modern blood novels not only expose this, they also unearth the primacy and precarity of gendered, marginalized lives. If the fiction of pure bloodlines provided immunity to those men of the elite castes – the material vacancy it papered over left them longing for a material reality elsewhere: bodies gendered feminine and not quite white. This provides a different explanation of the realist novel's "urgent need to construct its gallery of female protagonists" (Labayni, *Gender and Modernization* 416). These gendered bodies, as a kind of compensation, bear the brunt of materiality for the upper echelons of society. But "corporeality," Grosz urgently asserts, "must no longer be associated with one sex [gender] (or race), which takes on the burden of corporeality for it" (23).

In this book I have examined blood's enigmatic duality: the ethereal quality of bloodlines and the visceral reality of bloodshed. Spanish realism's persistent return to the bleeding body gestures towards realism's own discursive limitations. Ultimately, attending to the materiality of blood suggests that matter is not a "passive product of discursive practices" (Heckman 104). As bleeding is gendered feminine, this further illuminates that gender is not construed through representation alone, that is, discursively. Crucially, material blood only makes itself visible in moments of great precarity, if not death. Galdós's realism in particular suggests that *life* may be discursively inflected, but it cannot be accounted for by discourse alone. This speaks to Claire Colebrook's assertation that "[t]he self may be performative – having no being that grounds its life other than its own doing – but those performances are materially constrained" (67). Likewise, what transpires from these blood novels, and the Galdosian realist aesthetic, especially, is the body as the material condition of possibility for culturally inscribed identities.

The physical body inflects, enables, but also interrupts – sometimes fatally – these identities. The materialism that takes shape in these blood novels registers the possibility of the gendered body's "resistance or recalcitrance to the process of cultural inscription" (Grosz 190). It underscores the material limitations that evidence the ensanguined body's socially determined precarity, which underwrites the vacuous but powerful discourse of blood purity that bestows the elite – particularly elite men – with immunity. Ultimately, blood novels illustrate with rich aesthetic detail how feminine bodies both materialize and perish in vivid evacuations of blood, narrating the unruly ways in which gender comes to matter.

Notes

Preface

1 I want to thank Manuel Cuellar for introducing me to this book.

Introduction: Realism's Blood

1 In her book *The Moment of Racial Sight*, Irene Tucker argues that the concept of "skin-based race," which emerged in the Enlightenment, sought to "make likeness visible instantaneously" (76). The notion that race is immediately and visually discernable is not entirely operative in the works I examine where bloodlines function as a subcutaneous and immutable marker of identity.

2 Eventually, the ideology of *limpieza de sangre* spread to colonial Latin America, producing there a hierarchical system of classification based on proportions of Spanish, Indigenous, and African blood.

3 Valis does not provide the details of these blood-purity requirements.

4 This persistence of blood-based hierarchies may be explained, in part, by the relatively "late" emergence of a Spanish middle class. See Jesus Cruz for a detailed study of the rise of the Spanish middle class.

5 Here, I am thinking of Miguel de Unamuno's writings on *lo castizo*: "Se usa más a menudo el calificativo de *castizo* para designar a la lengua y al estilo. Decir en España que un escritor es castizo, es dar a entender que se le cree más español que a otros" ("The qualifier *castizo* is used more frequently to designate language and style. To say in Spain that a writer is *castizo* is to suggest that they are considered more Spanish than others"; *En torno al casticismo* 27–8).

6 See Peter Bly's recent discussion on medical doctors in the works of Alas and Galdós.

7 Goode does not identify those that countered this viewpoint.

8 And beyond the nation, as Edward Said has provocatively argued, novels provided European readers with a "consolidated vision … of the globe" (*Culture* 74).

9 Anne McClintock makes this argument in the context of American colonial encounters.

10 Jennifer Smith describes Pacheco as a "healthy racial hybrid" in constrast to the *gitana*, who figures as a "threatening racial other" ("The Gypy's Curse" 466). Akiko Tsuchiya, for her part, notes that Asis "constructs an image of her future lover on the basis of his racial (and implicitly 'national') features" (142).

11 One of the most fascinating depictions of material blood in Pardo Bazán's works (one that falls outside the scope of this project) occurs in *Madre Naturaleza* when the narrator refers to cow's milk destined for human consumption as "sangre blanca" ("white blood"; 306).

12 When compared to the novels studied here, women's bleeding seems notably missing in Pardo Bazán. In Joyce Tolliver's excellent analysis of Pardo Bazán's short story "Exangüe" ("Exsanguine," literally bloodless), we see that blood is oddly and materially absent in a story of colonial violence and torture. For Tolliver, "Exangüe" ironically exposes "the reduction of flesh-and-blood women to mere image" as they become "icons pressed into service for the family, for the nation, or for artistic delectation" (298).

13 Burk does not provide the source for the citation from Margaret Greer.

1. The Colour of Blood: Racializing Illegitimacy in *Doña Luz*

1 Omi and Winant define "racial formation" as *the sociohistorical process by which racial identities are created, lived out, transformed, and destroyed* (109; emphasis in original).

2 Within Latin American Studies, there has been significant debate around the usage of "caste" versus "race" in the colonial period, with similar claims to historicity. Some scholars see caste and race as discrete categories pertaining to different historical periods, with race crystallizing at some point in the nineteenth century when the concept becomes more explicitly biologized. See, for example, Ruth Hill. As Daniel Nemser succinctly explains: "According to this view, difference in colonial Latin America should be understood as 'cultural' (or perhaps 'socioracial') and therefore fluid. Only in the 'modern' period does it become truly 'racial,' meaning 'biological' and fixed. Yet this argument takes at face value the language of nineteenth-century race scientists without acknowledging the complexities of racial thought even during that period" (9).

3 For Bhabha, colonial mimicry enfolds the power to disrupt colonial
discourse. This is what Bhabha terms the "menace" of mimicry (126). Roy,
however, remains sceptical of its subversive potential.

4 Lisa Surwillo's groundbreaking monograph *Monsters by Trade: Slave
Traffickers in Modern Spanish Literature and Culture* (2014) was the first book-
length study to examine the role of the "negrero" ("slave trafficker") in
modern Spanish literature.

5 Fedorchek translates "fiereza" as "hauteur," which erases the animality or
savagery implicit in the description of Luz's excessive pride.

6 Dirt or mud as a metaphor for morally suspect behaviour gets further
developed by Leopoldo Alas in *La Regenta* to signify unchaste behaviours.
See chapter two.

7 Much of the work on Juan Valera's oeuvre gravitates towards *Pepita
Jiménez*, while less scholarly attention has been given to *Doña Luz*. Joan
Torres-Pou examines the question of orientalism in Juan Valera's work,
focusing mostly on his final novel, *Morsamor*. His brief commentary on
Doña Luz establishes Valera's familiarity with Hinduism and notes its
influences in the novel (see chapter 1, "El Oriente en la obra de Juan
Valera," pp. 23–58 in *Asia*), but no study, to my knowledge, explicitly
examines this novel through the lens of empire.

8 Here I borrow a concept that Lisa Lowe develops in her essay "The
Intimacies of Four Continents." For Lowe, the term "intimacies"
characterizes the interdependencies and linkages between Europe,
America, Africa, and Asia through colonialism. Lowe is particularly
interested in the unevenness in the representation of these intimacies and
focuses on the absence of the figure of the Chinese coolie and the erasure
of Asia in the historiography of the early Americas. For Lowe, it is through
"the intimacies of the four continents" that the conditions upon which
modern humanism and a racialized division of labour were produced.
She develops the concept of the intimate as a polyvalent term having
three central meanings: The first meaning of intimacy is the idea of spatial
proximity, the second is the idea of privacy in contrast to the bourgeois
public sphere of work and politics, and the third refers to the "volatile
contact of colonized peoples" (203). I use the term "intimacy" adopting
Lowe's first definition: to refer to both the imagined and real proximity
and interconnectedness between Spain, Asia, Africa, and the Americas,
which is projected through representation of these spaces in Valera's novel.

9 The original Syrian manuscript source for Galland's translation only
contained 281 nights, so Galland supplemented the original with tales
from other sources with Arabic originals. As a result, stories including
Ali Baba, Aladdin, and likely the tale of Prince Ahmed were added to his
problematic translation (Johnson et al. 245).

10 Cheng asserts that "Orientalism is a critique, ornamentalism a theory of being" (18).

11 See Megan C. Thomas's book *Orientalists, Propagandists, and Ilustrados: Filipino Scholarship and the end of Spanish Colonialism.* In chapter two, "Locating Orientalism and the Anthropological Sciences: The Limits of Postcolonial Critiques," Thomas advances a nuanced, historicized understanding of the "unusual contours" of Spanish orientalism and anthropology, which have been obscured by contemporary critiques of orientalist thought.

12 This tension between surface and depth function as a trope in this novel – indexed by words like "velar" ("to veil"), "revelar" ("to reveal"), and "desvelar" ("to unveil"). These are further developed by Galdós and Alas. See chapters two and four.

13 See Valera's collection of essays *A vuela pluma*, published in 1897.

14 Joan Torres-Pou, writing about Valera's orientalism in *Morsamor*, asserted that his "literary exoticism disappears when he talks about America and Europe, places which he knew well" ("The Exotic as Subversive" 255). This paradigm, however, does not neatly map onto *Doña Luz*, which presents less clear-cut lines between Europe, the Orient, and the colonial.

15 John Blanco uses *Respublica Christiana*, a term associated with medieval thought, to refer to the imperial project of the evangelizing, i.e., sovereign rule through Christianization. Blanco focuses in particular on the unique circumstances that gave clergy greater authority in the Philippines and on the notion of native consent as part of the conversion process. He explains, "By the very choice of labels ('republic' as opposed to 'monarchy' or 'aristocracy'), we can see that such an order had to be based from the beginning on native consent – same force that the state tried to marshal in its project of Bourbon reform. This is because religious conversion to Christianity implies both the initiate's freedom to choose (or not choose) Christianity and to recognize that freedom is tied to an order or rationality that is primarily theological and only secondarily political" (24–5).

16 See Bridget Aldaraca *El ángel del hogar* 88–117, and Alison Sinclair, "Luxurious Borders" 212–14. I find Sinclair's discussion particularly useful, framing it as a problem of female excess and containment. The prostitute and her desires exceed the boundaries of bourgeois social order.

17 In *Pepita Jiménez*, Luis remarks: "En cuanto a Pepita Jiménez, que imaginaba yo que vendría también en burra con jamugas, pues ignoraba que montase, me sorprendió apareciendo en un caballo tordo muy vivo y fogoso, vestida de amazona, y manejando el caballo con destreza y primor notables ... Pepita me miraba compasiva, al ver la facha lastimosa que sobre la mula debía yo de tener" ("With regard to Pepita Jiménez, whom I had imagined would also arrive riding sidesaddle on a donkey, of course I

didn't know that she rode, she surprised me by appearing on a strong and fiery dapple-gray horse, dressed like an Amazonian woman and directing the horse with notable skill and ability"; Valera, *Pepita Jiménez* 98–9).

18 "Se llama también el distinto linaje de los caballos y otros animales, porque vienen de padres conocidos por su lealtad, fiereza u otra circunstancia, señalados y particulares"

  ("It is also used for the distinct lineage of horses, bulls and other animals, because they come from known parents because of their loyalty, ferocity, or other identified and particular circumstances"; *DRAE* "casta" 1792). In contrast to the black horses in Valera, Clarín associates a white horse with Ana Ozores in *La Regenta*. Tellingly, this horse is characterized as "de pura raza española" ("of pure Spanish race") (78).

19 See Martin-Marquéz "Arabism and the Reconsideration of Spanish History and Identity in the Nineteenth Century" 27–38, in *Disorientations*.

20 Eric Calderwood's recent monograph *Colonial Al-Andalus: Spain and the Making of Modern Moroccan Culture* examines how the history of Muslim medieval Iberia – Al-Andalus – was deployed to justify Spain's colonization of Morocco in the twentieth century.

21 I am grateful to Julie Ward for helping me see this.

22 Torres-Pou argues that Valera's use of the exotic subverts literary orientalist techniques. As evidence, he cites the following quote from "Sobre Dos Acusaciones Contra España": "Casi todo esto contiene un arabismo u orientalismo hechicero y de color de rosa, tan creado por nosotros (los españoles), que bien se puede asegurar que no hay Árabe ni moro que aunque se le tradujera en su lengua, entendiese palabra de ello" ("Nearly all of this contains a spellbinding and rose-colored Arabism or orientalism, very much created by us (the Spanish) such that one can be sure that there is no Arab or moor that could understand a single word of it, even if it were translated into their language"; Valera 115). Taken out of context, Torres-Pou interprets this passage as a nod to Valera's understanding of the constructed and literary nature of Orientalism. However, an examination of the complete essay makes clear that Valera is attempting to centre Spanish authorial power as the originator of culture in response to Draper's accusations. In other words, any cultural contribution that could be identified as "oriental" is actually a Spanish creation that Arabs and moors would not be sophisticated enough to comprehend. Arabic poetry written by Spaniards, Valera argues, "casi de seguro no hubiera nacido jamás en el alma de un moro de África ó de un beduino de Arabia" ("almost certainly would never have been born in the soul of an African moor or an Arab Bedouin"; 115). Ergo his claim that "los árabes y los moros no eran sabios cuando vinieron á España, ni trajeron sabios consigo, de suerte que los sabios y la sabiduría que hubo más tarde

entre ellos, no deben tenerse por arábigas sino por españolas" ("Arabs and moors were not learned when they came to Spain, nor did they bring wisemen with them, the happenstance of wisemen and wisdom they had much later among them, ought not to be considered Arabic but rather Spanish"; 117).

2. From Blood to Flesh: Avowing Material Pleasure in *La Regenta*

1 Eric Hobsbawm defines the bourgeoisie as "a body of persons of power and influence, independent of the power and influence of traditional birth and status" (244) (qtd. in Stoler 103). For her part, Valis observes, "The middle classes prized newness, progress, and individual achievement, but in Spain, as elsewhere in Europe, many of them also looked to the aristocracy as social and cultural models. They looked, that is, to the past" (*Culture of Cursilería* 49). This nostalgic, aspirational positioning reveals the ongoing influence of Spain's aristocratic, early modern mores in the loosely woven social fabric of the bourgeoisie.

2 While it is possible to argue that the townspeople of Vetusta demonstrate a naturalist perspective in viewing inheritance as a significant factor in determining Ana's destiny, the pervasive discourse of blood purity and the novel's engagement with early modern gender ideals provide overwhelming evidence that this deterministic viewpoint precedes the tenets of naturalism. Scholars have long grappled with the issue of determinism in *La Regenta*. For a succinct overview of the literature on this topic, see Lou Charnon-Deutsch's article "Between Agency and Determinism."

3 While Alas employs the term "class" here, the blood-based exclusivity of its membership more closely aligns it with caste.

4 See Lisa Surwillo "Speaking of Race in *Don Álvaro*" for a discussion the significance of the *pura raza española* ("purebred Spanish") horse, which was initially reserved for the use of royalty and the nobility.

5 Spain's American empire is also alluded to throughout the novel. An enclave of *indianos* reside in a new part of the city known as *la colonia* ("the colony"), brightly coloured – the narrator tells us – like an American bird or "una india brava adornada con plumas y cintas de tonos discordantes" ("a savage Amerindian woman adorned with feathers and ribbons of clashing colors"; 160; Rutherford 30). The lecherous town priest views *la colonia* as a miniature Peru and himself as a spiritual Pizarro (161). "The past," Noel Valis writes of *La Regenta*, "consistently intrudes as a subtle and sometimes not so subtle reminder of what was once the splendor of imperial Spain" ("Romantic Reverberation" 41–2). For a postcolonial reading of *La Regenta*, see Pablo García.

6 Joan Ramon Resina does not explicitly mention menstruation, but does write that "Ana suffers her first nervous crisis when she reaches puberty" (235).

7 See Beth Bauer for a detailed analysis of the hermeneutics of confession in *La Regenta*.

8 Evidencing this point, Monlau referred to priests as "médicos del alma" ("doctors of the soul"; *Higiene* vi).

9 For D.A. Miller, the novel enacts a disciplinary or policing function. For example, Miller argues that in regard to *Nana*, "Zola wants to register the Parisian *fille* no less than the police. *Nana* is the title of a file, referring both to the prostitute who resists the record and to the novel whose representational practice has already overcome this resistance" (21). One might advance a similar argument in regard to *La Regenta*, whose narrative gaze so frequently takes on a voyeuristic quality. For Charnon-Deutsch, this voyeuristic gaze takes on pornographic qualities ("Voyeurism, Pornography, and 'La Regenta'"). While the narrative at times takes an objectifying stance, on the whole, the gaze is ambivalent at best – shifting between moments of objectification and identification with the protagonist.

10 See Armstrong, Flint, and Tsuchiya.

11 Along these lines, Valis argues, in the context of Ana's mysticism, that Ana "never attains self-knowledge in *La Regenta*: she maintains a confused perception of her feelings and motivations throughout the novel" (*Decadent Vision* 98).

3. Social Blood: The Aesthetics of the Crowd in *La desheredada*

1 See Gabrielle Miller for a historical analysis of prostitution in *La desheredada*.

2 The negative social connation of leeches is an interesting point of contrast to the curative power attributed to leeches in medicine. In my research on leeches, I was struck by the reverence with which the medical community treated them – as precious commodities and delicate animals that are often misused and abused by laypeople. See, for example, *Historia natural y médica de las sanguijuelas* (1828) by J.L. Derheims.

3 Clark translates "sangre social" as "the blood of society." I prefer to preserve the term social here, as it captures the interactive nature of the crowd.

4 Aurélie Vialette's recent book *Intellectual Philanthropy: The Seduction of the Masses* presents an original account of the fear around working-class uprisings in Spain and the philanthropists' attempt to quash their political power.

5 See Bridget Aldaraca *El ángel del hogar* 88–117, and Alison Sinclair "Luxurious Borders" 212–14.

6 Maite Zubiaurre and Luis Cesta discuss this concept in contrast to what López Bago referred to as "la novela bonita" – Valera's *Pepita Jimenez* being the prime example of this. They do not specify the source of this concept.

7 It should be noted that Pablo Sánchez León traces the notion of the menacing crowd to the Enlightenment (16), though so-called crowd science is squarely a product of the late nineteenth century.

8 Ortega y Gasset's idea of the *hombre-masa* ("mass-man") echoes earlier writings by Gustave Le Bon in which he asserts that "The disappearance of conscious personality and the turning of feelings and thoughts in a different direction, which are the primary characteristics of a crowd about to become organised [*sic*], do not always involve the simultaneous presence of a number of individuals on one spot. Thousands of isolated individuals may acquire certain moments, and under the influence of certain violent emotions – such, for example, as a great national event – the characteristics of a psychological crowd" (44). Thomas Mermall notes that critics such as Francisco Zamora "acusa a Ortega la falta de precisión y rigor científico y denuncia *La rebelión* diciendo que es un pastiche de las ideas de Le Bon" ("accuses Ortega of lacking precision and scientific rigor and denounces *La rebelión*, saying that it's a pastiche of the ideas of Le Bon"; 10–11).

9 Zola's *Germinal* (1885) is often cited as representing an anxious vision of working-class crowds. While his *Au Bonheur des Dames* (1883) depicts a crowd of female consumers, it is important to note that *La desheredada* obviously predates both Zola's novel as well as the works of Le Bon and Ortega y Gasset. We see the fear of modern crowds in Spain beginning as early as Monlau. Moreover, other canonical European novels predating Zola already register this fear, including Elizabeth Gaskell's *Mary Barton* (1848) and *North and South* (1854–5), Victor Hugo's *Les misérables* (1862), Charles Dickens's *A Tale of Two Cities* (1859), and George Eliot's *Felix Holt, the Radical* (1866). Galdós, at the very least, would have been familiar with Dickens's treatment of crowds.

10 For an extensive discussion on *lo cursí*, see Noël Valis's *Culture of Cursílería*.

11 In "Family Romance," Freud writes that "the imagination of girls is apt to show itself much weaker" (156). By contrast, novelists of the nineteenth century seem to gender unwieldy imaginations feminine. Galdós's *Isidora* and Flaubert's *Madame Bovary* serve as prime examples of modern, feminine rewritings of *Don Quijote*.

12 These formal elements in Galdós raise important questions about gender and genre since an excess of detail (like ornamentation) has been historically gendered feminine. See Luisa Elena Delgado's "'Más estragos que las revoluciones': Detallando lo femenino en 'La de Bringas.'"

13 For a discussion on the formal function of frames in Galdós, see Labanyi "The Problem of Framing in *La de Bringas.*" For a broader analysis of literary framing in Galdós, see Hazel Gold's *The Reframing of Realism: Galdós and the Discourses of the Nineteenth-Century Novel.*

14 See note 13.

15 "Final de otra novela" is interesting from a gender perspective given that it has a masculine protagonist. I often ask my students how we would read *La desheredada* differently had its protagonist been Tomás Rufete, and this often feels like futile exercise. Feminine beauty and male heterosexual desire play such a decisive role in this novel that it becomes nearly impossible for students to imagine that there would be anything worth narrating if the embittered civil servant took her place.

16 La Casa de Dementes de Santa Isabel en Leganés was inaugurated in 1851 by Melchor Ordoñez, Spain's minister of government (*ministro de gobernación*) (Villasante 34).

17 For an extensive discussion on confinement in the novel, see Liana Ewald.

18 Olga Villasante's research on Leganés also confirms that the institute was named after Isabell II.

19 Thiers was the chief executive of the French national government in 1871 and sent the orders for the repression of the revolutionary government.

20 Ortega y Gasset talked about the crowd as possessing "coincidencias de deseos" ("coinciding of desires"; 132). Similarly, Freud in *Group Psychology and the Analysis of the Ego* employed the term *liebe* to discuss the emotive bond of crowds.

21 This statement appears informed by the widely held beliefs in the medical community around the power of imitation within crowds. In *Higiene Pública*, Monlau warned: "Los pueblos, considerados en masa, tienen el instinto de imitación casi tan fuerte como los niños. Las modas y las opiniones, los sistemas y las sectas, la reacciones y los cismas, llevan ya arrebatados como un torrente á [*sic*] millones de individuos, cuando la razón y el exámen apenas ha formado todavía un prosélito. Y es que el poderosísimo instinto de imitación obra como una especia de simpatía, y con una velocidad eléctrica. En una reunión bosteza uno, y á [*sic*] los dos minutos bostezan ciento" ("people, considered as a mass, have an instinct for imitation almost as strong as those of children. Trends and opinions, systems and sects, reactions and schisms, arrive already half-baked like a torrent to millions of individuals, when reason and examination have scarcely formed a proselyte. And this extremely powerful instinct for imitation works like a kind of sympathy, and with electric velocity. One person yawns in a meeting, and two minutes later one hundren yawn"; 673). Later, in 1890, the French criminologist Gabriel Tarde would author the influential book *Les lois de l'imitation.*

22 Liana Ewald's essay "Confinement, Consolation, and Confession
in Galdós's *La desheredada*" explores in great detail the imagery of
confinement in *La desheredada* as a metaphor for Galdós's disillusionment
with the novel form, noting that he hoped the middle class would become
the raw material for a new, more expansive literary form. Ewald does not
engage with the gendered aspect of confinement, which seems central to
the author's work both in *La desheredada* and in other works, most notably
Tristana.

23 Leigh Mercer argues that the ideology of domesticity operates differently in
Spain as compared to other European literary traditions. The Spanish novel,
Mercer argues, shows a preference for "open social spaces as a means
to explore and define the female bourgeoisie" (17). Thus promenades,
museum visits, and shopping can be framed as "visual practice[s]" that
figured as part of the repertoire of bourgeois femininity (66).

24 See Beth Bauer for an extensive discussion on anagnorisis in *La desheredada*.

25 It bears mentioning that Amadeo is a foreign king – not of the blood of the
Spanish monarchy. Thus, the Restoration, instantiated by Alfonso XII's
reign, is also a restoration of blood.

26 In Spanish fiction, the figure who indulges in pleasure most forcefully is
the fallen woman. Amanda Anderson, in her study on the Victorian novel,
argues the male author needs to ward off the fallen woman. As a kind
of constitutive other, she remains diametrically opposed to "normative
masculine identity seen to possess the capacity for autonomous action,
enlightened rationality, and self-control" (13).

27 For Miller, Balzac's *Une ténébreuse affiare* (1841) is a prime example of this
super-vision by which the narrator "assumes a fully panoptic view of the
world it places under surveillance" (23).

4. Transfusions: Queering Kinship in *Fortunata y Jacinta: Dos historias de casadas*

1 Noting that Galdós's mother died shortly before he finished writing
Fortunata y Jacinta, John Sinnigen argues that "Todo eso se manifiesta
en los fuertes personajes femeninos (reconocidos casi unánimemente
por la crítica como más interesantes que los masculinos) que sustentan
la tendencia feminocéntrica de la novelística galdosiana. Galdós
utiliza la ficción para intentar penetrar, representar y apropriarse de
lo femenino" ("All of this manifests in the strong female characters
(recognized almost exclusively in the criticism as more interesting
than the male ones) that sustain the woman-centric tendency in
Galdosian novels. Galdós uses fiction to try to penetrate, represent, and
appropriate the feminine"; 117).

2 For Tsuchiya, gender deviance lies at the heart of social marginality, and this certainly holds true for Fortunata, Mauricia, and Maxi. All exhibit characteristics that prevent them from conforming to bourgeois notions of what men and women should be. Another way to think of these characters and their tragic ends is through the concept of freedom. Julio Rodríguez Puértolas points to the fact that "En *Fortunata y Jacinta* mueren o desaparecen todos los personajes que creen en la libertad (Mauricia y Fortunata como ejemplos máximos), y son asimilados de modo apropiado los que bien pueden llamarse pseudolibertarios (José Izquierdo, genialmente transformado por Galdós en modelo de cuadros históricos tradicionales; Juan Pablo Rubín, convertido por la Restauración en gobernador de una provincia). Por otro lado, quienes ejercen alguna clase de autoridad, aunque sea en mínimas parcelas, lo hacen de tal modo que se consideran infalibles" ("In *Fortunata y Jacinta*, the characters that believe in freedom all die or disappear [Mauricia and Fortunata are prime examples], and the ones that we might call pseudo-liberal are assimilated in an appropriate way [José Izquierdo, ingeniously transformed by Galdós into the image of traditional historical paintings. Juan Pablo Rubín, converted by the Restoration into the governor of a province.] By contrast, those who exercise some type of authority, however minimal, do it in a way that is considered infallible"; 111).
3 Interestingly, Moreno-Isla, the anglophile seducer who falls in love with Jacinta, dies of a blood-related cause: "Se ahogaba. En la región cardiaca, o cerca de ella, más al centro, sentía el golpe de la sangre con duro y contundente compás. Era como si un herrero martillase junto al mismo corazón, remachando a fuego una pieza nueva que se acababa de echar" ("He felt asphyxiated. In the area around his heart, or nearby, close to the center, he could feel the blood surging in a sharp, forceful rhythm. It was as if a blacksmith were hammering right next to his very heart, riveting a new piece onto it, in the fire"; *FJ* II 569; Moncy Gullón 673). He does not occupy the social periphery of the novel, and, befittingly, his death results from a stoppage or blockage of blood flow rather than its drainage or exposure.
4 Commenting on the significance of the post-revolutionary period, Sinnigen explains that "aunque la burguesía luego renuncia a determinadas metas progresistas y busca la estabilidad y la garantía de su parcela del poder mediante la formación de una alianza con la aristocracia terrateniente, el período revolucionario no dejó de ser una fisura en el bloque de poder, en el orden establecido y en las ideologías dominantes, una fisura que dejó vislumbrar nuevos horizontes que incluyeron cierta modernización y un importante impulso para mujeres y obreros" ("even though the bourgeoisie would later renounce certain progressive objectives and

look for stability and the guarantee of their share of power through the formation of an alliance with the landed aristocracy, the revolutionary period did not cease to be a fissure in the block of power, in the established order and in the dominant ideologies, a fissure that allowed new horizons, which included a kind of modernization and an important push for women and workers, to come the fore"; 116).

5 In her article "Family Ties and Tyrannies: A Reassessment of Jacinta," Harriet Turner astutely notes that sterility has been "assigned to [Jacinta], it is construed as a physical impairment *she* must bear" (16), when we ought to consider that she in fact lives a "sterile life" (17) that makes conception highly improbable. When describing Jacinta as sterile, my intention is not to reproduce the patriarchal logic that shoulders Jacinta with the sole burden of perpetuating the caste. Instead, I am interested in how the narrative presents Jacinta as sterile, likely in relation to the multigenerational practice of incest within the two families.

6 When Jacinta first learns of Juan's past affair with Fortunata, she exclaims: "El hombre bien criado y la mujer ordinaria no se emparejan bien. Pasa la ilusión, y después ¿qué resulta? Que ella huele a cebolla y dice palabras feas … A él … como si lo viera … se le revuelve el estómago y empiezan las cuestiones. El pueblo es sucio, la mujer de la clase baja, por más que se lave el palmito, siempre es pueblo. No hay más que ver las casas por dentro. Pues lo mismo están los benditos cuerpos" ("A well-bred man and a common woman aren't compatible. When his ardor cools, what's left? She smells of onions and uses foul language. And as for him, I can almost see it: he's revolted, and then the quarrels start. The common people are dirty. No matter how much she scrubs herself, a low-class woman is always low class. All you have to do is see the insides of their houses. Their bodies are just the same"; *FJ* I 314; Moncy Gullón 61).

7 Elsewhere in the novel, the narrator registers the perturbing power of the consumption of bloody animal flesh: "Instó mucho al *maestro* a que tomara un *biftec*; pero don José lo rehusó, aunque buenas ganas tenía de aceptarlo. De sólo oler la carne y ver la sangre de ella y la grasa en el plato de sus amigos, le parecía que se trastornaba" ("He urged the maestro to have a steak, but Don José declined – although it wouldn't have pained him to accept. Just smelling the meat and seeing the juice [blood] run out of it into the grease on his friends' plates was enough to upset him"; *FJ* II 695; Moncy Gullón 755).

8 This argument nuances John Sinnigen's obsveration that "[d]ebido fundamentalmente a su papel en el ciclo reproductivo, las mujeres están más identificadas con el proceso natural y con el cuerpo, y por tanto están desvaloradas por los artífices de la cultura que quieren transcender la naturaleza mediante la razón" ("due fundamentally to their role in the

reproductive cycle, women are more closely identified with the natural process and with the body, and for this reason they are devalued by architects of culture that want to transcend nature via reason"; 119). Over the course of the novel, we see that it is the socially marginalized, those that remain excluded from the elite caste, who are consigned to the bloody realm of corporeality.

9 Mauricia is also consigned to the status of thingness when she is compared to a hunted animal after her injury: "– Pues esa buena pieza … fue recogida en la calle por los protestantes" ("This great catch … was picked up off the street by the Protestants"; *FJ* II 372; my translation).

10 The bird motif has been explored by several critics. See Stephen Gilman, Roger Utt, Agnes Moncy Gullón, and Stephen Hart.

11 For a discussion on the fetish of infantilism, see Anne McClintock's chapter "Imperial Leather: Race, Cross-Dressing, and the Cult of Domesticity" in *Imperial Leather: Race, Gender, and Sexuality in the Colonial Context*.

12 I thank Emilie Bergmann for helping me see this.

13 It is worth noting that in medieval and early modern Spain, following Galenic theories of medicine, breast milk was thought to be derived from blood that flowed from the uterus. Crucially, breast milk was treated as a source of religious and racial contamination in the context of blood purity both in Spain and the New World.

14 Here we might recall that Isabel Cordero imports fabrics of "género blanco" ("white materials"; *FJ* I 255; Moncy Gullón 29) anticipating new infrastructure that would bring public water to Madrid.

15 I am reminded here of the transformative power of ink in *El amigo manso* as the first-person narrator and protagonist narrates his own creation: "Creo que me zambulló en una gota de tinta; que dio fuego a un papel; que después fuego, tinta y yo fuimos metidos y bien meneados en una redomita que olía detestablemente á azufre y otras drogas infernales … Poco después salí de una llamarada roja, convertido en carne mortal. El dolor me dijo que yo era un hombre" ("I think he plunged me into a drop of ink; set fire to a sheet of paper; and then the fire, the paper, and I were put into a little bottle which had an awful stench of pitch, sulfur, and other infernal concoctions … A bit later I emerged from a flash of red flame, transformed into a mortal flesh. The pain I felt told me I was a man"; Galdós 145–6; Russell 3).

16 Noël Valis in her study on *cursilería* observes that the desire for social distinction through self-fashioning has a particular history in Spain rooted in its religious past in which *limpieza de sangre* created a caste system based on blood. Valis remarks that this "notion of distinction that blood ties symbolized found a middle-class substitution in cultural distinction as

sought in the artifacts, dress, and manners of the socially superior class" (*The Culture of Cursilería* 50). *Fortunata y Jacinta*, however, evidences that dress and decorum were faulty indicators of caste identity and that "the symbolics of blood" persisted through the modern era as a modality of distinction in this long transition to the modern.

17 Here we might recall Maxi's persistent attempts to correct Fortunata's speech as an attempt to make her appear more educated.

18 These are Judith Butler's words, taken from an interview with Gayle Rubin.

Coda: The Bleeding Body

1 The article appeared in *Anales de la Sociedad Ginecológica Española*. The pagination is erroneous in the original, jumping from 17 to 258.

2 Some women, Cortejarena goes on to say, even improve their health after several rounds of bleeding ("evacuaciones sanguíneas") (17).

3 It worth noting, however, that while Cortejarena seems to point to the effect of cultural inscription on the body, he does this while still reifying sexual difference by concluding that women tolerate all forms of blood loss better than men, precisely because their bodies sustain monthly menstruation.

4 Jameson develops this argument in his recent book *Antinomies of Realism*. See Chapter 5, "Pérez Galdós, or, the Waning of Protagonicity," 95–113.

Works Cited

Ahmed, Sara. *The Cultural Politics of Emotion*. Routledge, 2004.

– *Living a Feminist Life*. Duke UP, 2017.

Alaimo, Stacy, and Susan Hekman. "Introduction: Emerging Models of Materiality in Feminist Theory." *Material Feminisms*, edited by Stacy Alaimo and Susan Heckman, Indiana UP, 2008, pp. 1–19.

Alas, Leopoldo. "La desheredada." *Leopoldo Alas: Teoría y crítica de la novela española*. Editorial Laia, 1972, pp. 225–39.

– *La Regenta*, edited by Juan Oleza, vol. 1, Cátedra, 2008.

– *La Regenta*, edited by Juan Oleza, vol. 2, Cátedra, 2009.

– *Su Único Hijo*, edited by Juan Oleza, Cátedra, 1990.

Aldaraca, Bridget. *El ángel del hogar: Galdós and the Ideology of Domesticity in Spain*. U of North Carolina P, 1992.

Álvarez Junco, José. *La comuna en España*. Siglo XXI de España Editores, 1971.

– "Los rojos." *La comuna en España*. Siglo XXI de España Editores, 1971, pp. 127–31.

Amann, Elizabeth. "Metaphor, Metonymy and Inheritance: Representing Revolution in Galdós's *La desheredada*." *Revista de Estudios Hispánicos*, vol. 37, no. 3, 2003, pp. 437–62.

Anderson, Amanda. *Tainted Souls and Painted Faces: The Rhetoric of Fallenness in Victorian Culture*. Cornell UP, 1993.

Anderson, Benedict. *Imagined Communities: Reflections on the Origin and Spread of Nationalism*. Verso, 2006.

Anidjar, Gil. *Blood: A Critique of Christianity*. Columbia UP, 2014.

Apte, Vaman Shivaram. *The Student's English Sanskrit Dictionary*. Jainendra Press, 1963.

Armstrong, Nancy. *How Novels Think: The Limits of Individualism from 1719–1900*. Kindle ed., Columbia UP, 2006.

Auerbach, Nina. *Woman and the Demon: The Life of a Victorian Myth*. Harvard UP, 1982.

"Baba." *Diccionario de la lengua castellana*. Real Academia Española, 1884, http://ntlle.rae.es/ntlle. Accessed 15 October 2019.

Barker-Benfield, G.J. *The Culture of Sensibility: Sex and Society in Eighteenth-Century Britain*. U of Chicago P, 1992.

Barrows, Susanna. *Distorting Mirrors: Visions of the Crowd in Late Nineteenth-Century France*. Yale UP, 1981.

Bauer, Beth Wietelmann. "Confession in *La Regenta*: The Secular Sacrament." *Bulletin of Hispanic Studies*, vol. 70, no. 3, 1993, pp. 313–23.

– Introduction. *Doña Luz: A Novel*, translated by Robert M. Fedorchek, Bucknell UP, 2002, pp. 13–24.

– "Isidora's Anagnorisis: Reading, Plot, and Identity in *La desheredada*." *Anales Galdosianos*, vol. 24, 1989, pp. 43–52.

Beusterien, John. "The Celebratory Conical Hat in *La Celestina*." *Crime and Punishment in the Middle Ages and Early Modern Age: Mental-Historical Investigations of Basic Human Problems and Social Responses*, edited by Albrecht Classen and Connie L. Scarborough, De Gruyter, 2012, pp. 403–14.

Bhabha, Homi K. *The Location of Culture*. Routledge, 2004.

Biddick, Kathleen. "The Cut of Genealogy: Pedagogy in the Blood." *Journal of Medieval and Early Modern Studies*, vol. 30, no. 3, 2000, pp. 449–62.

Blanco, Alda. "Spain at the Crossroads: Imperial Nostalgia or Modern Colonialism?" *A Contracorriente: Una Revista de Historia Social y Literatura en América Latina*, vol. 5, no. 1, 2007, pp. 1–11.

Blanco, John D. *Frontier Constitutions: Christianity and Colonial Empire in the Nineteenth-Century Philippines*. U of California P, 2009.

Bly, Peter A. "The Physician in the Narratives of Galdós and Clarín." *Imagined Truths: Realism in Modern Spanish Literature and Culture*, edited by Mary L. Coffey and Margot Versteeg, U of Toronto P, 2019, pp. 111–43.

Brooks, Peter. *Reading for the Plot: Design and Intention in Narrative*. Vintage Books, 1985.

– *Realist Vision*. Yale UP, 2005.

Burk, Rachel L. "Metamateriality and Blood Purity in Cervantes's Alcaná de Toledo." *The Cultural Politics of Blood, 1500–1900*, edited by Kimberly Anne Coles et al., Palgrave Macmillan, 2015, pp. 25–44.

Butler, Judith. *Bodies That Matter: On the Discursive Limits of "Sex."* Routledge, 1993.

– *Undoing Gender*. Routledge, 2004.

Calderwood, Eric. *Colonial Al-Andalus: Spain and the Making of Modern Moroccan Culture*. Harvard UP, 2018.

"Cándido/a." *Diccionario de la lengua castellana de la Real Academia Española*, 1884, http://ntlle.rae.es/ntlle. Accessed 15 October 2019.

Canetti, Elias. *Crowds and Power*. Viking Press, 1963.

"Castizo/a." *Diccionario de la lengua castellana de la Real Academia Española*, 1884, http://ntlle.rae.es/ntlle. Accessed 15 October 2019.

"Casta." *Diccionario de autoridades*, 1729, http://ntlle.rae.es/ntlle. Accessed 15 October 2019.

"Casto." *Diccionario de autoridades de la Real Academia Española*, 1729, http://ntlle.rae.es/ntlle. Accessed 15 October 2019.

"Casto/a." *Diccionario de la lengua castellana de la Real Academia Española*, 1884, http://ntlle.rae.es/ntlle. Accessed 15 October 2019.

Cervantes Saavedra, Miguel de. *Entremeses*. Taurus, 1981.

Chang, Julia H. "'Aquellos neófitos indios, chinos y anamitas': Asia in the Imperial Imaginary of *Doña Luz*." *Arizona Journal of Hispanic Cultural Studies*, vol. 18, 2014, 235–46.

– "Between Intimacy and Enmity: Spain and the Philippines Post-Suez." *Journal of Spanish Cultural Studies*, vol. 17, no. 4, 2016, pp. 305–22.

Charnon-Deutsch, Lou. "Between Agency and Determinism: A Critical Review of Clarín Studies." *Hispanic Review*, vol. 76, no. 2, 2008, pp. 135–53.

– "Voyeurism, Pornography, and *La Regenta*." *Modern Language Studies*, vol. 19, no. 4, 1989, pp. 93–101.

Cheng, Anne Anlin. *Ornamentalism*. Oxford UP, 2019.

Cifuentes, Luis Fernández. "Signs for Sale in the City of Galdós." *Modern Language Notes*, vol. 103, no. 2, 1988, pp. 289–311.

Clark, Lester, translator. *The Disinherited*. By Benito Pérez Galdós, Phoenix House, 1999.

Coffey, Mary L., and Margot Versteeg. Introduction. *Imagined Truths: Realism in Modern Spanish Literature and Culture*, edited by Mary L. Coffey and Margot Versteeg, U of Toronto P, 2019, pp. 3–38.

Colebrook, Clare. "On Not Becoming Man: The Materialist Politics of Unactualized Potential." *New Materialism*, edited by Stacy Alaimo and Susan Hekman, Indiana UP, 2008, pp. 52–84.

Coles, Kimberly Anne, et al., editors. Introduction. *The Cultural Politics of Blood, 1500–1900*, Palgrave Macmillan, 2015, pp. 1–24.

Connor, Laura. "Framing Women: Frame, Perspective and Interpretation in *Fortunata y Jacinta*, *Grand Bal*, and *Madeleine*." *Hispanic Review*, vol. 83, no. 2, 2015, pp. 165–86.

Cortejarena, Francisco. "Ligeros apuntes acerco del efecto de las evacuaciones sanguíneas de la mujer." *Anales de la Sociedad Ginecológica Española*, 1875, pp. 17–259.

Cruz, Jesus. *The Rise of Middle-Class Culture in Nineteenth-Century Spain*. Louisiana State UP, 2011.

Cruz Martes, Camille. "El espacio ambiguo de la muerte en *Fortunata y Jacinta*." *Pórtico: Revista de Estudios Hispánicos del Recinto Universitario de Mayagüez*, vol. 1, 2006. pp. 141–73.

Deleuze, Gilles, and Félix Guattari. *A Thousand Plateaus: Capitalism and Schizophrenia*. U of Minnesota P, 1987.

Delgado, Luisa Elena. "Más estragos que las revoluciones: Detallando lo femenino en *La de Bringas*." *Revista Hispánica Moderna*, vol. 48, no. 1, 1995, pp. 31–42.

Delgado, Luisa Elena, et al. Introduction. *Engaging the Emotions in Spanish Culture and History*, edited by Luisa Elena Delgado et al., Vanderbilt UP, 2016, pp. 1–20.

Derheims, J.L. *Historia natural y médica de las sanguijuleas*. Translated by J.Y. and R.M.F. Vallés y Compañía, 1828.

Dickens, Charles. *Charles Dickens's A Tale of Two Cities*, edited by Harold Bloom, Chelsea House Publishers, 1987.

Dopico Black, Georgina. *Perfect Wives, Other Women: Adultery and Inquisition in Early Modern Spain*. Duke UP, 2001.

Douglas, Mary. *Purity and Danger: An Analysis of Concepts of Pollution and Taboo*. Praeger, 1966.

DuPont, Denise. *Writing Teresa: The Saint from Ávila at the* fin-de-siglo. Bucknell UP, 2012.

Eliot, George. *Felix Holt, the Radical*, edited by Fred C. Thomson, Oxford UP, 1998.

Ewald, Liana. "Confinement, Consolation, and Confession in Galdós's *La desheredada*." *Hispanic Review*, vol. 76, no. 4, 2008, pp. 361–86.

Fanon, Frantz. *Black Skin, White Masks*. Grove Press, 2008.

Fedorchek, Robert M., translator. *Doña Luz*. By Benito Pérez Galdós, Bucknell UP, 2002.

Felski, Rita. *The Gender of Modernity*. Harvard UP, 1995.

Flaubert, Gustave. *L'éducation sentimentale: Histoire d'un jeune homme*, edited by Edouard Maynial, Garnier, 1964.

– *Madame Bovary*, edited by Bair Lowell and Leo Bersani, Bantam Books, 1981.

Flint, Kate. *The Woman Reader: 1837–1914*. Clarendon, 1993.

Foucault, Michel. *The History of Sexuality*. Vol. 1, Vintage Books, 1990.

Frank, Jason. "The Living Image of the People." *Theory & Event*, vol. 18, no. 1, 2015, Project MUSE, muse.jhu.edu/article/566086. Accessed 15 October 2019.

Frankenberg, Ruth. "The Mirage of an Unmarked Whiteness." *The Making and Unmaking of Whiteness*, edited by Birgit Brander Rasmussen, Duke UP, 2001, pp. 72–96.

Freud, Sigmund. "Family Romances." *Theory of the Novel: A Historical Approach*, edited by Michael McKeon, Johns Hopkins UP, 2000, pp. 156–9.

– *Group Psychology and the Analysis of the Ego*. Empire Books, 2011.

Gallagher, Patrick L. "Juan Valera and the Irony of Beauty in 'Doña Luz.'" *The Journal of the Midwest Modern Language Association*, vol. 33, no. 1, 2000, pp. 74–96, JSTOR, www.jstor.org/stable/1315119. Accessed 15 October 2019.

García, Pablo. "Vetusta Imperial: América y la Colonia en *La Regenta* de Leopoldo Alas." *Revista Hispánica Moderna*, vol. 56, no. 2, 2003, pp. 269–84.

García Sarría, Francisco. *Clarín, o la herejía amorosa*. Gredos, 1975.

Gaskell, Elizabeth Cleghorn. *Mary Barton*, edited by Shirley Foster, Oxford UP, 2006.

– *North and South*, edited by Easson Aungus and Sally Shuttleworth, Oxford UP, 1998.

Gerrard Lisa. "The Feminist Dimension of La Regenta." *Letras Femeninas*, vol. 13, no. 1/2, 1987, pp. 91–9.

Gill, Hélène. *The Language of French Orientalist Painting*. Edwin Mellen Press, 2003.

Gilman, Sander L. "Black Bodies, White Bodies: Toward an Iconography of Female Sexuality in Late Nineteenth-Century Art, Medicine, and Literature." *Critical Inquiry*, vol. 12, no. 1, 1985, pp. 204–42.

Gilman, Stephen. "The Birth of Fortunata." *Anales Galdosianos*, vol. 1, 1966, pp. 71–80.

– *Galdós and the Art of the European Novel, 1867–1887*. Princeton UP, 1981.

Godón, Nuria. "La singular prostitución de *La Regenta*." *Hispania*, vol. 98, no. 2, 2015, pp. 252–63.

Gold, Hazel. *The Reframing of Realism: Galdós and the Discourses of the Nineteenth-Century Spanish Novel*. Duke UP, 1993.

Goode, Joshua. *Impurity of Blood: Defining Race in Spain, 1870–1930*. Louisiana State UP, 2009.

Greer, Margaret Rich, et al., editors. *Rereading the Black Legend: The Discourses of Religious and Racial Difference in the Renaissance Empires*. U of Chicago P, 2007.

Grosz, Elizabeth. *Volatile Bodies: Toward a Corporeal Feminism*. Indiana UP, 1994.

Gullón, Agnes Moncy, translator. *Fortunata and Jacinta: Two Stories of Married Women*. By Benito Pérez Galdós, U of Georgia P, 1986.

– "The Bird Motif and the Introductory Motif: Structure in *Fortunata y Jacinta*." *Anales Galdosianos*, vol. 9, 1974, pp. 51–74.

Gullón, Germán. "La mirada masculina y la conciencia en *La Regenta*." *Biblioteca Virtual de Cervantes*, 2005, http://www.cervantesvirtual.com/nd/ark:/59851/bmctq691. Accessed 15 October 2019.

Halberstam, Jack. *In a Queer Time and Place: Transgender Bodies, Subcultural Lives*. New York UP, 2005.

Hart, Stephen. "Galdós's *Fortunata y Jacinta*: An 'Inoffensive Hen'?" *Forum for Modern Language Studies*, vol. 22, no. 4, 1986, pp. 342–53.

Hekman, Susan. "Constructing the Ballast: An Ontology for Feminism." *New Materialism*, edited by Stacy Alaimo and Susan Hekman, Indiana UP, pp. 85–119.

Hering Torres, Max S. "Purity of Blood: Problems of Interpretation." *Race and Blood in the Iberian World*, edited by Max S. Hering Torres et al., Lit Verlag, 2012, pp. 11–38.

Hering Torres, Max S., et al. Editorial. *Race and Blood in the Iberian World*, edited by Max S. Hering Torres et al., Lit Verlag, 2012, pp. 1–10.

Hill, Ruth. *Hierarchy, Commerce and Fraud in Bourbon Spanish America: A Postal Inspector's Exposé*. Vanderbilt UP, 2005.

Hobsbawm, Eric. *The Age of Capital: 1845–1878*. Scribner, 1975.

Hugo, Victor. *Les Misérables*. Literary Guild of America, 1954.

Jaffe, Catherine. "In Her Father's Library: Women's Reading in *La Regenta*." *Revista de Estudios Hispánicos*, vol. 39, 2005, pp. 3–26.

Jagoe, Catherine. *Ambiguous Angels: Gender in the Novels of Galdós*. U of California P, 1994.

– "Sexo y género en la medicina del siglo XIX." *La mujer en los discursos de género: textos y contextos en el siglo XIX*, edited by Catherine Jagoe et al., Icaria, 1998, pp. 305–67.

Jagor, Fedor. *Travels in the Philippines*. Chapman and Hall, 1875.

Jameson, Fredric. *The Antinomies of Realism*. Verso, 2013.

Johnson, Rebecca Carol, et al. "The Arabian Nights, Arab-European Literary Influence, and the Lineages of the Novel." *Modern Language Quarterly*, vol. 68, no. 2, 2007, pp. 243–79.

Kant, Immanuel. *Anthropology from a Pragmatic Point of View*. Translated by Victor L. Dowdell, Southern Illinois UP, 1978.

Kelly, Megan L. "Subir, subir siempre: Representing Death as Presentiment in *Fortunata y Jacinta*." *Anales Galdosianos*, vol. 50, 2015, pp. 11–25.

King, Sarah E. "Food Imagery in *Fortunata y Jacinta*." *Anales Galdosianos*, vol. 18, 1983, pp. 78–88.

Kristeva, Julia. *Powers of Horror: Essays on Abjection*. Columbia UP, 1982.

Labanyi, Jo. *Gender and Modernization in the Spanish Realist Novel*. Oxford UP, 2000.

– "The Political Significance of *La desheredada*." *Anales Galdosianos*, vol. 14, 1979, pp. 51–7.

– "The Problem of Framing in *La de Bringas*." *Anales Galdosianos*, vol. 25, 1990, pp. 23–34.

Larsen, Kevin S. "Ido del Sagrario's Alimentary Madness." *Science, Literature, and Film in the Hispanic World*, edited by Jerry Hoeg and Kevin S. Larsen, Palgrave Macmillan, 2006, pp. 151–74.

Le Bon, Gustave. *The Crowd*. Routledge, 1995.

"Limpio/a." *Diccionario de la lengua castellana*. Real Academia Española, 1884, http://ntlle.rae.es/ntlle. Accessed 15 October 2019.

López Bago, Eduardo. *La prostituta*, edited by Pura Fernández, Seville, Renacimiento, 2005.

– *El Cura: (Caso de incesto). Novela médico-social,* edited by Maite Zubiaurre and Luis Cesta, Stockero, 2013.

Lowe, Lisa. "The Intimacies of Four Continents." *Haunted by Empire: Geographies of Intimacy in North American History,* edited by Ann Laura, Duke UP, 2006, pp. 191–212.

Mandrell, James. "Malevolent Insemination: *Don Juan Tenorio* in *La Regenta.*" *"Malevolent Insemination" and Other Essays on Clarín,* edited by Noël Valis, Michigan Romance Studies, 1990, pp. 1–28.

Mariscal, George. "The Role of Spain in Contemporary Race Theory." *Arizona Journal of Hispanic Cultural Studies,* vol. 2, 1998, pp. 7–22.

Martínez, María Elena. *Genealogical Fictions: Limpieza de sangre, Religion, and Gender in Colonial Mexico.* Stanford UP, 2008.

Martin-Márquez, Susan. *Disorientations: Spanish Colonialism in Africa and the Performance of Identity.* Yale UP, 2008.

McClintock, Anne. *Imperial Leather: Race, Gender, and Sexuality in the Colonial Conquest.* Routledge, 1995.

McKinney, Collin. *Mapping the Social Body: Urbanisation, the Gaze, and the Novels of Galdós.* U of North Carolina P, 2010.

Mercer, Leigh. "'A primera sangre': The Duel as Bourgeois Battleground in Nineteenth-Century Spain." *Journal of Spanish Cultural Studies,* vol. 9, no. 1, 2008, pp. 61–74.

– *Urbanism and Urbanity: The Spanish Bourgeois Novel and Contemporary Customs (1845–1925).* Bucknell UP, 2013.

Mignolo, Walter. Afterward. *Rereading the Black Legend: The Discourses of Religious and Racial Difference in the Renaissance Empires,* edited by Margaret R. Greer et al., U of Chicago P, 2007, pp. 312–24.

Miller, D.A. *The Novel and the Police.* U of California P, 1988.

Miller, Gabrielle. "Contextualizing Prostitution in Benito Pérez Galdós's *La desheredada* (1881)." *Romance Notes,* vol. 58, no. 3, pp. 403–14.

Monlau, Pedro Felipe. *Elementos de higiene privada ó arte de conservar la salud del individuo.* 4th ed., Manuel Rivadeneyra, 1870.

– *Elementos de higiene pública.* D. Pablo Riera, 1847.

– *Elementos de obstetrecia.* J. Verdaguer, 1833.

– *Higiene del matrimonio ó el libro de los casados.* Estereotª. y Galvanopª. de Aribauª y Oª, 1876.

Morrison, Toni. *Playing in the Dark: Whiteness and the Literary Imaginary.* Vintage Books. 1992.

Muñoz, Sara. *'Andando se hace el camino': Calle y subjetividades marginales en la España del siglo XIX.* Iberoamericana, 2017.

Murray, N. Michelle, and Akiko Tsuchiya, editors. *Unsettling Colonialism: Gender and Race in the Nineteenth-Century Global Hispanic World.* State U of New York P, 2019.

Nemser, Daniel. *Infrastructures of Race: Concentration and Biopolitics in Colonial Mexico*. U of Texas P, 2017.

Nye, Robert A. *The Origins of Crowd Psychology: Gustave Le Bon and the Crisis of Mass Democracy in the Third Republic*. Sage Publications, 1975.

Omi, Michael, and Howard Winant. *Racial Formation in the United States*. 3rd ed., Routledge, 2014.

Ortega y Gasset, José. *La rebelión de las masas*, edited by Thomas Mermall, Castalia, 1998.

Outes-León, Brais. "'En aquella hora sublime': Ana Ozores o la trascendencia estético-religiosa en *La Regenta*." *Anales Galdosianos*, vol. 46, no. 1, pp. 67–86.

Pardo Bazán, Emilia. *Insolación: Historia Amorosa*, edited by Ermitas Penas Varela, Cátedra, 2001.

– *La madre naturaleza*, edited by Ermitas Penas Varela, Castalia, 2014.

– *Los pazos de Ulloa*, edited by María de los Ángeles de Ayala, Cátedra, 1997.

Parsons, Deborah L. *Streetwalking the Metropolis: Women, the City and Modernity*. Oxford UP, 2003.

Pastor, Nuria S. "'No quiero morirme sin hacerle a usted una fineza': La circulación de bienes y personas en *Fortunata y Jacinta*." *Bulletin of Hispanic Studies*, vol. 89, no. 3, 2012, pp. 255–69.

Pennington, Eric. "Structuring Empire in the Opening Chapter of *La Regenta*." *Romance Notes*, vol. 49, no. 2, 2009, pp. 167–76.

Pérez Galdós, Benito. *El amigo Manso*, edited by Francisco Caudet, Cátedra, 2001.

– *Fortunata y Jacinta: Dos historias de casadas I*, edited by Francisco Caudet, Cátedra, 2011.

– *Fortunata y Jacinta: Dos historias de casadas II*, edited by Francisco Caudet, Cátedra, 2011.

– *La de Bringas*, edited by Alda Blanco and Carlos Blanco Aguinaga, Cátedra, 2007.

– *La desheredada*, edited by German Gullón, Cátedra, 2009.

Perrot, Philippe. *Fashioning the Bourgeoisie: A History of Clothing in the Nineteenth Century*. Princeton UP, 1994.

Pick, Daniel. *Faces of Degeneration: A European Disorder, c.1848–c.1918*. Cambridge UP, 1989.

Pope, Randolph. "Embodied Minds: Critical Erotic Decisions in *La Regenta*." *Imagined Truths: Realism in Modern Spanish Literature and Culture*, edited by Mary L. Coffey and Margot Versteeg, U of Toronto P, 2019, pp. 236–58.

Porter, Roy. "Sex in the Head." *London Review of Books*, vol. 10, no. 18, 1988, https://www.lrb.co.uk/the-paper/v10/n13/roy-porter/sex-in-the-head. Accessed 15 October 2019.

Ragan, Robin. "'Desarreglos propios del sexo': Advertising Sexual Disorders and Regulating Women in *fin-de-siglo* Spain." *Decimonónica: Revista de producción cultural hispánica decimonónica*, vol. 7, no. 1, 2010, pp. 40–60.

Ramberg, Lucinda. "Troubling Kinship: Sacred Marriage and Gender Configuration in South India." *American Ethnologist*, vol. 40, no. 4, 2013, pp. 66–75.

Resina, Joan Ramón. "Ana Ozores's Nerves." *Hispanic Review*, vol. 71, no. 2, 2003, pp. 229–52.

Ribbans, Geoffrey. *Conflicts and Conciliations: The Evolution of Galdós's* Fortunata y Jacinta. Purdue UP, 1997.

– *History and Fiction in Galdós's Narratives*. Clarendon Press, 1993.

Robert, Marthe. "From Origins of the Novel." *Theory of the Novel: A Historical Approach*, edited by Michael McKeon, Johns Hopkins UP, 2000, pp. 160–77.

Rodríguez, Juana María. *Queer Latinidad: Identity Practices, Discursive Spaces*. New York UP, 2003.

Rodríguez Puértolas, Julio. "*Fortunata y Jacinta*, entre la libertad y el orden." *Verba Hispanica*, vol. 15, no. 1, 2007, pp. 103–20.

Roof, Judith. *Come as You Are: Sexuality and Narrative*. Columbia UP, 1996.

Roy, Parama. *Indian Traffic: Identities in Question in Colonial and Postcolonial*. U of California P, 1998.

Rubin, Gayle. "The Traffic in Women." *Toward and Anthropology of Women*, edited by Rayna Reiter. NY Monthly Review Press, 1975, pp. 157–210.

– Interview by Judith Butler. "Sexual Traffic: Interview." *differences: A Journal of Feminist Cultural Studies*, vol. 6., no. 2–3, 1994, pp. 62–99.

Ruiz Salvador, Antonio. "La función del trasfondo histórico en *La desheredada*." *Anales Galdosianos*, 1966, pp. 53–61.

Russell, Robert, translator. *Our Friend Manso*. By Benito Pérez Galdós, Columbia UP, 1987.

Rutherford, John, translator. *La Regenta*. By Leopoldo Alas, Penguin Books, 2005.

Said, Edward W. *Culture and Imperialism*. Knopf, 1993.

– *Orientalism*. Pantheon Books, 1978.

Sánchez León, Pablo. *Popular Political Participation and the Democratic Imagination in Spain: From Crowd to People, 1766–1868*. Palgrave Macmillan, 2021.

Seth, Vanita. *Europe's Indians: Producing Racial Difference, 1500–1900*. Duke UP, 2010, http://dx.doi.org/10.1215/9780822392941.

Sheeran, Amy. "The Fictions of Blood in *La fuerza de la sangre*." *Cervantes: Bulletin of the Cervantes Society of America*, vol. 37, no. 1, 2017, pp. 33–61.

Siebers, Tobin. *Disability Aesthetics*. U of Michigan P, 2010.

Sieburth, Stephanie Anne. *Reading* La Regenta: *Duplicitous Discourse and the Entropy of Structure*. Benjamins, 1990.

Sinclair, Alison. *Dislocations of Desire: Gender, Identity, and Strategy in* La Regenta. U of North Carolina Department of Romance Languages, 1998.

– "Luxurious Borders: Containment and Excess in Nineteenth-Century Spain." *A Companion to Spanish Women's Studies*, edited by Xon de Ros and Geraldine Hazbun, Tamesis, 2011, pp. 211–33.

– "The Regional Novel: Evolution and Consolation." *The Cambridge Companion to the Spanish Novel: From 1600 to the Present*, edited by Harriet Turner and Adelaida López de Martínez, Cambridge UP, 2003, pp. 49–64.

Sinnigen, John H. *Sexo y política: Lecturas galdosianas*. Ediciones de la Torre, 1996.

Smith, Jennifer. "The Gypsy's Curse: Race and Impurity of Blood in Pardo Bazán." *Revista Canadiense de Estudios Hispánicos*, vol. 39, no. 2, 2015, pp. 459–82.

– "The Wet Nurse and the Subversion of the *Angel Del Hogar* in Medical and Literary Texts from Nineteenth-Century Spain." *Hispanic Journal*, vol. 31, no. 1, 2010, pp. 39–52.

Smith, Paul. "Juan Valera and the Illegitimacy Motif." *Hispania*, vol. 51, no. 4, 1968, 804–11.

Smith, Paul Julian. *The Body Hispanic: Gender and Sexuality in Spanish and Spanish American Literature*. Clarendon Press, 1989.

Sobejano Esteve, Gonzalo. "Sentimientos sin nombre en *La Regenta*." *Insula: Revista de Letras y Ciencias Humanas*, no. 451, 1984, pp. 1–6.

Sommer, Doris. *Foundational Fictions: The National Romances of Latin America*. U of California P, 1991.

Spenser, Edmund. *A View of the Present State of Ireland*. 1596. Edited by W.L. Renwick, Clarendon, 1970.

Spivak, Gayatri Chakravorty. "Three Women's Texts and a Critique of Imperialism." *Critical Inquiry*, vol. 12, no. 1, 1985, pp. 243–61.

Steinlight, Emily. *Populating the Novel: Literary Form and the Politics of Surplus Life*. Cornell UP, 2018.

Stoler, Ann Laura. *Race and the Education of Desire: Foucault's History of Sexuality and the Colonial Order of Things*. Duke UP, 1995.

– "Racial Regimes of Truth." *Duress: Imperial Durabilities of Our Times*, Duke UP, 2016, pp. 237–65.

Surwillo, Lisa. *Monsters by Trade: Slave Traffickers in Modern Spanish Literature and Culture*. Stanford UP, 2014.

– "Passing Counterfeit Whiteness and Mulatta Wealth in *Los misterios de Barcelona*." *Journal of Spanish Cultural Studies*, vol. 10, no.1, 2009, pp. 75–87.

– "Pituso en *Blackface*: Una mascarada racial en *Fortunata y Jacinta*." *Hispanic Review*, vol. 78, no. 2, 2010, pp. 189–204.

– "Speaking of Race in Don Álvaro." *Revista Hispánica Moderna*, vol. 63, no. 1, 2010, pp. 51–67.

Tanner, Tony. *Adultery in the Novel: Contract and Transgression*. Johns Hopkins UP, 1979.

Taussig, Michael T. *What Color Is the Sacred?* U of Chicago P, 2009.

Thomas, Megan C. *Orientalists, Propagandists, and Ilustrados: Filipino Scholarship and the End of Spanish Colonialism.* U of Minnesota P, 2012.

Tompkins, Kyla Wazana. *Racial Indigestion: Eating Bodies in the 19th Century.* New York UP, 2012.

Tarde, Gabriel de, and Elsie Worthington Clews Parsons. *The Laws of Imitation.* H. Holt and Company, 1903.

Tolliver, Joyce. "Over her Bloodless Body: Gender, Race, and the Spanish Colonial Fetish in Pardo Bazán." *Revista canadiense de estudios hispánicos,* vol. 34, no. 2, pp. 285–301.

Tolstoy, Leo. *Anna Karenina.* Edited by Marian Schwartz and Gary Saul Morson, Yale UP, 2014.

Torres-Pou, Joan. *Asia en la España del Siglo XIX: Literatos, viajeros, intelectuales y diplomáticos ante Oriente.* Rodopi, 2013.

– "The Exotic as a Subversive Element in Juan Valera's *Morsamor.*" *Romanische Forschungen,* vol. 106, 1994, pp. 254–9.

Tsuchiya, Akiko. *Marginal Subjects: Gender and Deviance in Fin-de-siècle Spain.* U of Toronto P, 2011.

Tsuchiya, Akiko, and William G. Acree, editors. *Empire's End: Transnational Connections in the Hispanic World.* Vanderbilt UP, 2016.

Tucker, Irene. *The Moment of Racial Sight: A History.* U of Chicago P, 2012.

Turner, Harriet S. "'Afterlives': Experiences of Space and Time in the Spanish Realist Novel." *Anales de la literatura española contemporánea,* vol. 41, no. 4, 2016, pp. 1147–64.

– *Benito Pérez Galdós, Fortunata and Jacinta.* Cambridge UP, 1992.

– "Family Ties and Tyrannies: A Reassessment of Jacinta." *Hispanic Review,* vol. 51, no. 1, 1983, pp. 1–22.

– "Metaphor and Metonymy in Galdós and Tolstoy." *Hispania,* vol. 75, no. 4, 1992, pp. 884–96.

– "The Realist Novel." *The Cambridge Companion to the Spanish Novel: From 1600 to the Present,* edited by Harriet Turner and Adelaida López de Martínez, Cambridge UP, 2003, pp. 81–101.

Unamuno, Miguel. *En torno al casticismo.* Cátedra, 2005.

– *Tres novelas ejemplares y un prólogo.* Espasa-Calpe, 1931.

Urey, Diane F. *The Novel Histories of Galdós.* Princeton UP, 1989.

Utt, Roger L. "'El pájaro voló': Observaciones sobre un leitmotif en *Fortunata y Jacinta.*" U of Texas P, 1974.

Valdivia, Pablo. Introduction. *Tristana* by Benito Pérez Galdós, 1892, Manchester UP, 2016, pp. 1–36.

Valera, Juan. *Doña Luz,* edited by Enrique Rubio Cremades, Espasa-Calpe, 1990.

– *Pepita Jiménez,* edited by José B. Monleón, Ediciones Alkal, 1998.

– "Sobre dos acusaciones tremendas contra España, del anglo-americano Draper." *A vuela pluma*, Fernando Fé, 1897, pp. 103–48.

Valis, Noël Maureen. *The Culture of Cursilería: Bad Taste, Kitsch, and Class in Modern Spain*. Duke UP, 2002.

– *The Decadent Vision in Leopoldo Alas: A Study of* La Regenta *and* Su único hijo. Louisiana State UP, 1981.

– "Romantic Reverberation in *La Regenta*: Hugo and the Clarinian Decay of Romanticism." *The Comparatist*, vol. 3, 1979, pp. 40–52.

– *Sacred Realism: Religion and the Imagination in Modern Spanish Narrative*. Yale UP, 2010.

Vialette, Aurélie. *Intellectual Philanthropy: The Seduction of the Masses*. Purdue UP, 2018.

Villasante, Olga. "Dossier: El manicomio nacional de Leganés: una aproximación histórica a partir de su archivo clínico." *Frenia*, vol. 3, 2008, pp. 33–68.

Viota y Soliva, Eduardo. *Memoria histórica del hospital de dementes de Santa Isabel de Leganés*. A. Barrial, 1896.

Weil, Kari. "Purebreds and Amazons: Saying Things with Horses in Late-Nineteenth-Century France." *differences: A Journal of Feminist Cultural Studies*, vol. 11, no. 1, 1999, pp. 1–37.

White, Joseph Blanco. *Letters from Spain*. H. Colburn, 1822.

Wilson, Elizabeth. "The Invisible Flâneur." *New Left Review*, vol. 1, no. 191, 1992, https://newleftreview.org/I/191/elizabeth-wilson-the-invisible-flaneur. Accessed 15 October 2019.

Zola, Émile. *Au Bonheur des Dames*. Hachette, 1980, http://hdl.handle.net/2027/coo.31924011565540. Accessed 15 October 2019.

– *Germinal*, edited by Colette Becker, Presses universitaires de France, 1984.

– *Nana*. Classiques Garnier Numérique, 2005.

Index

Toronto Iberic